Locke

'an admirable introduction . . . written by a real philosopher with
a real philosophical interest in Locke.'
Andrew Pyle, Bristol University, UK

'a wonderful contribution to the understanding of Locke
by non-specialists.'
Dan Kaufman, University of Colorado, Boulder, USA

Routledge Philosophers

Edited by Brian Leiter
University of Texas, Austin

Routledge Philosophers is a major series of introductions to the great
Western philosophers. Each book places a major philosopher or thinker
in historical context, explains and assesses their key arguments, and
considers their legacy. Additional features include a chronology of major
dates and events, chapter summaries, annotated suggestions for further
reading and a glossary of technical terms.

An ideal starting-point for those new to philosophy, they are also essential
reading for those interested in the subject at any level.

Hobbes	A. P. Martinich
Leibniz	Nicholas Jolley
Locke	E. J. Lowe
Hegel	Frederick Beiser
Rousseau	Nicholas Dent
Schopenhauer	Julian Young
Freud	Jonathan Lear

Forthcoming:

Spinoza	Michael Della Rocca
Hume	Don Garrett
Kant	Paul Guyer
Fichte and Schelling	Sebastian Gardner
Husserl	David Woodruff Smith
Rawls	Samuel Freeman

E. J. Lowe

Locke

Routledge
Taylor & Francis Group

LONDON AND NEW YORK

First published 2005
by Routledge
2 Park Square, Milton Park, Abingdon, Oxon OX14 4RN

Simultaneously published in the USA and Canada
by Routledge
270 Madison Ave, New York, NY 10016

Routledge is an imprint of the Taylor & Francis Group

Typeset in Joanna MT and Din by
RefineCatch Ltd, Bungay, Suffolk
Printed and bound in Great Britain by
TJ International Ltd, Padstow, Cornwall

British Library Cataloguing in Publication Data
A catalogue record for this book is available from the British Library

Library of Congress Cataloging in Publication Data
Lowe, E. J. (E. Jonathan)
    Locke / E. J. Lowe.
        p. m. – (The Routledge philosophers)
    Includes bibliographical references (p.   ) and index.
    ISBN 0-415-28347-7 (hardcover) – ISBN 0-415-28348-5 (pbk.)
    1. Locke, John, 1632–1704. I. Title. II. Series.
    B1297.L69 2005
    192 – dc22
                                                      2004017847

ISBN 0-415-28347-7 (hbk)
ISBN 0-415-28348-5 (pbk)

Preface

My aim in this book is to expound and evaluate a representative sample of John Locke's philosophical views, focusing on certain major areas of his work that I judge to have been of lasting interest and importance. Owing to the great size of Locke's literary output and the broad scope of his philosophical concerns, I concentrate on the central core of his intellectual system: his theory of knowledge, his metaphysics, his philosophy of mind, and his philosophy of language – as they are developed in the *Essay Concerning Human Understanding* – and his political philosophy, as it is represented in his *Second Treatise of Government*. However, I also make mention of some of Locke's other influential works in Chapter 1 and, where appropriate, in later chapters. For example, I discuss his extensive published correspondence with Edward Stillingfleet in Chapter 3, in view of the important light that it throws upon some of Locke's metaphysical opinions. And I discuss his first *Letter on Toleration* in Chapter 6, in the context of Locke's political theory. I should emphasize that the present study has no pretension to being a comprehensive account of Locke's philosophy, even with regard to the areas of his work that it covers. I considered it preferable to discuss certain selected issues in some depth rather than try to cover many more superficially. At the same time, by selecting the issues in question from quite widely differing areas of his work and showing how Locke's treatments of them are none the less closely interrelated, I hope to convey something of the systematicity of his approach to philosophy in general. I have also used parts of Chapters 1 and 7 to give a broader overview of his work.

There have been several good studies in recent years of specific aspects of Locke's philosophy as well as some dealing with his life and work more generally. The present book is distinctive in a number of respects. First, it includes an account of Locke's personal history and intellectual development which does not presume that its readers will already be familiar with the general circumstances of English political and intellectual life in the seventeenth century. Second, it does not assume an extensive acquaintance with present-day philosophical debates, doctrines and terms that are relevant to the evaluation of Locke's philosophy. Third, on many particular issues the interpretation of Locke's views that it advances differs significantly from those of other recent commentators and scholars. It is not in any sense a rival to my own earlier book, *Locke on Human Understanding* (London and New York: Routledge, 1995), although it does complement that book in various ways. The earlier book focuses exclusively on the *Essay Concerning Human Understanding* and is intended to guide its readers through that particular text. In the present book, I am also concerned with other aspects of Locke's work, notably his political philosophy, while at the same time being more selective in my choice of topics on which to concentrate. However, I do take the opportunity here to develop, modify or further defend some of the interpretations of Locke's views that I advanced in the earlier book, as well as to present in an accessible form the results of other work that I have done on Locke's philosophy since that book appeared.

My primary intention is that this book should provide something specifically suited to the needs of students and general readers who are newcomers to Locke's philosophy with little specialized knowledge of recent developments in academic philosophy or Locke scholarship. Thus it may serve as a general introduction to Locke's thought for undergraduate students of philosophy and related disciplines. At the same time, I include material which will,

I hope, be of some interest to Locke scholars, historians of philosophy and philosophers concerned with the current debates that Locke's thought has influenced. For the benefit of non-specialist readers, I have included a glossary of philosophical terms at the end of the book. This explains the meanings of certain important terms which recur frequently or figure prominently in Locke's writings or in discussions of Locke's philosophy. Following each chapter, I have provided some suggestions for further reading. A consolidated bibliography appears at the end of the book.

Acknowledgements

In writing this book, I have in various places drawn upon, adapted or developed work of mine that has appeared in print elsewhere in recent years, mostly in journal articles which some readers of the book may not find easily accessible. I am indebted to the editors and publishers concerned for permission to do this. In Chapter 3, I adapt material from my articles 'Locke, Martin and Substance', *The Philosophical Quarterly* 50 (2000), pp. 499–514, and 'Identity, Individuation and Unity', *Philosophy* 78 (2003), pp. 321–36. In Chapter 4, I build upon an account of Locke's views about language that I first advanced in Chapter 6 of my *Subjects of Experience* (Cambridge: Cambridge University Press, 1996). In Chapter 5, I draw upon my article 'Locke: Compatibilist Event-Causalist or Libertarian Substance-Causalist?', *Philosophy and Phenomenological Research* 68 (2004), pp. 688–701.

I am grateful to Brian Leiter, the series editor, and to Tony Bruce of Routledge for encouraging me to write this book, and to them as well as to three anonymous readers for very helpful suggestions concerning its content.

1632	Locke is born in Wrington, Somerset.
1647	Locke is admitted to Westminster School.
1649	Charles I is executed in London.
1652	Locke enters Christ Church, Oxford.
1656	Locke graduates as a Bachelor of Arts of the University of Oxford.
1658	Locke graduates as a Master of Arts of the University of Oxford.
1660	The House of Stuart is restored to the throne with Charles II, and Locke is elected Lecturer in Greek at Christ Church.
1662	Locke is elected Lecturer in Rhetoric at Christ Church.
1663	Locke is elected Censor of Moral Philosophy at Christ Church.
1665	Plague breaks out in London; Locke is appointed secretary to the diplomatic mission of Sir Walter Vane to Brandenburg.
1666	The Great Fire of London occurs; Locke meets Anthony Ashley Cooper, Chancellor of the Exchequer and later first Earl of Shaftesbury.
1667	Locke takes up residence in Shaftesbury's household at Exeter House in London; Locke begins to collaborate with the eminent physician, Thomas Sydenham.
1668	Locke oversees an important liver operation on Shaftesbury; Locke is elected a Fellow of the Royal

	Society; Locke becomes Secretary to the Lords Proprietors of Carolina.
1671	Locke begins work on early drafts of the *Essay Concerning Human Understanding*.
1673	Locke is appointed Secretary to the Council of Trade; Shaftesbury is dismissed as Lord Chancellor by Charles II.
1675	Locke is awarded the degree of Bachelor of Medicine by the University of Oxford.
1675–9	Locke travels in France.
1679	Shaftesbury briefly returns to public office as Lord President of the Council.
1680	Sir Robert Filmer's *Patriarcha* is published posthumously; the Exclusion Bill is rejected by the House of Lords.
1681	Shaftesbury is arrested for high treason and imprisoned in the Tower of London, but is later released.
1682	Shaftesbury flees to exile in the Netherlands.
1683	Shaftesbury dies in the Netherlands; the Rye House plot is discovered; Locke escapes to the Netherlands.
1684	Locke is expelled from his Studentship at Christ Church.
1685	Charles II dies and is followed on the throne by his brother, James II.
1688	James II is removed from the throne and replaced by William of Orange and his wife Mary in the Revolutionary Settlement.
1689	Locke returns to England from the Netherlands; *An Essay Concerning Human Understanding*, *A Letter on Toleration* and *Two Treatises of Government* are published.
1691	Locke moves to Oates in Essex, the house of Sir Francis and Lady Masham.
1693	*Some Thoughts Concerning Education* is published.
1695	*The Reasonableness of Christianity* is published.
1696	Locke is appointed a Commissioner of the Board of Trade.

1697   *A Letter to the Bishop of Worcester* (Edward Stillingfleet) is published.

1700   Locke resigns as a Commissioner of the Board of Trade; the fourth edition of *An Essay Concerning Human Understanding* appears.

1704   Locke dies at Oates and is buried in the churchyard of High Laver, Essex.

One

Life and Work

Why should we today be at all interested in the life and philosophical works of John Locke, when the writings of so many of his long-forgotten contemporaries now gather dust on library shelves and seventeenth-century English history has been reduced in the public imagination to a few glamorous or bloody incidents? One very good reason is that, despite his relatively obscure beginnings, Locke's influence on his own and later generations of thinkers has been immense and is particularly strong today – so much so, in fact, that many current philosophical disputes cannot be properly understood except in the light of his work and its impact. Another is that Locke's solutions to a number of important philosophical problems are still, very arguably, amongst the best that we possess. These are claims that I shall try to substantiate in the later chapters of this book. But in the present chapter I shall focus on Locke's life and times, setting his work in its historical context.

Locke led a remarkably full and interesting life. For, despite his relatively humble origins, he had the good fortune not only to live through some of the most momentous episodes and developments of English political and intellectual history but also to make significant contributions to many of them. Undoubtedly, his intelligence, curiosity, perspicacity, ambition, sense of duty and strength of character equipped him unusually well for such a role. But good luck also inevitably had a hand in his success, for the times in which he lived and the circles in which he moved were perilous ones, continually beset by the dangers of war, disease, religious strife and political intrigue. That he found time to write so much of lasting philosophical value is remarkable and it is our own good fortune that so much of what he did write has been preserved, including a great deal of his extensive correspondence, much of it with some of the leading intellectual and political figures of his day. I shall say more about the scope and contemporary impact of Locke's literary output in due course, but first I shall outline the major events and circumstances of his life.

LOCKE'S LIFE AND TIMES

John Locke was born in the south-west of England in 1632, in the small village of Wrington in the county of Somerset. His parents were John (1606–61) and Agnes (1597–1654). The small house in which he was born was the home of his maternal grandmother and no longer exists, having been demolished towards the end of the nineteenth century. However, the house in which he grew up, some miles away from his birthplace, was larger and set in its own grounds. His father was a person of moderately comfortable means, being an attorney and minor landowner. The family lands brought in rents which helped Locke in later times to maintain a private source of income, but which never made him wealthy, even when supplemented by his other earnings. Locke was careful with money all his life, not because he was miserly but because he valued the freedom conferred by independent means.

At the time of Locke's birth, Charles I (1600–49) of the House of Stuart was King of England – as well as of Scotland, the two thrones having been united in the person of Charles's father, James I (1566–1625) – and English politics was entering a turbulent period which would not be brought to a close until shortly before Locke's death in 1704. In due course, Locke himself was to play an important role in political developments, as we shall soon see. But this could scarcely have been predicted when, supported by the patronage of a powerful ally of his father, Locke secured a place at Westminster School, then the foremost school in the country.

Locke was at Westminster School when, in 1649, Charles I was beheaded in nearby Whitehall – an event which the pupils were, however, forbidden from attending. Locke's education at Westminster was rigorous but narrow, consisting mainly in the intensive study of Latin and Greek. The regime was harsh and punishments were severe, including regular beatings. But Locke was an assiduous pupil and secured a scholarship at Christ Church, Oxford, becoming a Student of that college. Locke was to retain this status – equivalent to that of a Fellow at other colleges – and an entitlement to rooms and board in Christ Church until his explusion in 1684 at the behest of Charles II (1630–85).

Throughout this period of English history, politics and religion were inextricably intertwined as a consequence of the upheavals engendered by the Reformation in the previous century and the fragile hold of the Stuarts on the English throne. Locke inherited from his parents a strong Protestant faith, which was to exercise a large influence on his future intellectual development and political allegiances. It was these allegiances that were to cost him his Studentship at Christ Church and to result in his exile from the country between 1683 and 1689. But it was also this period of exile that was most productive for Locke as a philosopher, culminating as it did in the publication of his three greatest works, *An Essay Concerning Human Understanding*, the *Second Treatise of Government* and *A Letter on Toleration*, all of which made their first appearance in print in 1689.

Locke was awarded the degree of Bachelor of Arts by the University of Oxford in 1656, following a traditional course of study centring once more on the ancient languages and their literature. Remaining in Oxford, Locke then became more deeply engaged in philosophical and theological studies, when not carrying out teaching and administrative duties for his college. At this time, his political views were still markedly more conservative and less liberal than they were later to be. Gradually, his intellectual interests broadened to include medicine, his fascination with which was later deepened by his association with the eminent physician,

Thomas Sydenham (1624–89). Oxford was then becoming a centre of scientific innovation, inspired by the empirical methods and discoveries of continental astronomers and physicists, such as the Italian Galileo Galilei (1564–1642) and the Dutchman Christiaan Huygens (1629–93). This was despite, rather than thanks to, the attitude of the university authorities at the time, who were firmly traditional in their conception of the proper concerns of academic life and higher education. The chemist Robert Boyle (1627–91) and the microscopist and polymath Robert Hooke (1635–1703) were amongst the scientists based in Oxford, and Boyle in particular became a close associate of Locke. Boyle and Hooke were members of the Royal Society of London, instituted to foster innovative work in experimental science. Locke himself became a member in 1668, taking a close concern in its proceedings for the rest of his life. By these means, he became a good friend of the greatest scientist of the age, Isaac Newton (1642–1727), Lucasian Professor of Mathematics at the University of Cambridge. Although Locke's own scientific interests lay chiefly in medicine and he had little knowledge of mathematics, he was evidently fascinated by scientific discoveries of all kinds, as well as by the reports of the many explorers who were then travelling to exotic parts of the world hitherto unknown to Western Europeans.

Locke long aspired to become a Doctor of Medicine but was not prepared to submit to the outdated requirements of the University of Oxford for the award of this degree. He was eventually awarded the lesser degree of Bachelor of Medicine in 1675. By that time, however, his knowledge of medicine had already led to a profound change in his circumstances and prospects. This came about as a result of his encountering, quite by chance, the leading Whig politician of the day, Anthony Ashley Cooper (1621–83). They first met in 1666 – a time at which the parliamentary party division between Whigs and Tories, which was to dominate English political life for several generations to come, was coming into being. Lord Ashley, as he then was, was Chancellor of the Exchequer at the time, a man of considerable intelligence and political guile who had risen to become one of the most powerful figures in the land. Lord Ashley, struck by Locke's evident good sense and knowledgeability, invited him to become his medical adviser and to take up residence in his imposing London house. This Locke did in 1667, remaining there until 1675. In 1668 Locke was responsible for overseeing a serious liver operation on Lord Ashley. This involved the insertion of a silver tube in the patient's abdomen to drain an abscess – a potentially hazardous intervention before the modern age of antiseptic medicine. Fortunately for Locke, Lord Ashley made an excellent recovery and thereafter regarded Locke as one of his closest friends and confidants.

Locke's association with Lord Ashley – soon to become, in 1672, the first Earl of Shaftesbury – was undoubtedly the most momentous development in his career. Shaftesbury's influence at the court of Charles II was very great until the king dismissed him in 1673, although he was briefly to return to public office in 1679. From this time onwards English politics were greatly disturbed by the problem of the succession to the throne. For Charles II had no legitimate child and his brother and heir, James II (1633–1707), was notorious for his openly admitted allegiance to Roman Catholicism. Whig politicians like Shaftesbury and his circle, which included Locke in a minor capacity, wanted an Act to be passed by Parliament excluding James from succession to the throne – a move very much opposed by Charles II and his court, concerned to perpetuate the Stuart line and the independence of the throne from Parliament. At this time royal power was still very considerable and opposition like Shaftesbury's extremely dangerous. Shaftesbury himself escaped to the Netherlands in 1682 after a charge of treason had been levelled against him, but died soon after his arrival, early in 1683.

At this time Locke, who had been travelling abroad in France during 1675–9 and had not resumed his membership of Shaftesbury's household upon his return, was nevertheless still closely associated with Shaftesbury's circle and hence in considerable personal danger himself. Government spies kept a close watch on his activities, particularly looking for any evidence of compromising letters or seditious writings. Locke, however, was very careful to cover his tracks. In the summer of 1683 matters came to a head with the Rye House plot, when leading members of Shaftesbury's circle – Algernon Sidney (or Sydney, 1622–83), Lord William Russell (1639–83) and the Earl of Essex (1631–83) – were implicated in an attempt to kidnap and assassinate Charles II and his brother and were all three arrested for treason, two of them subsequently being executed. Algernon Sidney was convicted and executed partly on the strength of a political treatise that he had secretly written, questioning the divine right of kings to rule over their subjects – a theme on which Locke himself had been working at this very time, leading eventually to the publication of his two *Treatises of Government* in 1689. Locke, although not directly involved in the Rye House plot, was now even more under suspicion and escaped to the Netherlands in September 1683. From there he did not return to England until 1689, but he managed to spend his period of exile usefully and, it seems, relatively happily, engaged in his philosophical projects when not travelling about the country, writing letters, or conversing with fellow intellectuals. Following the Revolutionary Settlement of 1688, which removed James II from the throne after a disastrous reign of three years, the throne passed jointly to the Dutch Prince of Orange, William (1650–1702) – a grandson of Charles I – and his wife Mary (1662–94), James II's elder daughter. With the reign of the Protestant William and Mary began the long period of Whig ascendancy in English politics, a regime very much in line with Locke's own political and religious convictions.

During his last years, from his return to England in 1689 until his death in 1704, Locke enjoyed much public esteem and royal favour, in addition to great intellectual fame as the author of *An Essay Concerning Human Understanding*, which was published late in 1689. He

performed a number of official duties, notably as a Commissioner
of the Board of Trade, in which capacity he was responsible for
affairs in the American colonies and contributed significantly to
economic and monetary reform. However, the need to attend meet-
ings in Westminster took a toll on his health, as he suffered from
chronic asthma which was severely aggravated by the polluted air
and winter fogs of seventeenth-century London. Besides, flattered
though he was by the distinction of public office and pleased by the
substantial salary attached to it, his greatest desire in the closing
years of his life was to pursue his scholarly and intellectual interests. His international fame also brought him an ever-growing bur-
den of correspondence.

Eventually Locke retired permanently to Oates, the Essex home
of his friends Sir Francis and Lady Masham, who in 1692 offered
him accommodation in a part of the country with a more salubri-
ous climate than London's, but still within a day's coach-ride from
the capital. Lady Masham (1658–1708) was born Damaris Cudworth, daughter of the eminent Cambridge philosopher Ralph
Cudworth (1617–88), and was someone who could engage with
Locke on terms of intellectual parity as well as friendship, being the
author of a number of published works herself. After some years of
progressively failing health and at the age of seventy-two, Locke
died with great composure of mind, in his room at Oates in 1704.
He is buried at a local church, where his epitaph bears a modest
inscription in Latin, composed by himself. The house where he
died was long ago demolished.

Locke never married, although he had many female friends like
Damaris Cudworth and had an esteem for the intellectual qualities
of women which was unusual in men of the time. Without children of his own, he was nonetheless very fond of them and was
influential in promoting more humane and rational attitudes
towards their upbringing and education – never forgetting,
it seems, the severe treatment that he had experienced at Westminster School. In character he was a little introverted and

hypochondriacal, but he by no means disliked company. He enjoyed good conversation but was abstemious in his habits of eating and drinking. He was a prolific correspondent and had a great many friends and acquaintances, on the continent of Europe as well as in Britain and Ireland. If there was a particular fault in his character, it was a slight tetchiness in response to criticism of his writings, even when that criticism was intended to be constructive. Although academic in his cast of mind, Locke was strongly moved by his political and religious convictions – especially by his concern for liberty and toleration – and had the good fortune to live at a time when there was no great divide between the academic pursuit of philosophical interests and the public discussion and application of political and religious principles. He thus happily lived to see some of his strongest convictions realized in public policy, partly as a consequence of his own writings and involvement in public affairs.

LOCKE'S WRITINGS

Locke's greatest intellectual achievement was undoubtedly *An Essay Concerning Human Understanding*. It was first published in full in December 1689, although the title page of the first edition bears the date 1690. Locke worked on the manuscripts on which it was based from the early 1670s onwards, but most intensively during his period of exile in the Netherlands between 1683 and 1689. He continued to revise the *Essay* after its first appearance, supervising three further editions of it before his death. The fourth edition of 1700 accordingly represents his final view and is the version most closely studied today.

The *Essay* is chiefly concerned with issues in what would today be called epistemology or the theory of knowledge, metaphysics, the philosophy of mind, and the philosophy of language. As its title implies, the book's purpose is to discover, from an examination of the workings of the human mind, just what we are capable of understanding about the universe in which we live. Locke's contention is that all of the 'materials' of human knowledge arise from experience – that is, from what he calls our *ideas* of sensation and reflection. Sensation provides us with ideas of external things and their qualities, while reflection – nowadays more often called introspection – provides us with ideas of our own mental activities. These ideas, Locke thinks, are then worked upon by our powers of abstraction and reason to produce such real knowledge as we can hope to attain. Beyond that, he allows, we have other sources of belief – for instance, the testimony of other people and, perhaps, divine revelation – but beliefs of these kinds he regards as having only some degree of probability, which falls short of the certainty that he takes to be necessary for genuine knowledge.

It may help at this point if I briefly sketch the structure of the *Essay*. The whole work is made up of four books, each containing many chapters which are subdivided into numbered sections, so that it has become a standard practice to locate passages in the work in terms of the book, chapter and section in which they appear – for example, 'Book II, Chapter VIII, section 6' or, more briefly, 'II, VIII, 6' – and this is the method that I shall adopt. Book I, 'Of Innate Notions', is devoted to an attack on the doctrine of innate ideas, which implies – contrary to Locke's own view – that much of our knowledge is independent of and prior to experience. In Book II, 'Of Ideas', Locke attempts to explain in detail how sensation and reflection can in fact provide all of the materials of our understanding, including even such seemingly abstruse ideas as those of substance, identity, and causality, which many of Locke's opponents took to be self-evidently innate. In Book III, 'Of Words', Locke develops an account of how language, as he sees it, both helps and hinders us in the communication of our ideas. Finally, in Book IV, 'Of Knowledge and Opinion', Locke proposes ways in which processes of abstraction and reason operate upon our ideas to produce genuine knowledge and explains why, in his view, such knowledge differs from mere probable opinion. At the same time he tries to locate the proper boundary between the province of reason and experience on the one hand and that of revelation and faith on the other.

Locke's view of our intellectual capacities is clearly a modest one. At the same time, he held a firm personal faith in the truth of Christian religious principles. This may seem to conflict with the mildly sceptical air of some of his epistemological doctrines. In fact, he himself perceived no conflict here – unlike some of his contemporary religious critics – although he did regard the modest extent of our intellectual capacities as providing a strong ground for religious toleration. Reason, he thought, does not in general con-flict with religious faith, but when religious questions arise to which reason supplies no definitive answer he considers it both irrational and immoral to enforce conformity of belief by means of legal or political power. Interestingly enough, indeed, it appears that what originally motivated Locke to pursue the inquiries that were to culminate in his writing the *Essay* was precisely a concern to settle how far reason and experience could take us in establishing moral and religious truths. His considered answer is that they can-not take us very far where religious truths are concerned, for although he thinks that we can know – in fact, that we can *prove* – that God exists, he does not think that we can in the same way know where truth lies in disputes between the advocates of differ-ent monotheistic religions and creeds. On the other hand, Locke believes that *moral* truths are as demonstrable as truths of mathematics.

Locke's concern with morality and religion, both intimately bound up with questions of political philosophy in the seventeenth century, was one which dominated his thinking throughout his intellectual and public career – although he published no substan-tial work exclusively devoted to morality in the way that many other major philosophers have done, so that his mature views on this subject must be gleaned from writings whose chief focus may seem to lie elsewhere. His earliest works, unpublished in his own lifetime, were the *Two Tracts on Government* (1660 and 1661) and the

Essays on the Law of Nature (1664), all but the first of the *Two Tracts* being written in Latin, although now available in English translation. The position on issues of political liberty and religious toleration which Locke adopted in those early works was, however, considerably more conservative than the one that he was later to espouse, following his association with Shaftesbury. This was to find expression in *A Letter on Toleration* and *Two Treatises of Government* – both published anonymously in 1689, the former in both Latin and English and the latter in English. The *Second Treatise* explicitly recognizes the right of subjects to overthrow even a legitimately appointed ruler who has abused his trust and tyrannizes over his people – a doctrine which would almost certainly have led to an accusation of sedition had the manuscript been discovered by government spies. The *First Treatise* was an extended attack upon an ultra-royalist tract written by Sir Robert Filmer (d. 1653), entitled *Patriarcha, or the Natural Power of Kings Asserted* and published in 1680, in which the divine right of kings was defended as proceeding from the dominion first granted by God to Adam. Algernon Sidney, one of the Rye House plot conspirators, had been convicted of sedition partly on the strength of a manuscript he had written attacking Filmer's work, so one can well understand Locke's secrecy and caution in the years immediately preceding his flight to the Netherlands.

In addition to the works already mentioned, Locke published a good many other writings, notably on religious and educational topics. *Some Thoughts Concerning Education* (1693) was the product of advice he had offered in correspondence, over a number of years, to his friends Edward and Mary Clarke, concerning the upbringing of their children. This work went into many editions, proving to be very popular and influential with more enlightened parents for a long time to come. Locke's interest in the intellectual development of children is also plain to see in the *Essay* itself, where it has a direct relevance to his empiricist principles of learning and concept-formation. *Some Thoughts Concerning Education* is a classic work on the subject, giving Locke a prominent position in a tradition of enlightened thinkers about the upbringing of children which includes Michel Montaigne (1533–92) before him and Jean-Jacques Rousseau (1712–78) after him. Even so, some of Locke's remarks in this work have a quaint and mildly alarming ring to those who read it today, as when he asserts that 'The first Thing to be taken care of, is, that Children be not too *warmly clad or cover'd*, Winter or Summer . . . 'Tis Use alone hardens [the body], and makes it more able to endure the Cold' (section 5). Humane though he was by the standards of his time, Locke was strongly opposed to overindulging the young. That he was concerned primarily with the education of 'young Gentlemen', though perfectly understandable in the historical context, also distances him somewhat from our currently more egalitarian outlook on matters educational.

Locke's explicitly religious writings include The Reasonableness of Christianity (1695) and the Paraphrase and Notes on the Epistles of St Paul (published posthumously, 1705–7). The former was published anonymously – like a good many of Locke's other writings – and encountered hostility from conservatively minded critics, to some of whom Locke responded in print. He also wrote on economic and monetary issues connected with his various involvements in public and political affairs, notably concerning the harmful effects on trade of restrictions on the rate of interest and concerning measures to rectify the debasement of the coinage. Amongst his lesser-known philosophical works is a critique of the views of the French philosopher Nicolas Malebranche (1638–1715) – a proponent of the doctrine of occasionalism, according to which all created things possess no real causal powers of their own and God alone is the immediate cause of their behaviour and of our knowledge of them. This work of Locke's is entitled An Examination of Pere Malebranche's Opinion of Seeing All Things in God. Part of its interest lies in the fact that there are some affinities between Malebranche's views and those of George Berkeley (1685–1753), who was later to be a major critic of Locke's own system (see McCracken 1983). Other items included in Locke's collected *Works* – which have run to many editions – are his lengthy replies to Edward Stillingfleet (1635–99), then the Bishop of Worcester, answering hostile criticisms raised by Stillingfleet against the view of substance defended by Locke in the *Essay*. The religious significance of this dispute was that Locke's view was suspected of threatening the doctrine of the Holy Trinity. There is also amongst Locke's collected *Works* a long piece entitled 'Of the Conduct of the Understanding', which was originally intended for inclusion in a later edition of the *Essay*.

From this brief survey of Locke's writings, we can see that although his most important works were published during his fifties and sixties, within a comparatively short period beginning in 1689, his final views were the result of a very long process of maturation stretching back at least thirty years before that. At the same time, despite the breadth of Locke's intellectual interests, it seems fair to say that the *Essay* was the cornerstone of all his work, providing the epistemological and methodological framework for almost everything else he wrote. Certainly, although editions of Locke's collected *Works* run to many volumes and a remarkably extensive corpus of his original manuscripts and letters has survived, it is on the *Essay* that his reputation as the greatest English philosopher principally stands. Of all his other works, the only one which comes close to it in stature is his *Second Treatise of Government*, of which I should now say a little more.

As I mentioned earlier, the *Two Treatises of Government* were first published, anonymously, in 1689, very soon after Locke's return from the Netherlands. Locke never openly admitted his authorship of the work in his lifetime, although there is no question that it is his, as a codicil to his will makes clear. It appears that these treatises were intended to be parts of a larger work, the rest of which was unfortunately lost. The *First Treatise*, attacking Filmer's *Patriarcha*, may seem rather archaic today, because Filmer's views now look absurdly antiquated. But we should remember that Filmer and Locke were writing at a time when educated opinion in Europe still embodied the unquestioned assumption that the entire world had been created by God only a few thousand years previously and that Adam was the first man, in accordance with the biblical account given in Genesis. We should also remember that the question of whether or not Christian monarchs had a divinely ordained right to exercise absolute rule over their subjects was then a political issue of the first importance.

Because the *Two Treatises* appeared in 1689, shortly after the Revolutionary Settlement of 1688, it has sometimes been supposed that they were intended as a vindication of that event and of the institution of a constitutional monarchy, in which the power of the king was restricted by that of Parliament. However, it is now known that Locke was working on the manuscript much earlier in the 1680s, when political factions were in dispute over the suitability of Charles II's Roman Catholic brother, James, to be heir to the throne. The *Two Treatises* should, then, be seen in that context and as a direct response to Filmer's absolutist tract, which had been provocatively published in 1680 – many years after its author's death – as a justification of the divine right of kings to rule by familial descent from Adam and with the supposedly unfettered authority of a father over his children.

Interesting though these historical points are, it remains the case that the *Second Treatise* is the one that has been of lasting philosophical significance. It is sometimes suggested that it has even exercised momentous political influence by providing the ultimate inspiration for the Constitution of the United States of America, which was framed nearly one hundred years later. However, it is difficult to substantiate this idea in detail, even if it is true to say that many of the views defended by Locke in the *Second Treatise* had by then become common currency amongst liberal-minded politicians and political theorists, many of whom were at least broadly familiar with its principal themes and doctrines. That Locke's writings on government and toleration were cited by some leading figures during the American Revolution, in support of such principles as the separation of church and state and no taxation without representation, hardly suffices to show that Locke's work directly inspired or influenced the thinking of such individuals (see Dunn 1969a). After all, politicians often seek to give added weight or authority to their views by selectively citing the works of illustrious thinkers – and by the end of the eighteenth century Locke certainly had that status, though more on account of the fame of the *Essay* than anything else. Certainly, it is far from clear that Locke himself would have considered the American Revolution justified on his own principles. However, these cautionary observations should not in any way be seen as belittling the importance of the *Second Treatise* as a contribution to liberal political philosophy, because similar observations might be made about almost any other classic work of political theory. The historical significance of such works rarely lies in any direct influence they have on the thoughts of individual politicians and statesmen, who are typically more concerned with practical issues of short-term political strategy and everyday decision-making than with lofty philosophical principles. Rather, it lies in the contribution they make to the formation of a general climate of opinion, in which political policies that are in tune with their ideas are able to gain some purchase with the people at large.

THE CONTEMPORARY IMPACT OF LOCKE'S WORK

Locke's *Essay* aroused widespread attention from the moment it first appeared. One reason for this was the excellent publicity that it received in the leading intellectual journals of the day – at a time when academic journals were still a comparatively recent phenomenon. By this stage of Locke's career, he had built up a widespread network of important European connections during his lengthy stays in France and Holland, when he took the opportunity to travel extensively and meet some of the most eminent philosophers, scientists and theologians of the time. He kept up a regular correspondence with a number of these influential people and consequently had already acquired an international reputation as an important thinker before any of his views appeared in print.

An abridged version of the *Essay*, prepared by Locke himself, appeared in 1688 – a year before the full text was published – in an internationally renowned journal, the *Bibliothèque Universelle*. Many contemporary philosophers, including Leibniz, became acquainted with Locke's work by this means. The first edition of the full text was published in London late in 1689, and soon received appreciative reviews in various widely read journals. Between 1689 and 1700, Locke was to prepare three further, extensively revised editions of the *Essay*. A French translation by Locke's friend Pierre Coste (1668–1747) appeared in 1700, soon followed by a Latin translation, both of which were vitally important in disseminating Locke's ideas amongst European intellectuals. It is clear, then, that from the very beginning the *Essay* was widely recognized as being a major work of philosophy.

In these early years, reaction to the *Essay* was divided, some critics praising it highly while others were deeply hostile. For a time, the hostility mounted, but later it subsided as broadly Lockean views in epistemology and metaphysics began to be more widely accepted. The initial hostility was largely directed at features of the *Essay* thought by some to be damaging to religion and, by implication, to morality – notably, its apparently sceptical air and its repudiation of the doctrine of innate ideas. Although Locke himself had a firm Protestant faith, he was suspected by some of favouring Socinianism, an unorthodox variety of Christian belief which involved a denial of the doctrine of the Trinity – the doctrine that God is three persons in one, Father, Son, and Holy Ghost – and thereby a denial of the divinity of Jesus Christ. There seems to have been some substance to this charge, even though Locke never explicitly admitted its truth. Indeed, Locke's theological views were taken to have some affinity with the deism that was later to become widespread amongst enlightened intellectuals in the eighteenth century. Deism was a rationalistic version of monotheism which attempted to eliminate all of the more mysterious and miraculous features of traditional Christian belief – and was itself to develop in due course into the wholly secular, atheistic world-view that is, for better or worse, apparently taken for granted in many Western intellectual circles today.

Locke cannot be held responsible for this gradual slide to atheism and there is no doubt at all about the sincerity of his own Christian faith, but his early critics may well have been right in seeing dangers to their conception of religion in the emphasis that Locke laid upon reason and experience in the foundations of human knowledge. Of this sort of critic, Edward Stillingfleet, the Bishop of Worcester, was perhaps the most formidable. He and Locke engaged in a series of lengthy published exchanges, about which I shall have more to say in Chapter 3.

It is perhaps hard for us today to see Locke as a particularly sceptical philosopher, especially when we compare him with David Hume (1711–76), whose *Treatise of Human Nature* of 1739 was quite self-consciously sceptical in its approach – and indeed sceptical about most of the claims central to Locke's realism concerning the world of material objects. Locke was in fact not so much sceptical as anti-dogmatic, notably about religious claims based on revelation rather than on reason and experience. But to the religious dogmatists of his time, this would indeed have appeared dangerously sceptical. Locke's attack on the doctrine of innate ideas undoubtedly added to these suspicions. Adherents of that doctrine held that the concept of God, together with certain moral and religious principles, were planted in our minds from birth by God himself, giving us no excuse for denying their veracity. To repudiate the doctrine therefore struck many as opening the floodgates to atheism and immorality. In fact, nothing could have been further from Locke's intention. His motive for attacking the doctrine of innate ideas – quite apart from the fact that he thought it was simply false and unfounded – was that he saw it as a socially and intellectually pernicious buttress for all sorts of obscurantist and authoritarian views. In Locke's opinion, God gave mankind sense organs and a power of reason in order to discover such knowledge – including moral knowledge – as we need to have, thus rendering innate ideas quite unnecessary. And in matters of faith which go beyond the reach of reason and experience, he thought, revelation is a ground only for private, individual religious belief, which it would be morally as well as intellectually wrong to make enforceable universally by the authority of church or state.

Amongst the contemporary philosophical – as opposed to religious – critics of the *Essay*, two deserve special mention: the Irishman George Berkeley, Bishop of Cloyne, and the German polymath Gottfried Wilhelm Leibniz (1646–1716). Much of Berkeley's philosophy, notably his *Principles of Human Knowledge* of 1713, can be seen as a reaction to Locke's. Berkeley was like some other Christian critics of the *Essay* in attacking what he saw as its potential for scepticism, but unlike them he focused on what Locke himself would have regarded as the least sceptical aspect of his position – his realism concerning the world of material objects. Berkeley saw the real threat to religion in Locke's position as lying in its advocacy of a material world existing independently of any mind – including, at least potentially, the mind of God. He also thought that to regard the 'real' world as being somehow divested of all the sensible qualities of colour, sound, taste and smell which characterize our immediate experience of things – apparently making it a lifeless realm of material atoms moving in the void – was just to invite doubts about the very existence of anything beyond our own private experience. Berkeley's criticisms of Locke, although sometimes based on what appear to be mistaken or uncharitable interpretations of Locke's views, do raise serious questions which are hard to answer – even if Berkeley's own 'idealist' alternative may strike us as still harder to defend.

Leibniz, unlike Berkeley, criticized Locke's views during Locke's own lifetime, both in his own work and in correspondence with other philosophers. Locke was acquainted with some of these criticisms, but appears not to have been much impressed by them, despite Leibniz's very considerable reputation in European intellectual circles at the time. Leibniz even wrote an extended work in dialogue form discussing the *Essay* chapter by chapter, entitled *New Essays on Human Understanding* – but he gave up plans to publish it upon learning of Locke's death in 1704. In due course this important work was, however, published and it contains many insightful criticisms of Locke's views, as well as clarifying Leibniz's own opinions on many matters. Some of Leibniz's most memorable criticisms are directed against Locke's attack on innate ideas. Leibniz – like René Descartes (1591–1650) before him – did not defend the doctrine of innate ideas in any spirit of authoritarian dogmatism or obscurantism, but rather because he considered that certain fundamental components of human knowledge and understanding simply could not be acquired, as Locke believed, from sense experience. In answer to Locke's challenge to explain in what sense knowledge of which an infant was apparently quite unaware could be said to be 'in' its mind, Leibniz was to adopt a strikingly modern conception of cognition as being in quite large measure a subconscious process – a view which, in our own post-Freudian age, may appear less contentious than it would have done to Locke's contemporaries, many of whom were sympathetic to Descartes's conception of the mind as being in every way transparent to itself.

In sum, we see that Locke's *Essay* received close attention by the very best minds of his time and rapidly achieved a reputation which it has never since lost amongst the classics of Western philosophy. Despite initially being discouraged in Oxford University as dangerous material for students to read, it soon became a standard text and lost its early notoriety as a radical and even revolutionary work. As often happens with revolutionary writings once their tenets have been absorbed into the prevailing orthodoxy, the doctrines of the *Essay* eventually began to appear quite conservative and themselves became targets for later intellectual revolutionaries, such as Hume.

I have concentrated on the contemporary reception of Locke's *Essay* both because of its timeless importance as a classic of Western philosophy and because the views that it contains will be the main focus of attention in the remaining chapters of this book. Furthermore, it was the *Essay* that secured Locke's reputation in his own day as one of Europe's leading thinkers. This is not to deny that in Locke's own time many of his other writings achieved fame or notoriety, as objects of praise or as targets for criticism – though it is hard to believe that some of them would have done so had they not been known or supposed to have been written by the author of the *Essay*. The *Two Treatises*, whose authorship Locke kept secret until his death, received far less attention than the *Essay* in the years immediately following its publication and even for quite some time after that (see Dunn 1969). In any case, while writings such as the first *Letter on Toleration* and the *Second Treatise of Government* continue to be widely read as seminal texts in the history of philosophy, it is more difficult for present-day readers to understand the excitement and discussion stimulated at the time by the publication of a work such as Locke's *The Reasonableness of Christianity*, or the speculation that it provoked as to the identity of its author. This is simply a reflection of the very different intellectual climate in which we now live, partly as a consequence of the changed conception we have of our cognitive capacities and the physical universe that we inhabit – a change which Locke's *Essay* helped in no small measure to bring about. I shall be examining some of these longer-term effects of Locke's views in the final chapter of this book.

SUMMARY

How can one summarize a life so multi-faceted as Locke's, or a literary output as varied and influential as his? It is scarcely possible to imagine a similar figure emerging in present-day Western society, where most politicians and philosophers are career professionals narrowly focused on their own spheres of activity, whether by choice or by economic and institutional necessity. From relatively humble beginnings, he rose to be one of the foremost European philosophers of his time and the close confidant and adviser of some of England's leading politicians. His writings on epistemology, metaphysics and political theory have been of lasting significance, changing the course of European thought and justly earning him the title of England's greatest philosopher. He was the first Western philosopher in modern times to focus his inquiries on the structure and formation of the human mind in order to gain insight into the objects and extent of human knowledge. The subsequent projects of David Hume in the *Treatise of Human Nature* and Immanuel Kant (1724–1804) in the *Critique of Pure Reason* would, very arguably, have been unthinkable without the precedent set by Locke's great masterpiece, *An Essay Concerning Human Understanding*.

FURTHER READING

Ayers, Michael 1991: *Locke* (London & New York: Routledge).

Chappell, Vere (ed.) 1994: *The Cambridge Companion to Locke* (Cambridge: Cambridge University Press).

Chappell, Vere (ed.) 1998: *Locke* (Oxford: Oxford University Press).

Cranston, Maurice 1957: *John Locke: A Biography* (London: Longman).

Fuller, Gary, Stecker, Robert and Wright, John P. (eds) 2000: *John Locke: An Essay Concerning Human Understanding in Focus* (London & New York: Routledge).

Hall, Roland (ed.) 1970–2000: *The Locke Newsletter*.

Hall, Roland (ed.), 2000–: *Locke Studies*.

Hall, Roland & Woolhouse, Roger 1983: *Eighty Years of Locke Scholarship* (Edinburgh: Edinburgh University Press).

Harris, Ian 1998: *The Mind of John Locke*, revised edn (Cambridge: Cambridge University Press).

Jolley, Nicholas 1999: *Locke: His Philosophical Thought* (Oxford: Oxford University Press).

Lowe, E. J. 1995: *Locke on Human Understanding* (London & New York: Routledge).

Rogers, G. A. J. (ed.) 1994: *Locke's Philosophy: Content and Context* (Oxford: Clarendon Press).

Stewart, M. A. (ed.) 2000: *English Philosophy in the Age of Locke* (Oxford: Clarendon Press).

Yolton, John W. 1956: *John Locke and the Way of Ideas* (Oxford: Clarendon Press).

Yolton, John W. (ed.) 1969: *John Locke: Problems and Perspectives* (Cambridge: Cambridge University Press).

Two

Knowledge and Experience

Locke is customarily classified as an 'empiricist' philosopher and, while this label – like all philosophical labels – carries with it the danger of distortion, it does serve to characterize an important aspect of his theory of knowledge or epistemology. Locke held that all of the 'materials' – as he put it – of human knowledge and understanding arise from experience, in the form of what he calls 'ideas'. In maintaining this, he aligned himself with some of the leading experimental scientists of his day and firmly against a dominant philosophical doctrine of the time, the doctrine of innate ideas. According to this doctrine, certain fundamental components of human knowledge are inborn rather than acquired by processes of observation, learning and reasoning – inborn because they are part of the very frame of the human mind as God designed it. In virtue of their supposedly divine source, these components of human knowledge were not to be questioned or doubted, in the view of upholders of the doctrine – many of whom had vested interests of a religious or political character which could, by this device, be placed beyond the scope of publicly acceptable criticism. Locke's fierce opposition to the doctrine of innate ideas was undoubtedly motivated, at least in part, by his hatred for the cloak that it provided for obscurantist and authoritarian dogmas. More importantly, however, it stimulated him to inquire into the mechanisms by which human knowledge is in fact generated, thereby giving rise, in the shape of his *Essay Concerning Human Understanding*, to the first sustained and systematic account of human cognitive psychology composed in modern times. After explaining and evaluating Locke's philosophical objections to the doctrine of innate ideas, I shall try to capture and evaluate the central features of his positive epistemological project in the *Essay*.

LOCKE'S REJECTION OF INNATE IDEAS

According to the doctrine of innate ideas, as it was widely understood and endorsed in the seventeenth century, God 'imprints' on the human soul at the very beginning of its existence some fundamental ideas of a logical, metaphysical and moral nature – including the idea of himself – in virtue of which human beings are able to have certain knowledge of God's existence, his moral law and many features of his created world. But Locke was a devoted Christian with a firm belief in God's existence. Why, then, was he so hostile to the doctrine of innate ideas? One reason is that he was convinced that the great experimental scientists of his day – men like Isaac Newton, Robert Boyle, Robert Hooke and Christiaan Huygens – had developed by far the most fruitful method of discovering truths about the natural world, namely, the method of systematic observation and experimentation. The early members of the Royal Society had, by the time of Locke's *Essay*, already made considerable headway in unlocking nature's secrets by just such careful empirical investigation. Newton, the greatest mathematician and scientist of the age, explicitly recognized the need for mathematical theories of nature to be answerable to observational evidence and experimental confirmation. Locke saw his own role as a philosopher as that of a mere 'under-labourer', clearing the way for scientists like Newton to uncover the workings of the natural world by empirical means and to formulate general mathematical principles for predicting natural phenomena in reliable ways (see the opening 'Epistle to the Reader' in the *Essay*). He had no faith in Descartes's ambition to provide an a priori metaphysical foundation for natural science.

Another reason for Locke's hostility to the doctrine of innate ideas was the threat that he saw in it to freedom of thought and inquiry, not only in science but also in matters of morality, religion and politics. In contrast to Descartes, who kept his political and religious opinions to himself, Locke was a champion of individual liberty and rights at a time when these were – at least in England – beginning to prosper, even if still rather precariously. Absolute monarchy in the shape of the Stuarts had received a rebuff during the Civil War, only to be revived in a milder form with the Restoration in 1660. Locke was on the victorious side when the last Stuart king was finally removed in 1688–9 with the so-called Glorious Revolution, but the future of political and religious liberty still hung in the balance. He was acutely aware that the docrine of innate ideas is liable to be exploited by conservative and reactionary forces, because it is only too easy to appeal to supposedly God-given principles of morality and religion in order to silence challenges to prevailing authority and vested interests. This potential of the doctrine for abuse by illiberal forces undoubtedly weighed heavily with Locke in determining him to oppose it.

Locke's main aim in the Essay is to explain and vindicate empiricism, by showing how all of the 'materials' of human thought and knowledge can have their origin in experience – by which he means not only sensory experience, but also the kind of introspective experience that we enjoy through what he calls reflection on 'the internal Operations of our Minds' (Essay, II, I, 2). According to Locke, then, it is ultimately to experience alone that we owe all of our ideas, none of which is consequently innate. It is these ideas of sensation and reflection that he is referring to when he speaks of the 'materials' of our thought and knowledge.

But what, exactly, does Locke mean by the term 'idea'? Locke himself defines an idea as being 'Whatsoever the Mind perceives in itself, or is the immediate object of Perception, Thought or Understanding' (Essay, II, VIII, 8). This definition may leave the present-day reader rather puzzled, partly because the word 'idea' – which was ubiquitous in philosophical writings in the seventeenth and eighteenth centuries – has now entirely dropped out of use as a technical philosophical term. Perhaps the nearest that we have to it in current philosophical usage is the word 'concept'. It may strike us as odd to speak of the mind as *perceiving* concepts, as Locke speaks of it as perceiving ideas – but this is because the word 'perceive' has also undergone a considerable change of meaning since Locke's day, at least as philosophers and psychologists understand it. We now prefer to speak of people 'understanding' or 'grasping' concepts. Another problem is that Locke uses the word 'idea' not only in contexts in which today's philosophers would speak of 'concepts', but also in other contexts in which they would prefer to use instead a word such as 'percept'. Thus, the word 'idea' in Locke's usage is meant to denote something which can on the one hand be an ingredient or component of a *thought*, but which can on the other hand equally well be an ingredient or component of a sensory or introspective *experience*. Indeed, that ideas can play both of these roles is crucial to Locke's empiricist thesis that all of the 'materials' of our thought originate in experience.

I shall return to the question of what Locke takes ideas to be later in this chapter, but it is now time to look at his arguments against the doctrine that at least some of our ideas are innate, rather than having an origin solely in experience. First, some preliminary distinctions need to be made concerning the views that Locke was attacking. Although loosely an attack on the doctrine of innate ideas, Locke's onslaught is mainly aimed against supposedly innate *principles* and only secondarily against innate ideas or 'notions', as he also calls them. A principle is something propositional in form, as Locke makes clear by two of his favourite examples – 'those magnified Principles of Demonstration, *Whatsoever is, is;* and *'Tis impossible for the same thing to be, and not to be*' (*Essay*, I, II, 4), which would nowadays be called, respectively, the law of identity and the law of non-contradiction. By contrast, an idea, notion, or concept is only an ingredient or component of a proposition – such as the concept of identity, which figures in both of those laws and is commonly expressed by the word 'same'.

Another distinction deserving some comment is the one that Locke draws between *speculative* and *practical* principles. The former are logical and metaphysical principles – like the two already cited – whereas the latter concern morality, that is, our duties to each other and to God. Our attention in what follows will be focused on the former, although it is clear that in terms of the danger to freedom posed by innatist doctrines, innatism regarding the principles of morality, politics and religion must have been of more urgent concern to Locke.

For all his confident rhetoric and heavy sarcasm, Locke's explicit arguments against innatism are not quite as compelling as he seems to think they are, even if they do carry considerable weight. These arguments focus on the issue of 'universal assent' – or, as he also sometimes calls it, 'universal consent'. Locke seems to presume three things. First, that the proponents of innate principles believe that these principles are universally assented to by all mankind, without exception. Second, that such universal assent is supposed by them to provide clear proof of the innate status of the principles in question. And third, that there is no other sort of evidence that is or could be offered in support of the innateness of any principle. In characterizing his opponents' position in this somewhat restricted and uncharitable way, Locke is perhaps already guilty of setting up something of a straw man as his target.

For example, Locke remarks at one point that '[Even] if it were true in matter of Fact, that there were certain Truths, wherein all Mankind agreed, it would not prove them innate, if there can be any other way shewn, how Men may come to that Universal Agreement' (*Essay*, I, II, 3). Here Locke rather unfairly assumes that innatism must be an explanation of the last resort, inherently inferior to any credible alternative explanation – including, of course, his own empiricist alternative. Even more problematically, Locke contends that the innatist's argument from universal assent may actually be inverted, so as to generate an incontrovertible argument *against* innatism. Confident – for reasons which I shall come to shortly – that there are in fact no principles which receive universal assent, Locke claims that this, in conjunction with the argument from universal assent, demonstrates that there are after all no innate principles: '[T]his Argument of Universal Consent, which is made use of, to prove innate Principles, seems to me a Demonstration that there are none such: Because there are none to which all Mankind give an Universal Assent' (*Essay*, I, II, 4). But what Locke really needs to secure his conclusion here is something to which innatists need not necessarily be committed – although Locke himself explicitly assumes that they are – namely, that 'universal Assent . . . must needs be the necessary concomitant of all innate Truths' (*Essay*, I, II, 5). This is certainly not something that is implied by the innatist's argument from universal assent, even if Locke is correct in supposing that the innatists of his day assumed it to be the case. For, from the supposition that if a truth is universally assented to, it is therefore innate, it does not follow that if a truth is innate, it is therefore universally assented to. So Locke is at best misleading in his assertion that the 'Argument of Universal Consent . . . to prove innate Principles . . . [is] a Demonstration that there are none such' (cf. Lowe 1995, pp. 24–5).

Commenting on this criticism of Locke, Halla Kim correctly notes in a recent paper that Locke assumes, on behalf of the innatist, that any innate truth would have to be universally assented to and that, in conjunction with Locke's own claim that there are no truths that are universally assented to, this implies that there are no innate truths (Kim 2003, pp. 23–4). I have no quarrel with either Locke or Kim on this score, beyond pointing out, as I did a moment ago, that innatists need not in fact accept the assumption that Locke imputes to them. My criticism of Locke is that he mistakenly supposes that the argument from universal assent *itself* can be turned into a demonstration that there are no innate truths, once it is established that no truths are universally assented to. For Locke quite explicitly takes the argument, as advanced by innatists, to be this:

> that there are certain Principles both *Speculative* and *Practical* . . . universally agreed upon by all Mankind: which therefore they argue, must needs be constant Impressions, which the Souls of Men receive in their first Beings, and which they bring into the World with them.
>
> (*Essay*, I, II, 2)

It is this argument that Locke immediately goes on to call 'This Argument, drawn from *Universal Consent*' (*Essay*, I, II, 3) and 'this Argument of Universal Consent' (*Essay*, I, II, 4). And the argument, it is clear, employs only the assumption that if a truth is universally assented to, then it is innate – *not* the other assumption that Locke imputes to the innatist, that if a truth is innate, then it is universally assented to. Kim maintains that *both* assumptions are implicated in what Locke calls 'the Argument of Universal Consent' (Kim 2003, p. 19), but this seems to me quite unwarranted by the text of the *Essay*.

However, we have still to address the crucial question of whether or not any principles *are* in fact universally assented to. Against this claim, Locke makes the preliminary observation (*Essay*, I, II, 5) that ' 'tis evident, that all *Children*, and *Ideots*, have not the least Apprehension or Thought of' the principles claimed to be innate – principles such as the law of identity and the law of non-contradiction. This remark is not, however, immediately compelling, because 'assent' need not always be explicit. Indeed, as we shall see in Chapter 6, in his *Second Treatise of Government* Locke himself makes extensive use of the notion of *tacit* consent. All that is 'evident', perhaps, is that children and 'idiots' do not *expressly affirm* the principles in question. But that is not enough to show that they do not in any way apprehend – and in that sense, 'assent to' – those principles. All that Locke has to offer in response to this suggestion is the rather blustering comment that it seems to him 'near a Contradiction, to say, that there are Truths imprinted on the Soul, which it perceives or understands not' (*Essay*, I, II, 5). But what he *needs* to argue at this stage is, rather, that the soul – in particular, that of a child or an idiot – cannot perceive or understand a truth which it is incapable of expressly assenting to.

It is, of course, incumbent upon the innatist to say what sort of evidence would point to a child's 'tacit' assent to, for example, the law of non-contradiction. One proposal which Locke considers is that evidence of this is provided by the fact that young people *do* eventually give express assent to such a law, when asked, *upon attaining the use of reason*. But he makes light work of dismissing this suggestion as vacuous, on the grounds that no distinction could then be made between supposedly innate principles and a host of other obvious truths – such as that white is not black – to which immediate assent will also be expressly given by a child who has reached a sufficient age. It is worth remarking that Locke's presumption here seems to be that very young infants do *not* in fact engage in reasoning. But this too seems questionable. For, again, we should not confuse the possession of an intellectual capacity with an ability to exhibit it verbally.

Locke purports to offer another challenge to the innatist when he claims that 'No proposition can be said to be in the Mind, which it never yet knew, which it was never yet conscious of' (*Essay*, I, II, 5). Clearly, Locke is here allowing that we do not need to be *presently* conscious of every proposition that is in some sense 'in' our mind. Some truths of which we are not presently conscious we can 'call to mind', because they are stored in our memory. But, according to Locke, we must have been conscious of them at *some* past time in order for them to have been 'stored' in the first place. However, this seems to presuppose the truth of empiricism and so is question-begging from the innatist's point of view. Why should the *only* way for a truth to be stored in my mind be the one that Locke allows – namely, by being deposited in my memory following an episode in which I first become consciously aware of it?

Even so, there is an important lesson that can be drawn from Locke's critique of innatism. This is that it will not be enough for the innatist simply to say that a proposition can be innately 'in' the mind in virtue of the mind's having a *capacity* to understand it. For, as Locke remarks, by that standard, 'all Propositions that are true, and the Mind is capable ever of assenting to, may be said to be in the Mind' (*Essay*, I, II, 5), rendering the innatist's thesis trivial. This may be seen as Locke's reply to those of his contemporaries, like Descartes, who thought of innate knowledge as somehow being a *latent* or *dormant* state requiring only the mind's maturation and exposure to appropriate experience for its release or activation. Descartes, in his *Comments on a Certain Broadsheet* (Descartes 1984), suggests the analogy of a congenital disease, present from birth, whose symptoms emerge only later in life. Leibniz offers instead the analogy of a block of marble in which a yet-to-be-formed statue is prefigured by faults and veins in the stone. However, the trouble with both of these models of innate knowledge is that they fail adequately to distinguish between the presence of an innate *capacity* for knowledge – which Locke by no means wishes to deny – and the presence of *actual* knowledge in the mind of an infant from birth. Only the latter properly deserves to be called innate knowledge, Locke would claim.

Here it may be objected that Locke's complaint does not really work against Leibniz – who was, it should be noted, writing in direct response to Locke, in the *New Essays on Human Understanding*, his commentary on Locke's *Essay*. This is what Leibniz himself says:

> I have also used the analogy of a veined block of marble, as opposed to an entirely homogeneous block of marble, or to a blank tablet – what the philosophers call a *tabula rasa*. For if the soul were like such a blank tablet then truths would be in us as the shape of Hercules is in a piece of marble when the marble is entirely neutral as to whether it assumes this shape or some other. However, if there were veins in the block which marked out the shape of

Hercules rather than other shapes, then that block would be more
determined to that shape and Hercules would be innate in it, in a
way, even though labour would be required to expose the veins . . .
This is how ideas and truths are innate in us – as inclinations,
dispositions, tendencies, or natural potentialities, and not as
actions.

(Leibniz 1981, p. 52)

But it may be urged that when Locke complains that, in a merely
dispositional sense, 'all Propositions that are true, and the Mind is
capable ever of assenting to, may be said to be in the Mind', he is
unfairly conflating two different notions of dispositionality or capacity – two notions between which Leibniz himself distinguishes in
the quoted passage, as Alexander Miller has remarked (Miller 1995,
p. 144). In a weak sense, the unveined block of marble is disposed
to take on the form of Hercules, but is equally disposed to take on
any other form – whereas in a stronger sense, only the veined block
is disposed to take on the form of Hercules in *preference* to any other
form. And what Leibniz is suggesting is that certain ideas and principles are 'in' the mind from birth in the *stronger* dispositional sense,
not merely in the trivial weaker sense. However, Locke himself is
not in fact implying that the mind is infinitely malleable with
respect to the truths that it is capable of assenting to. He would
readily acknowledge that our capacities for intuition and reason
equip us to recognize some truths more easily than others, as we
shall see later. He would object, I think, to Leibniz's example by
saying that the mind of a newborn infant no more actually *contains*
knowledge already, in virtue of its inborn cognitive capacities, than
the veined block of marble already *contains* a statue in virtue of the
pattern of veins in it. Those cognitive capacities, he would say, are
precisely capacities to *acquire* knowledge – and what needs to be
acquired is not already possessed.

Although Locke's arguments against innate ideas and principles
are perhaps not entirely compelling, it is nonetheless incumbent

upon his opponents to explain in what sense such ideas and principles may be said to be 'in' the mind of a person even at a time
when that person is incapable of giving explicit expression to them.
It is likewise necessary for these opponents to tell us what sort of
evidence supports their view and why it does. If nothing else,
Locke's critique of innatism presents its adherents with some
important challenges and it seems fair to say that the sort of
innatism that was widely taken for granted in his day did not
already contain the resources with which to answer those challenges. At the very least, we may say, present-day advocates of
innatism have benefited by having to face up to certain difficulties
threatening it which Locke was the first person to see clearly. I shall
briefly return to this topic in Chapter 7.

LOCKE'S VERSION OF EMPIRICISM

I now need to say something about the view that Locke wants to put
in place of the doctrine of innate ideas – a view that we may go on
calling, for want of a better word, 'empiricism'. But first we must
return to Locke's use of the word 'idea', for a correct understanding
of this is crucial to a proper appreciation of his position.

We saw earlier that when Locke defines an idea as 'Whatsoever
the Mind perceives in itself, or is the immediate object of Perception, Thought or Understanding' (Essay, II, VIII, 8), he may seem to
be running together two quite distinct types of mental phenomena
– percepts and concepts. When we enjoy sensory experiences of our
physical environment – for instance, when we open our eyes and
look at surrounding objects – we are conscious of being subject to
states of perceptual awareness with distinctive qualitative features.
For example, when a normally sighted person sees a pair of apples
in ordinary daylight, one of them red and the other green, he or she
will enjoy certain characteristic features of colour experience
which will be absent from the perceptual experience of a colour-
blind person in the same circumstances. Locke seems at least sometimes to be using the term 'idea' to refer to such experiential

features. However, he also uses the term at times to refer to what we would now call *concepts*, that is, the meaningful components of thoughts that we may entertain about the world and attempt to communicate to one another in language – such as the thought that this apple is red and that one green. But, as I also indicated earlier, it would be unfair simply to accuse Locke of a confusion between percepts and concepts, because it is part of Locke's very project in the *Essay* to forge a link between our conceptual resources and features of our perceptual experience. The dual role played by ideas in Locke's kind of empiricism is essential to this project.

Many present-day philosophers, it must be said, regard this aspect of Lockean empiricism as utterly untenable for various reasons. One is that such philosophers are often dubious about the epistemological status or even the very existence of sensory features in perceptual experience and therefore regard ideas in this sense as an unpromising starting-point for the philosophy of perception and the theory of knowledge. Another reason is that they consider it a naive mistake to regard concepts as introspectible mental phenomena which are the materials or ingredients of thought. Rather, they hold, concepts are better understood as sets of interrelated cognitive *abilities* – for instance, abilities to discriminate between and recognize features of our physical and social environments, together with linguistic abilities to deploy certain words appropriately in successful interpersonal communication concerning such features. To know the meaning of a word, on this model, is not to be privately acquainted with some Lockean idea: rather, it is knowing how to *use* the word correctly according to intersubjective standards of public communication. My own opinion is that, when it is properly understood, there is more to be said for Locke's view than these present-day critics allow, as I shall explain in Chapter 4. For the time being, however, I shall set aside the worries of such critics and fall in with Locke's own usage of the word 'idea'.

Even setting aside such worries, however, there is another issue that we need to confront here. This is the question of what precisely

Locke means by describing ideas as being the 'immediate objects' of mental processes – both what he understands by 'immediacy' and what he intends by 'object' in this context. In calling ideas *objects*, should he be construed as regarding them as mental *images* – as mental 'pictures', so to speak, available for scrutiny by the mind's 'inner eye'? Again, in speaking of ideas as *immediate* objects, is he implying that our perception of other, 'external' objects is *mediated by* our perception of ideas, which thus constitute some sort of screen or veil between us and those other objects? And if so, does Locke's view harbour sceptical problems which serve to promote the cause of idealism? My answer will be that Locke need not necessarily be interpreted as regarding ideas as images, but that in any case this issue has no real bearing on the problem of scepticism, which arises equally for the so-called 'direct realist'.

We are now in a position to characterize Locke's particular version of empiricism more clearly. Locke's empiricism is at once *atomistic* and *constructivist* in character. In calling it 'atomistic', I mean that Locke regards ideas as falling into two classes, *simple* and *complex*, with complex ideas being analysable into simple components. For instance, the idea of a perceptible quality like redness is, for Locke, simple: our idea of redness cannot be analysed into any simpler elements – unlike, for example, our idea of a horse, which can. In calling Locke's doctrine 'constructivist', I mean this: while he holds that all of our ideas ultimately derive from experience, he doesn't hold that in order to possess a given complex idea we must actually have enjoyed a corresponding experience, since he thinks it suffices for us to have enjoyed experiences involving the various simple ideas into which that complex idea is analysable. Thus, he would say, we can possess the idea of a unicorn despite never having perceived such a creature, because it is analysable in terms of simpler ideas – those of a horse and a horn – which have either featured in our experience themselves or else are further analysable in terms of other ideas which have.

In the course of the *Essay*, Locke attempts to make good his claim to provide an alternative to innatism by analysing some of the key ideas – like those of *substance* and *causal power* – which innatists held to be innate and endeavouring to show how their simple ingredients might be acquired from experience and then put together by the mind. I shall be examining his proposed analyses of some of these ideas in later chapters of this book, partly with a view to evaluating how far Locke succeeded in achieving the empiricist goals that he set himself.

LOCKE'S THEORY OF SENSE PERCEPTION

We have just seen that at least sometimes Locke uses the word 'idea' to refer to what might nowadays be called *percepts*, conceived as being repeatable and recombinable sensory elements or ingredients of our perceptual experiences. Certainly, he considers that ideas are intimately involved in the processes of sense perception whereby we see, hear, smell, taste and feel physical objects in our environment and thereby come to acquire perceptual knowledge of their properties and relations. By no means all present-day philosophers and psychologists would agree with Locke about this. According to one school of thought, perceiving an object – for example, seeing a green apple – is not really a *sensory* activity at all, in the way that feeling pain or warmth is. Perception is instead considered just to be a special way of acquiring beliefs about one's physical environment. And while beliefs must indeed have meaningful propositional contents – and thus involve 'ideas' in the sense of *concepts* – there is, according to this view, no reason to suppose that any sort of sensory element is literally involved in perception. My own sympathies lie with Locke in this matter and, certainly, his theory of perception cannot be usefully discussed if one simply dismisses as completely mistaken this fundamental feature of it. According to Locke, whenever I perceive a physical object, such as an apple, I do so by having a perceptual experience which contains ideas of certain of that object's qualities, such as its greenness and roundness.

Another very important feature of Locke's theory of perception is that it is a *causal* theory. Ideas, he says, are 'produced in us . . . *by the operation of insensible particles on our Senses*' (*Essay*, II, VIII, 13). In the case of sight, these will be particles of light – photons, as physicists now call them – impinging upon the retinas of our eyes, thereby giving rise to activity in our optic nerves and subsequently in certain parts of our brain. What happens then – the production of 'ideas' in the mind – is, Locke concedes, something of a mystery, but one no greater than the mystery of how damage to a limb can give rise to a sensation of pain, with its subjective quality of intense unpleasantness.

Locke's advocacy of this sort of causal theory may appear to commit him to a denial of what is known as 'direct' realism – the view that the 'immediate' objects of perception are ordinary physical objects like apples, trees and rocks. But whether we can really say that depends on what we take to be his view of the nature of ideas – in particular, whether or not we take him to regard them as being mental 'images'. We shall see shortly that in this respect Locke's theory is in fact open to more than one interpretation. The issue is closely connected to one concerning Locke's conception of the relationship between perceptual experience and perceptual judgement. Consider the following passage:

> When we set before our Eyes a round Globe, of any uniform colour . . . 'tis certain, that the *Idea* thereby imprinted in our Mind, is of a Circle variously shadow'd, with several degrees of Lightness and Brightness coming to our Eyes. But we having by use been accustomed to perceive, what kind of appearance convex Bodies are wont to make in us . . . the Judgment presently, by an habitual custom, alters the Appearances into their Causes: So that from that, which truly is variety of shadow or colour . . . it makes pass for a mark of Figure, and frames to itself the perception of a convex Figure, and an uniform Colour; when the *Idea* we receive from thence, is only a Plain variously colour'd, as is evident in Painting.
>
> (*Essay*, II, IX, 8)

Here Locke appears to suggest that when we form a perceptual judgement concerning the properties of some perceived object, that judgement imposes an interpretation upon the ideas of sense produced in us by the object, very much in the way in which interpretation is involved in judging what properties objects are depicted as possessing in a painted scene. But how literally we should take this parallel will again depend upon what exactly we take Locke's conception of the nature of ideas to be. On the most simple-minded reading of the text, we might take him to be saying that ideas simply *are* mental 'pictures' or 'images', which we scrutinize inwardly and interpret in various ways. But, as I shall indicate later, other readings may also be available, which make Locke's view seem less problematic.

It may be tempting to suppose, in the light of passages like the one just quoted, that Locke and other seventeenth-century philosophers conceived of visual 'ideas' as inner, mental analogues of the retinal images formed by light rays at the back of our eyes. In Locke's day, the existence of such retinal images was a comparatively recent and surprising discovery. However, I believe that it is unduly simplistic to think of seventeenth-century philosophers as being drawn into an 'imagist' theory of perception by their supposed misconception of the role of retinal images in visual perception. In any case, while imagist theories may indeed be open to criticism, they are not – as we shall shortly see – as blatantly untenable and confused as some of their present-day critics have claimed them to be.

It is worth remarking, incidentally, that the passage just quoted above from the *Essay* immediately precedes Locke's answer to a famous question put to him by one of his many correspondents, the Irishman William Molyneux (1656–98). Molyneux had written to Locke asking him whether he thought that a man born blind but recently made able to see could, by sight alone, distinguish between a sphere and a cube, having previously been able to distinguish them only by touch. Having reported the question, Locke continues:

To which the acute and and judicious Proposer answers: *Not. For
though he has obtain'd the experience of, how a Globe, how a Cube
affects his touch; yet he has not yet attained the Experience, that
what affects his touch so or so, must affect his sight so or so; Or that
a protuberant angle in the Cube, that pressed his hand unequally,
shall appear to his eye, as it does in the Cube.* I agree with this
thinking Gent. whom I am proud to call my Friend, in his answer to
this his Problem.

(Essay, II, IX, 8)

If most people who have not reflected much on the question find
Molyneux's answer counterintuitive, Locke suggests that this is
merely indicative of the fact that the unreflective person is typically
unaware 'how much he may be beholding to experience,
improvement, and acquired notions, where he thinks, he has not
the least use, or help from them' (Essay, II, IX, 8). Thus Locke
ingeniously exploits the example to provide further support for his
empiricist epistemology.

WAS LOCKE AN INDIRECT REALIST?

I want now to return to the important question of whether Locke
conceived of ideas as mental *images*. According to one long-standing
tradition of Locke commentary – one which, perhaps, even
deserves to be called the 'orthodox interpretation' – Locke may
indeed be regarded as assuming an imagist conception of the role
of ideas in sense perception. On this interpretation, Locke holds
something like the following view. When I perceive an object –
such as a round, green apple – I do so in virtue of the fact that the
presence of the object causes me to experience a mental image,
certain parts or aspects of which represent corresponding properties of the object in question, such as the round shape and green
colour of an apple. Some of these aspects of the image represent
corresponding properties of the object because they actually *resemble*
them: for example, the *shape* of my mental image of the apple is

supposed to resemble, albeit perhaps only imperfectly, the shape of the apple. Properties represented in this way may be classified as *primary qualities*. But other aspects of the image represent corresponding properties of the object only because they are *regular concomitants* of such properties – that is to say, because the presence of an object possessing a given property regularly causes me to experience an image having a certain distinctive aspect. Supposedly, the *colour* of my mental image represents the 'colour' of an apple only in this way, rather by resembling it – and such properties of an object may be classified as *secondary qualities*. I shall return later to this distinction between primary and secondary qualities, for although Locke certainly endorses such a distinction, his understanding of its precise nature is as open to interpretation as is his theory of perception in general.

In calling ideas 'mental images', an advocate of this 'orthodox' interpretation of Locke's theory of perception is supposing that he takes them to be mental *objects* of a special kind, with perceptible properties of their own – just as an ordinary physical image, such as an oil painting of a landscape, is an object with perceptible properties of its own, which serve to represent various properties of the objects that it depicts. So, according to this interpretation, Locke holds that we literally *see* our visual ideas and, moreover, see them to possess various visible properties of colour and shape which serve to represent corresponding properties in the physical objects that we see – so-called 'external' objects such as apples, trees and rocks. Consequently, Locke is interpreted as holding an 'indirect realist' or 'representative' theory of perception, because he is taken to believe that we perceive external objects only 'indirectly', by perceiving 'internal' mental images which represent those objects.

Having set up Locke in this fashion, many critics then proceed to knock him down gleefully, pointing out all of the supposed absurdities and difficulties of the theory which they have attributed to him. Let us briefly consider what some of these alleged problems are and whether they really are unanswerable, before we discuss whether or not Locke did actually hold such a theory.

First of all, it may be protested that in saying, for instance, that one *sees* a tree by *seeing* a visual image of a tree, one has at best left the notion of seeing entirely unexplained and at worst embarked upon a vicious infinite regress. For if one needs to see a visual image in order to see a tree, does one not equally need to see *another* visual image in order to see the first one, and so on *ad infinitum*? I think not, for this is no better than arguing that if a surgeon needs to see television images in order to see what is happening inside someone's stomach, then he needs to see yet *other* television images in order to see the first ones. The crucial point here is that the circumstance that makes it necessary for the surgeon to look at television images in order to see certain events – namely, that these events are going on deep inside someone's body – does not apply to the television images themselves: for they are *not*, of course, located deep inside someone's body. The 'imagist' must, in all charity, be construed as taking a comparable view of the relevant differences between mental images and 'external' objects. He believes that there are reasons for supposing that 'external' objects cannot be seen 'directly', reasons that do not arise in the case of visual images themselves – though how *good* those reasons are is, of course, another matter. As for the complaint that this still leaves the notion of seeing entirely unexplained, it may be retorted that what has been left unexplained is in fact only the notion of *direct* seeing – and that this is a notion that stands in need of no 'explanation' in the sense in which the notion of 'indirect' seeing may plausibly be held to. Some notions, after all, must surely be explanatorily basic, and perhaps the notion of direct seeing has as good a claim to this status as any notion does. In any case, even if it is conceded that it is a failing to leave the notion of direct seeing unexplained, it may be urged that to explain the notion of *indirect* seeing – the sort of seeing that is supposedly involved in seeing 'external' objects such as trees – by appeal to the notion of direct seeing is still by no means vacuous and is certainly not simply circular.

There are other apparent problems for indirect realism. One difficulty that is often raised concerns the nature of the causal processes supposedly leading to the production of mental images in our minds. How, it may be asked, can a physical process – such as what Locke describes as 'the operation of insensible particles' – give rise to something so apparently different in kind as a mental image? Locke himself seems to concede that there is an element of mystery in this, though he also remarks (*Essay*, II, VIII, 13) that there is no reason why God should not have so ordered things that ideas are 'annexed' to certain physical operations in a systematic way. The mention of God here may make this look like a questionable appeal to a supernatural element in our make-up. But it could instead be seen as amounting to nothing more than a concession that certain aspects of human psychophysiology have to be accepted as 'brute facts', not susceptible to further explanation in physical terms. And this, very arguably, is not something that indirect realists are alone in having to concede.

By far the most serious charge that is commonly levelled against indirect realism, however, is that it is supposed to give rise to scepticism, by interposing a 'veil' of ideas between us and 'external' objects – so that instead of providing an account of how we can come to know the properties of those objects through perception, it actually implies that we *cannot* know them. If such objects are related to us merely as external *causes* of our ideas, it is complained, what reason can we have to suppose anything definite about the nature of those objects? In particular, how can we know that any of their properties really do *resemble* any properties of our ideas? Indeed, is it even intelligible to suppose that terms descriptive of ideas should also be applicable, in the very same sense, to objects supposedly so different in kind from ideas – for instance, that both a visual image and an external object could be 'square', in the very same sense of the word?

Now, I concede that this question about 'resemblance' is a difficult one for an indirect realist to handle satisfactorily. But the more general complaint that has just been raised – that indirect realism is especially conducive to scepticism – seems to me to be an exaggerated one. For it seems to me that *any* sort of 'realist' theory of perception – whether it be 'direct' or 'indirect' – is open to exploitation by a sufficiently ingenious sceptic. This is simply because any such theory must acknowledge that it is possible for our perceptual judgements to be mistaken. That is to say, any such theory must allow that it is possible for one to judge, quite sincerely, that one is perceiving an 'external' object of a certain kind and yet for that judgement to be false, perhaps because one is subject to some sort of perceptual illusion. The sceptic typically exploits this fact to try to persuade us that we might *always* be mistaken in our perceptual judgements. But it is not clear that the 'direct' realist is really any better equipped than the 'indirect' realist to resist this sort of sceptical move.

As I have already implied, the interpretation of Locke as being an 'indirect realist', or as assuming an 'imagist' conception of the role of ideas in sense perception, is not incontestable. It is arguable that he was a 'direct' realist of sorts, or at least that he did not commit himself definitely one way or the other over the question of whether we perceive physical objects 'directly'. One leading Locke scholar who seems to regard Locke as being, if anything, a direct realist is John Yolton, who contends that, for Locke,

> The way of ideas is Locke's method of recognising the mental features of seeing. It does not place the perceiver in some vale of ideas forever trying to break out into the world of physical objects.
>
> (Yolton 1970, p. 132)

Yolton goes on to remark, 'I see no evidence in the *Essay* that Locke thought of ideas as entities' (Yolton 1970, p. 134).

But what are we to suppose that Locke *did* think of ideas as being, if not mental 'entities' of a special kind – and, more specifically, mental images? There are at least two possible alternatives – and, indeed, these alternatives may not be mutually exclusive, as we shall shortly see. One is that when Locke talks of 'ideas' as being involved in processes of sense perception, he is simply talking about the various different *ways* in which physical objects affect us sensorily when we perceive them by means of our senses. So, for example, the way in which a red object typically affects me sensorily is different from the way in which a green object typically affects me, when I see both of them in normal lighting conditions. We might express this by saying that the red object affects me in the 'red' sort of way whereas the green object affects me in the 'green' sort of way – and that this is all that Locke means when he says that I experience an 'idea of red' in the one case and an 'idea of green' in the other. On this interpretation, he is not implying that these 'ideas' are themselves objects of any kind that I am seeing, with visible properties of their own which somehow correspond to the colour properties of physical objects. That being so, we can construe Locke as taking physical objects themselves to be the 'direct' objects of sense perception, because we are no longer taking him to suppose that we perceive those objects by means of perceiving other objects of a special kind, as the imagist account maintains. We are, of course, still regarding Locke as holding that, in order for us to perceive a physical object by means of our senses, that object has to affect us sensorily in some way – and, moreover, in a way of which we are conscious at the time – but that seems a perfectly sensible thing to say and, as Yolton remarks, does not seem to imply that we are somehow screened off by our ideas from physical objects. Even so, it must be confessed that this proposal is a little vague as it stands, because it has yet to be explained what exactly is to be understood by a 'way of being sensorily affected'. That is why I allowed, a moment ago, that this proposal may be compatible with a second possibility that I am about to describe.

The second possibility is that, in talking of 'ideas' as being involved in sense perception, Locke is adverting to the fact that when one perceives an object, one must perceive it 'as' an object of some kind, or at least 'as' possessing certain properties. So, for example, if I see a green apple, I may see it *as* an apple and *as* being green – but even if I do not, because I don't recognize it for the kind of object that it is, or suffer from red–green colour blindness, it seems that I must still see it as a thing of *some* kind and as possessing *some* property or other. For instance, I might just see it as a round piece of fruit. On this interpretation of Locke's use of the term 'idea' in his account of sense perception, to talk about the 'ideas' I have of a given object when I perceive it is to talk about what sort of thing I perceive the object as being and what properties I perceive it as possessing. Some present-day philosophers use the terms 'aspect' and 'aspectual' to capture this dimension of sense perception, particularly in the context of the perception of ambiguous figures, such as Ludwig Wittgenstein's famous 'duck-rabbit' figure (Wittgenstein 1958, p. 194), or the Necker cube diagram, which can be seen either as a cube tilted upwards or as a cube tilted downwards. When I see the cube as tilted upwards, I see it under one 'aspect', and when I see it as tilted downwards, I see it under another. Moreover, which aspect I see it under is not really subject to my voluntary control, although I can sometimes trigger a so-called 'Gestalt-switch' by focusing on a particular vertex of the cube. Because the aspects under which I perceive things are not subject to my voluntary control, they would appear to be dictated by the mechanisms of sense perception itself, rather than being determined by higher-level cognitive operations such as thought or judgement. And this is why it may seem appropriate to interpret Lockean 'ideas' of sense perception as approximating to perceptual 'aspects'.

An important feature of this interpretation is that it allows Locke to say that my perceptual 'ideas' of an object may be *inadequate* or *mistaken* in certain respects, although not completely so if I really am to perceive it. This in turn might enable us to understand what he could mean by saying that some of our ideas 'resemble' in certain ways the objects that we perceive – namely, by *not* being inadequate or mistaken. So, for example, when I see an object as being round and it *is* round, it might be said that my 'idea' of the object's shape and its actual shape resemble one another. But what, then, about Locke's suggestion that our ideas of colours and other so-called secondary qualities of objects *never* resemble those qualities? I shall return to this question shortly, but a quick answer is that he may be suggesting merely that, for example, our idea of a colour quality like redness misrepresents the true nature of the property in question, by representing it as being a surface feature of a physical object when in fact it is a *capacity* (or 'power') of an object to interact with light and thereby with our eyes in a certain way when we look at it.

In any case, the important point is that this interpretation of Locke's conception of perceptual 'ideas' once again enables us to regard him as a 'direct' realist. For it seems perfectly clear that we should not *reify* – that is, treat as things or, to use Yolton's expression, *entities* – the perceptual aspects under which we perceive objects. Thus, for example, when I see the Necker cube as tilted upwards, the upward-tilted aspect under which I see it is not *some further thing that I see*, in addition to the cube and its sides and vertices: rather, it is *how* I see the cube on this occasion. It is, to borrow Yolton's helpful manner of speaking, a 'mental feature of my seeing' – *mental* because the aspect in question is not an aspect of the cube itself, but only of how it appears to me.

As for the question of which, if either, of these direct realist interpretations is correct, I have no settled opinion on the matter – recalling that the two interpretations need not, in any case, be seen as being in direct competition with each other. If anything, I am inclined to judge that Locke himself did not clearly distinguish in his own mind between a non-imagist conception of perceptual ideas and an imagist one, much less have a specific non-imagist conception in view. This is not intended as a criticism of him, because we can hardly expect him to have been sensitive to distinctions that philosophers were not accustomed to making at the time at which he was writing and which have only been debated intensively during the last fifty years or so. I should, however, remark that of the two non-imagist accounts of the nature of perceptual ideas that I have offered, the second – attractive though it is in many ways – may appear to suffer from a certain difficulty, at least to the extent that it is proposed as being attributable to Locke himself. This is that it may seem to be inadequately equipped to accommodate the distinction between perceptual experience and perceptual judgement that I discussed earlier in connection with Locke's example of the perception of a uniformly coloured sphere or globe. For Locke suggests that my perceptual idea of the globe 'is only a Plain [i.e., plane] variously colour'd' – and yet I clearly perceive the globe *as* being convex and uniformly coloured, although with some parts of it highlighted and others in shadow. This might lead one to suppose that how I perceive the globe *as* being has, according to Locke, more to do with my perceptual *judgement* than it has to do with the content of my perceptual experience as such, as Locke seems to conceive of the latter.

However, perhaps the proposal can still be defended in the following terms. It may be suggested that what I have just referred to as 'the content of my perceptual experience as such' in the case of the globe is a matter of how I *would* perceive the globe as being, if I had not learned to interpret highlights and shadow as signs of convexity: for in the absence of such learning, perhaps I would indeed perceive – or, rather, misperceive – the globe as being flat and variously coloured. What I am proposing, then, is that Lockean 'ideas' of sense perception are not simply identifiable, quite generally, with what I earlier called perceptual 'aspects', but are, rather, identifiable only with what we might call 'untutored' perceptual aspects – those aspects under which we do or would perceive things in the absence of, or prior to, learning more about them through experience. However, I offer this proposal only as a suggestion which may help us to make sense of, amongst other things,

Locke's talk about a 'resemblance' or lack of it between our ideas and the perceptible qualities of things, without saddling him with an unattractive imagistic conception of ideas. If the proposal is considered to be unsatisfactory for any reason, we still have the other non-imagist interpretation of ideas to fall back on, for although that interpretation might be compatible with the 'aspectual' interpretation, it can also be developed in other ways – for example, along the lines of a so-called 'adverbial' theory of perceptual sensation. Since I have discussed that possibility quite extensively elsewhere (see Lowe 1995, pp. 42–7), I shall give only a brief sketch of it here.

Very briefly, then, what an adverbial theory of perceptual sensation proposes is that we should take quite literally our earlier talk of being sensorily affected in, for example, a 'red sort of way' or a 'green sort of way' – or, for short, of 'sensing *redly*' or 'sensing *greenly*', where it is the deployment of distinctive *adverbs* like these that gives the theory its name (see further Lowe 2000, pp. 114–19). Of course, everyday English does not in fact contain any such adverbs, but according to the adverbial theorist that is largely because ordinary speakers of the language have little need to describe the character of their sensory experiences as such, since most of the time they are much more concerned to describe the 'external' *objects* of sense perception. Ordinary English contains *adjectives*, such as 'red' and 'green', for this descriptive purpose and so it is unsurprising – so the adverbial theorist urges – that we should be tempted to exploit such adjectives in the relatively rare circumstances in which we are called upon to describe the character of the sensory experiences that we typically enjoy when we perceive red or green objects. Our mistake, however, is to go on deploying them as *adjectives*, albeit now as supposedly descriptive of 'inner' objects, or 'sense data', when in fact there are no such 'inner' objects to be described. The error, according to the adverbial theorist, may be corrected by transmuting the adjectives in question into adverbs characterizing the ways in which we are, typically, sensorily affected by perceptible objects describable by the adjectives in question. Thus sensing *redly*, for example, can be understood as sensing in that distinctive way in which one typically does when one sees a red object in normal lighting conditions. I shall not pretend that this sort of theory is free of all difficulties, but it undoubtedly has many attractions and may well be capable of being recruited in an attempt to understand how Locke himself thought of sensory 'ideas'. More particularly, it may help us to see how he may be interpreted as regarding sensory ideas not really as 'entities' that are themselves *sensed* but, in Yolton's words, as 'mental features' of sensory *processes*, such as the process of seeing ordinary, 'external' objects.

LOCKE'S DISTINCTION BETWEEN PRIMARY AND SECONDARY QUALITIES

In distinguishing between 'primary' and 'secondary' qualities of physical objects, Locke was following an already well-established tradition adopted by other seventeenth-century philosophers and scientists, including Descartes, Newton and Boyle. There was, however, some disagreement as to precisely how the distinction should be defined and consequently also some disagreement as to precisely which qualities fell into which category. Locke himself considered that the primary qualities of a body are those that are 'inseparable' from it (*Essay*, II, VIII, 9). A closely related notion is that the primary qualities of a body are its *intrinsic* properties – those which it could in principle possess even in the absence of any other body. Another is that the primary qualities are those which a physical body possesses purely by virtue of being *spatially extended*. However, rather than focus on the issue of how Locke and his contemporaries thought that the category of primary qualities should be defined, let us simply look at the list of them that Locke himself provides. They are, he says, 'Solidity, Extension, Figure, Motion, or Rest, and Number' (*Essay*, II, VIII, 9), to which he elsewhere adds 'Bulk' and 'Texture' (*Essay*, II, VIII, 10). The notion that *number* is a 'quality' or 'property' of objects, whether primary or secondary, may initially seem a little peculiar – but in fact I think that it is perfectly defensible, as I shall explain more fully in the next chapter. In any case, for present purposes I shall not question Locke's division of physical properties into primary and secondary qualities, but concentrate instead on his account of the nature of secondary qualities.

These secondary qualities, Locke tells us, are 'Powers to produce various Sensations in us' (*Essay*, II, VIII, 10) – indeed, he says, they are 'nothing but' such powers. Take the example of a colour quality, such as the redness of a red rubber ball. Now, we are naturally inclined to think of this redness as being (at least) a *surface feature* of the object possessing it, not fundamentally unlike such surface features as smoothness and roughness. (I say 'at least', because in some cases we may be further inclined to suppose that the feature in question does not lie merely on the surface of the object but penetrates below that to some depth, or even permeates the entire object.) When Locke asserts that such a secondary quality is really 'nothing but' a power in an object to produce certain sensations – that is, ideas – in us, he is implicitly rejecting this common-sense belief that a colour property such as redness is literally 'on' the surface of an object in the way in which it visibly appears to be. But let us be clear that Locke is *not* thereby denying that redness really is a quality or property of physical objects. He is simply saying that this quality, *as it is in the objects which possess it*, is just a 'power' – or, as we might now prefer to call it, a 'disposition' or 'capacity' – whose nature is not to be confused with that of the *idea* or *sensation* of redness which we typically enjoy upon being visibly confronted with red objects. Rather, the nature of that power is, he thinks, ultimately to be described in terms of the *primary* qualities of the particles composing an object's surface. For it is these, Locke supposes, that confer upon an object the power to cause sensations of redness in us.

This is not to say that Locke thinks that the word 'redness' can be defined as *meaning* something like 'power to produce sensations of redness in us', a definition that would in any case be circular. Indeed, Locke clearly regards the word 'red' as being undefinable, because he considers our *idea* of red to be a simple one – and for Locke the function of the word 'red' is to operate as a sign of this simple idea, as we shall see more fully in Chapter 4. Locke considers that anyone who has not enjoyed the experience of redness cannot really understand the word 'red' at all. This is the lesson that he intends us to draw from his famous anecdote concerning a blind man who, when asked what he thought scarlet was like, is said to have answered that he thought it was 'like the sound of a trumpet' (*Essay*, III, IV, 11).

Writing shortly after Locke's death, Berkeley raised a famous objection to Locke's thesis, mentioned earlier, that there is a 'resemblance' between primary qualities and our ideas of them which is absent in the case of the secondary qualities and their corresponding ideas. More than once Berkeley advances as a self-evident and fundamental principle that 'an idea can be like nothing but an idea' – for example, in his *Principles of Human Knowledge* (Berkeley 1975, p. 79) – the implication being that it is just unintelligible to suppose, as Locke seems to, that things as fundamentally different in nature as a lump of matter on the one hand and a mental idea on the other could in any sense resemble each other. Now it might be thought here that both Locke in maintaining the resemblance thesis and Berkeley in criticizing it are implicitly assuming what I earlier called an 'imagist' conception of ideas. For, on the one hand, an ordinary image, such as a painting, *can* meaningfully be said to resemble the thing that it depicts – for instance, a portrait can be said to resemble the person who sat for it. And yet, on the other hand, it may appear that the considerations which allow us to speak of such a resemblance in the case of a portrait and the person portrayed cannot come into play in the case of an idea of a physical object and the physical object of which it is the idea. For, clearly, we can establish the resemblance between a portrait and the person portrayed by looking at both of them together and comparing them, but we cannot in any analogous way 'compare' an idea with the physical object of which it is the idea because – at least according to Locke's theory of sense perception – the only way in which we can ever perceive a physical object is by experiencing an idea of it. So, it would seem, we can only ever 'compare' ideas with other ideas, not with physical objects. It is easy to see how this line of thought, amongst others, led Berkeley to reject altogether Locke's belief in a world of physical objects existing independently of our ideas and to defend instead the doctrine of idealism – the doctrine that nothing exists but minds and their ideas.

However, as I indicated earlier, there may be a way of making perfectly good sense of Locke's resemblance thesis, especially if we interpret him as being a 'direct' realist and not as being committed to an imagist conception of ideas. The suggestion is that when Locke maintains that our ideas of primary qualities 'resemble' those qualities in a sense in which our ideas of secondary qualities do not, he does not have in mind anything like the resemblance between a portrait and the person portrayed. Rather, it may be suggested, what he means to convey is his belief that our ideas of secondary qualities mislead us as to the real nature of those qualities in a way that our ideas of primary qualities do not – for our ideas of secondary qualities such as colour tempt us to think of them as being *categorical* rather than *dispositional* properties of the objects which possess them. Locke himself does not use these more modern terms 'categorical' and 'dispositional' to express the distinction at issue, but it seems perfectly clear that he did endorse the distinction because he contrasts what he calls 'powers' – that is, dispositional properties – with the primary qualities, such as shape and texture, which he takes to underlie and explain these powers. A categorical property is one which is precisely *not* a mere power to affect the properties of other objects in certain ways and it seems clear that there must be at least some such properties, because it apparently makes no sense to say that *every* property is merely a power to affect the properties of other objects in certain ways –

including the very properties that are supposed to be affected – for this seems to generate either a vicious infinite regress or a vicious circle. The suggestion is, then, that in his talk about 'resemblance' Locke is merely recording his conviction that, while our ideas of the primary qualities correctly represent them to us as being categorical in nature, our ideas of the secondary qualities misrepresent them to us as likewise being categorical in nature, when in fact they are mere dispositions or powers.

LOCKE'S ACCOUNT OF KNOWLEDGE

We have seen that Locke holds that all of the 'materials' of human knowledge – all of our 'ideas' – arise from experience, but we have yet to see what he takes knowledge itself to be and how he thinks that we arrive at it. Looking at Book IV of the *Essay*, we find that Locke there divides human knowledge into three kinds by reference to its basis in either intuition, reason or experience. This tripartite division was a traditional one, widely adopted by other seventeenth-century philosophers. But Locke combines it with a doctrine of his own that knowledge itself actually consists in our 'Perception of the Agreement, or Disagreement, of any of our Ideas' (*Essay*, IV, III, 1). He illustrates this thesis in the case of 'intuitive' knowledge in the following passage:

> [S]ometimes the Mind perceives the Agreement or Disagreement of two *Ideas* immediately . . . And this . . . we may call *intuitive Knowledge* . . . Thus the Mind perceives, that *White* is not *Black*, That a *Circle* is not a *Triangle*, That *Three* are more than *Two*, and equal to *One* and *Two*.
>
> (*Essay*, IV, II, 1)

Why are some things knowable by us 'intuitively' – such as that a circle is not a triangle – but others only 'demonstratively', or by means of *reason* in the form of deductive arguments or proofs? Locke himself offers the following explanation of our inability to know intuitively that, for instance, the three internal angles of a triangle equal two right angles:

> [T]he Mind being willing to know the Agreement or Disagreement in bigness . . . cannot by an immediate view and comparing them, do it . . . Because the three Angles of a Triangle cannot be brought at once, and be compared with any other one, or two Angles.
>
> (*Essay*, IV, II, 2)

The implication seems to be that our need to deploy reasoning in this sort of case reflects a limitation in our own cognitive capacities which would not afflict more powerful minds, especially the mind of God – after all, we can scarcely take Locke to suppose that not even *God's* mind could accomplish what, in this passage, he says the human mind is incapable of. So it would appear that the division between 'intuitive' and 'demonstrative' knowledge must be, for Locke, a merely relative one – relative, that is, to the cognitive capacities of the mind whose knowledge it is. This is, again, a view that was widely held by Locke's contemporaries, as was his contention that each step in a chain of demonstrative reasoning, together with the initial premises, must be perceived as intuitively certain:

> [I]n every step Reason makes in demonstrative Knowledge, there is an *intuitive Knowledge* of that Agreement or Disagreement, it seeks, with the next intermediate *Idea*, which it uses as a Proof . . . By which it is plain, that every step in Reasoning, that produces Knowledge, has intuitive Certainty.
>
> (*Essay*, IV, II, 7)

Locke's final category of knowledge – experiential knowledge, including knowledge by 'sensation' of the existence of physical things beyond ourselves – is rather more difficult to accommodate with his official definition of knowledge as the perception of the agreement or disagreement of our ideas. This is because, in sensation, the idea produced in us by an 'external' object does not appear to stand in any relevant relation of 'agreement' or 'disagreement' with other ideas we have, so much as a relation of 'agreement' or 'disagreement' with external reality. A danger here is that we may allow this consideration to persuade us – as it has evidently persuaded some of Locke's critics – that Locke's theory of sense perception, coupled with his theory of knowledge, presents him with an insoluble 'veil of perception' problem. However, as I indicated earlier, I think that it is a mistake to suppose that Locke's theory of sense perception, even if it is interpreted as a version of 'indirect realism', is inherently any more vulnerable to this kind of sceptical problem than is even the most explicit form of 'direct' realism. Moreover, we have also seen that his theory is in fact open to being interpreted as a version of direct realism. What is in any case clear is that Locke himself saw no genuine grounds for scepticism in the account of sensory knowledge that he provides:

> *The notice we have by our Senses, of the existing of Things without* us, though it be not altogether so certain, as our intuitive Knowledge . . . yet it is an assurance that *deserves the name of Knowledge.* If we persuade our selves, that our Faculties act and inform us right, concerning the existence of those Objects that affect them, it cannot pass for an ill-grounded confidence: For I think no body can, in earnest, be so sceptical, as to be uncertain of the Existence of those Things which he sees and feels.
>
> (*Essay*, IV, XI, 3)

Locke's critics naturally tend to pick upon passages in the *Essay* which invite a more sceptical reading, as when Locke says that 'the Mind knows not Things immediately, but only by the intervention of the Ideas it has of them' (*Essay*, IV, IV, 3). However, I suggest that all that this sort of passage really shows is that Locke recognized, very reasonably, that we can only acquire knowledge of things in the physical world to the extent that those things affect us in various ways of which we can be conscious. In response to his own question, as to how the mind shall know that its ideas 'agree with Things themselves' (*Essay*, IV, IV, 3), Locke answers as follows:

> [S]imple *Ideas*, which . . . the Mind . . . can by no means make to it
> self, must necessarily be the product of Things operating on the
> Mind in a natural way . . . and so . . . represent to us Things under
> those appearances which they are fitted to produce in us.
>
> (*Essay*, IV, IV, 3–5)

He elaborates this point using some examples of simple ideas of
secondary qualities, as follows:

> the *Idea* of Whiteness, or Bitterness, as it is in the Mind, exactly
> answering that Power which is in any Body to produce it there, has
> all the real conformity it can, or ought to have, with Things without
> us.
>
> (*Essay*, IV, IV, 4)

As for our *complex* ideas of 'substances', that is, of objects possessing many different properties or qualities, Locke remarks:

> Herein therefore is founded the *reality* of our Knowledge concerning
> *Substances*, that all our complex *Ideas* of them must be such, and
> such only, as are made up of such simple ones, as have been
> discovered to co-exist in Nature.
>
> (*Essay*, IV, IV, 12)

His contention, thus, is that sensation can provide us with knowledge not only of the existence of individual physical properties but
also of the existence of objects possessing various combinations of
those properties, at least to the extent that it can assure us that
certain combinations of properties regularly occur together in
nature. I shall say much more about Locke's account of substance in
the next chapter. But suffice it to say, for the time being, that Locke
is confident that his empiricist epistemology allows us to claim a
genuine knowledge of the natural world which, while it is
undoubtedly strictly limited in scope, possesses 'all the real conformity it can, or ought to have, with Things without us' (*Essay*, IV,
IV, 4).

Now, according to Locke, *belief* or *opinion* – which he contrasts sharply with knowledge – may be based on either *probability* or *faith*. Since, by Locke's account, the scope of our knowledge is 'very narrow' (*Essay*, IV, XV, 2), he thinks that in most everyday concerns we have to rely on probability, which is mere 'likeliness to be true' (*Essay*, IV, XV, 3), rather than certainty. One frequently reliable ground of probability, he considers, is *testimony*, on which he thinks we depend for a very large proportion of our firm beliefs, even in those matters which are capable of demonstration. Thus Locke gives an example of how a non-mathematician may firmly, and quite properly, *believe* that the three internal angles of a triangle add up to two right angles because a mathematician 'of credit' has told him that this is so, although it is only the mathematician who *knows* that it is so, having constructed a proof or demonstration of that proposition (*Essay*, IV, XV, 1). By contrast, in some matters of religion in which intuition, demonstration and sensation cannot provide us with knowledge, Locke thinks that we may justifiably ground our belief in what we take to be divine revelation – and assent of this sort Locke calls *faith*. However, he is emphatic that, rightly understood, reason and faith do not stand in opposition to one another, although he is also very critical of exaggerated and overly dogmatic claims of the scope of revelation:

> Whatever GOD hath revealed, is certainly true; no Doubt can be made of it. This is the proper Object of *Faith*: But whether it be a divine Revelation, or no, *Reason* must judge; which can never permit the Mind to reject a greater Evidence to embrace what is less evident, nor allow it to entertain Probability in opposition to Knowledge and Certainty.
>
> (*Essay*, IV, XVIII, 10)

In most of these matters, Locke was broadly representative of the enlightened intellectuals of his time. But perhaps the biggest gulf between his epistemology and that of present-day philosophers lies in his much more restrictive application of the term 'knowledge', to describe only that of which we are certain:

> And herein lies the *difference between Probability* and *Certainty*, *Faith* and *Knowledge*, that in all the parts of Knowledge, there is intuition; each immediate *Idea*, each step has its visible and certain connexion; in belief not so.
>
> (*Essay*, IV, XV, 3)

Today it would be regarded as very odd to say that we do not know that the earth is round, that the sun is millions of miles away from us, or that Napoleon lost the Battle of Waterloo – and yet, by Locke's standards, we cannot be said to 'know' these things, however justifiably assured we may be of their truth, whether through testimony or through scientific or historical research. Thus Locke is apt to sound unduly sceptical to modern ears. But we should not misconstrue as scepticism a view which merely deploys the term 'knowledge' in a much more restrictive sense than would be normal today. What *we* mean by saying that we 'know' that the earth is round is perhaps not so very different from what Locke would mean by saying that we merely 'believe' this, with a high degree of probability. Be that as it may, it is clear that Locke's conception of the relationship between knowledge and faith was immensely important for its bearing upon his attitude towards the question of religious toleration. But I must postpone discussion of that topic until Chapter 6.

SUMMARY

Locke's epistemological project in the *Essay* was to replace an account of human knowledge based on the doctrine of divinely instituted innate ideas and principles by one which sees human knowledge as the product of individual experiential and reasoning processes, originating in sensory perception and introspection and culminating in abstract thought about the natural world, God, and the principles of mathematics and morality. It is an account of knowledge which assigns responsibility for what is known to individual human beings rather than to God. As such, it is liberating but may at the same time provoke doubts and anxieties about the adequacy of our attempts to understand reality and ourselves. Locke does his best to allay such concerns and to reassure us that, if we use our mental capacities wisely, we can attain genuine knowledge in sufficient measure to meet our practical, moral and spiritual needs. He aligns himself with the great experimental scientists of the age, endorsing their conviction that by careful observation and judicious experimentation we can gradually disclose some of nature's secrets and turn that knowledge to our practical advantage in securing the comforts and conveniences of life, without undermining our faith in God and divine providence or our moral duties to each other as God's creatures. Some of Locke's contemporary critics were not so sanguine about the compatibility of his epistemology with traditional religious faith and perhaps their doubts were borne out by subsequent historical developments. But in Locke himself we seem to find a great mind in which religious faith and the scientific attitude lie in harmony with each other.

FURTHER READING

Alexander, Peter 1985: *Ideas, Qualities and Corpuscles: Locke and Boyle on the External World* (Cambridge: Cambridge University Press).

Ayers, Michael 1991: Locke, Volume I: *Epistemology* (London & New York: Routledge).

Morgan, Michael J. 1977: *Molyneux's Question: Vision, Touch and the Philosophy of Perception* (Cambridge: Cambridge University Press).

Wolterstorff, Nicholas 1996: *John Locke and the Ethics of Belief* (Cambridge: Cambridge University Press).

Yolton, John W. 1984: *Perceptual Acquaintance from Descartes to Reid* (Oxford: Blackwell).

Three

Substance and Identity

Since the first appearance of Locke's *Essay Concerning Human Understanding*, his account of the idea of *substance* has probably generated more criticism and disagreement than any other single topic in that book. If this seems strange from a present-day philosophical perspective, it is only because in recent times the idea of substance has played a much less prominent role in metaphysics than it did throughout the seventeenth century. Its philosophical importance at that time was intimately linked with its central place in theological thought, where it was invoked in accounts of the nature of God and the immortality of the soul. Thus the doctrine of transubstantiation – according to which bread and wine can become the body and blood of Christ – and the doctrine of the Trinity – according to which Father, Son and Holy Ghost are three distinct persons in one indivisible Godhead – both depend for their intelligibility on the idea of substance and accordingly risk being undermined if that idea is challenged. The surest way to protect the idea from criticism, it might seem, would be to declare it innate. Consequently, to the religious dogmatists of Locke's time, his attempt to provide the idea with a merely empirical foundation must have appeared extremely dangerous, inviting theological dissent and opening the door to atheism.

Locke himself clearly meant to defend, rather than to attack, the idea of substance, but it is not difficult to see why many of his contemporary readers should have regarded his defence as embarrassingly weak. And, certainly, it cannot be denied that subsequent criticisms of Locke's account of substance by prominent eight-eenth-century philosophers like Berkeley and Hume led to the almost complete eclipse of substance-centred metaphysics in Western philosophy throughout most of the ensuing two hundred years. Philosophers sympathetic to the idea of substance may accordingly feel, with some justification, that Locke has much to answer for in failing to provide a better defence of the idea. But I think that such a judgement would be unduly harsh and that genuine friends of the idea of substance should thank him for encouraging us to subject the idea to critical philosophical scrutiny and analysis. As we shall see, even if Locke was not completely successful in this part of his philosophy, there is much of value that we can learn from his account of the idea of substance. Later in the chapter, I shall turn to Locke's closely related accounts of the ideas of number, unity and identity and his application of the last of these in the special case of persons.

SUBSTANCE AND MODE IN LOCKE'S *ESSAY*

Our primary concern at present is with what Locke has to say about substratum, or pure substance in general − two terms that he uses more or less interchangeably. But to understand his use of these notoriously contentious terms, we must see how they relate to two other aspects of his talk about substance. On the one hand, we very often find Locke speaking of particular or individual substances. On the other, he scarcely less frequently talks about sorts of substances, with the implication that any particular substance may be said to belong to one or more of those sorts. Now, by a 'particular substance', Locke means pretty much what we would now call a particular or individual concrete thing or object − such as a particular man, a particular tree, or a particular rock. General terms like 'man', 'tree' and 'rock' − for which Locke himself coined the expression sortal terms − denote different sorts or kinds of particular substances. And, according to Locke, each of them does so by standing for, or signifying, a distinct abstract general idea (see Essay, III, III). Thus, for Locke, the abstract general idea signified by the sortal term 'tree' is a complex idea consisting in part of a combination of various simple ideas of qualities which the mind has observed 'to go constantly together' in experience. In Locke's opinion, when we classify a particular thing as being a *tree*, we do so because we find that its various observable qualities correspond to those whose ideas we have included in the abstract general idea that we take to be signified by the word 'tree'. This is Locke's much-disputed doctrine of classification by way of abstraction (for further discussion of which, see Lowe 1995, pp. 154–65). According to Locke, however, the abstract general idea of a certain sort of substance must always include, in *addition to* ideas of various qualities possessed by particular substances of that sort, the idea of something that 'supports' and unites those qualities – and this is the idea of *substratum*, or *pure substance in general*. But what exactly does Locke mean by saying this and why does he say it? And is what he says defensible, either on his own terms or in the light of present-day metaphysics and epistemology?

I should not approach these questions without first qualifying what I have just said concerning Locke's talk about particular substances, for in this matter he adopts both a stricter and a looser way of talking. According to the looser way of talking, ordinary middle-sized objects such as trees and horses can indeed be described as being 'particular substances'. But according to the stricter way of talking, it seems, Locke holds that in reality the only genuine substances are (1) individual material bodies – that is to say, individual material atoms and aggregates of such atoms – (2) individual 'finite spirits' or souls and (3) the infinite immaterial substance that, supposedly, is God. According to this account, as Locke himself puts it, 'all other things [are] but Modes or Relations ultimately terminated in substances' (*Essay*, II, XXVII, 2). And amongst 'all other things' here he clearly intends to include complex macroscopic individuals such as plants, animals and indeed human beings such as ourselves. To understand this proposal fully, however, we need to know what exactly Locke supposed a 'mode' to be.

In fact, Locke's use of the term 'mode' draws heavily upon a Scholastic metaphysical tradition that he was, in other respects, very much concerned to challenge. Although the triad of technical terms 'substance', 'attribute' and 'mode' was central to that tradition, it survived and prospered in seventeenth-century metaphysics, despite the growing hostility to Scholastic philosophy in general. According to prevailing usage at the time, *attributes* are universal characteristics necessarily common to all particular substances of the same very general kind, while *modes* are the different particular ways in which those attributes are instantiated in different particular substances. For example, a finite material substance or 'body' which – like all material bodies – necessarily exhibits the attribute of being spatially extended, must at any given time have a particular *shape*, which is a mode of that attribute. A word of caution at this point: in everyday language we often use 'particular' to mean merely 'specific' and may thus understand a 'particular shape' to be a specific, but still universal, characteristic capable of being shared by many different objects – such as, for example, *triangularity* or *squareness*. But a 'particular shape' in the sense now being discussed is supposed to be something that is itself a *particular*, rather than a universal, and as such uniquely possessed by just *one* particular substance, even if other particular substances may possess exactly similar shapes.

The particular shape of an extended, material thing is, then, itself just as much a 'real being' as is that thing – but it is not a *thing*, if by that is meant a particular *substance*. Rather, it is the particular *way* in which that thing is extended. As such, the shape is an *ontologically dependent* being, entirely depending for its existence and identity upon the thing whose shape it is – for it cannot exist without that thing and is distinguished from other, exactly resembling particular shapes only in virtue of being possessed by *that* thing rather than by any other thing. As Locke himself puts it: 'Modes . . . contain not in them the supposition of subsisting by themselves, but are considered as Dependences on, or Affections of Substances' (*Essay*, II,

XII, 4). Now, according to Locke's stricter way of talking, it seems, many of the middle-sized material beings that we are apt to classify as particular substances – notably, highly complex individuals such as plants and animals – are properly speaking only dependent entities, arising from the various complex ways in which the general attributes of matter are instantiated by large aggregates of material atoms. That is to say, they are strictly speaking only *modes*, or combinations of modes.

Since Locke largely relegates this stricter way of talking to the background of his discussion, so shall I, crucial though it is for a proper understanding of his metaphysical position as a whole. What is more immediately important for our present purposes is the fact that Locke is clearly committed to preserving the Scholastic distinction between substance and mode as a fundamental feature of his ontology. Thus, even if we treat something like a tree or a horse as being a particular substance, in accordance with Locke's looser way of talking, this still requires us, in Locke's eyes, to regard the particular *shape, colour, weight* and so forth of such a thing – in short, all of its particular *qualities* – as having the status of modes, that is, as being ontologically dependent beings. But *upon what* are they ontologically dependent? This is where the doctrine of substratum comes into play.

Locke clearly thinks that – precisely because we conceive of the qualities of a thing as having the status of modes, or dependent beings – we cannot help supposing, whenever we observe certain qualities to be coinstantiated in nature, that there is *something* upon which they depend for their existence and union: something in which they 'inhere' and which 'supports' them. The idea of such a 'something', he considers, is unavoidably included in our abstract general idea of any sort of substance, along with the ideas of various qualities which together serve to determine *which* sort of substance that abstract general idea is an idea of. But Locke is emphatic that this 'something' is 'something we know not what' – something of which we have no 'positive' idea, but only an obscure and 'relative' idea (*Essay*, II, XXIII, 3). In describing the idea of substratum as a 'relative' idea, Locke is adverting to the fact that, on his account, the idea is merely that of something which stands in the relation of *support* to particular qualities, albeit with the added assumption that this 'something' does not itself stand in need of any similar 'support'. But how far this aspect of Locke's account can survive philosophical scrutiny remains to be seen.

LOCKE'S CORRESPONDENCE WITH STILLINGFLEET

Although the *Essay* itself – and especially Chapter XXIII of Book II, 'Of the Complex Ideas of Substances' – constitutes our primary source for Locke's considered views concerning substance, his published correspondence with the Bishop of Worcester, Edward Stillingfleet, is also vitally important for purposes of interpretation. For here Locke explains and justifies his account of the idea of substance in the light of some very astute contemporary criticism. Stillingfleet, as a leading representative of the Church of England, was disturbed by what he saw as the dangerous theological implications of Locke's account, especially for the orthodox Christian doctrine of the Holy Trinity.

In his correspondence with Stillingfleet, Locke is at pains to argue that his account of the idea of substratum is not particularly revisionary and, indeed, that it pretty well coincides with the conception of substance that Stillingfleet himself adheres to. But Stillingfleet's most pressing charge, I think, is that Locke is not entitled, by his own lights, to espouse such an idea of substratum, because Locke cannot account for our acquisition of that idea by empiricist means. According to Locke, the idea of substratum is not itself a simple idea of sensation or reflection: nor could it be by his own account, for in his view all such simple ideas are ideas of various sensible qualities or mental operations – in short, they are all ideas of entities which belong to the ontological category of *mode*. Rather, the idea of substratum is a complex idea, which the mind supposedly constructs by processes of abstraction and reasoning. But how can it do so? – that is Stillingfleet's question.

Locke's answer to this question seems to run as follows. First, the mind finds that it cannot conceive how any collection of coinstantiated qualities – such as a particular shape, colour, weight, solidity and so forth – can exist and be united together without something to 'support' their existence and explain their union. That is to say, the mind finds the notion of a free-floating 'bundle' of compresent qualities to be incomprehensible. Consequently, reason prompts us to suppose the existence of *something* whose role it is to support and unite these qualities as the qualities of a single object. But, Locke wants to say, the mind already has the materials for such a reasoned supposition – and these materials are ultimately supplied by the simple ideas of sensation and reflection, as his empiricism requires. On the one hand, we have the general idea of *something* – that is, of an entity or being – by way of abstraction: for particular sensible qualities and mental operations, of which we do have simple ideas, are all entities or beings, and so provide exemplars upon which the process of abstraction can operate to form an abstract general idea of this type. On the other hand, we have the idea of the relation of *support*, again derived, by means of abstraction and comparison, from simple ideas of sensation and reflection, in accordance with Locke's doctrine concerning the formation of our ideas of relations more generally (see *Essay*, II, XXV–XXVIII). Then the mind can construct the idea of substratum as the idea of *something* which is the 'unknown' relatum of this relation of *support*, whose other relata are the various coinstantiated qualities deemed to stand in need of such 'support'.

However, there are some obvious objections to this account of the origin of our idea of substratum. For one thing, the relation of 'support' of which the mind supposedly acquires the idea by way of abstraction and comparison cannot, arguably, be the relation in which coinstantiated qualities are meant to stand to a substratum. For the latter relation is, by Locke's own principles, inscrutable to the senses, whereas any relation of support of which we can have formed an idea by way of abstraction and comparison will not be. We may speak, for example, of pillars *supporting* a roof or of a table *supporting* a book, but here the kind of support involved is an observable relation between things which are themselves classifiable as particular substances (at least according to Locke's looser way of talking about particular substances). It surely cannot be intelligible to suppose that substratum *supports* qualities in anything like this sense. Surely, talk of 'support' in the latter context at best involves a metaphorical use of the term as it is familiarly understood.

To be fair, it must be acknowledged that Locke himself is fond of appealing to etymology in his explanations of abstruse and technical terms – and the case of 'substance' is no exception. He repeatedly points out that it originates from the Latin words meaning 'under' and 'standing' (see, for example, *Essay*, II, XXIII, 2). But, even granting that much of our technical terminology involves what are sometimes called 'dead metaphors', it is not clear that this will get Locke off the hook in the present case. For the relation of substratum to qualities can really be *nothing at all* like the relation of a pillar to a roof. The latter relation is causal and contingent, whereas the former can apparently be neither – if, indeed, we can properly speak of a *relation* obtaining in that case at all. Locke does, it is true, sometimes speak of substratum as being a 'cause' of the union of a thing's qualities (see *Essay*, II, XXIII, 6), but this cannot plausibly be understood as involving the ordinary notion of *efficient* causation, implicated when we say that pillars 'cause' a roof to stay up. The relation between substratum and quality is plausibly not that of cause to effect, but, rather, one of *ontological dependency* – which, if it is really a relation at all, has an entirely non-contingent and metaphysical character. But how can the mind be supposed to have constructed an idea of this kind of relation merely by way of abstraction and comparison from simple ideas of sensation and reflection?

There is, besides, another problem for Locke's account of the origin of our idea of substratum, this time to do with the role which the idea of *something* plays in that account. Locke's suggestion, as we have seen, is that this is just a perfectly general idea of a *being* or *entity*, for which observable items such as sensible qualities can provide exemplars. But if, as Locke seems to suppose, the only entities which the mind can encounter in experience are ones which fall into the ontological category of *mode* – *'External Objects furnish the Mind with the Ideas of sensible qualities'* (*Essay*, II, I, 5) – how can he avoid the objection that abstraction performed on our ideas of such entities will only deliver a *restricted* idea of 'something', applying only to entities of this category? A dilemma seems to threaten Locke here. If the most general abstract idea that we can form by means of abstraction from our experience of particular sensible qualities is restricted to embrace only entities like these, then abstraction cannot serve to construct an idea of something that is *not* like a quality, as substratum is supposed not to be. On the other hand, if the abstract general idea of 'something' which we derive from our experience of sensible particulars is indeed perfectly general, why do we conceive of those particulars as standing in need of some kind of ontological 'support' – why don't we think of them simply as being *entities* or *beings*, without any presumption that they are somehow *non-self-subsistent* entities?

These problems point, I think, to the basic soundness of Stillingfleet's main charge against Locke – that he cannot adequately explain, in his own empiricist terms, how we come to possess the idea of substratum that he says we possess. The implication would seem to be that, if we do indeed possess it, the idea must simply be *innate*. That being so, either Locke should have abandoned the idea of substratum, or he should have given a different account of it, or else, finally, he should have withdrawn his opposition to the doctrine of innate ideas. The last option, I assume, he would never have been prepared to contemplate. However, we shall see shortly that it may instead be possible to modify Locke's account of substratum in a way which renders it both compatible with his empiricism and independently defensible.

FURTHER DIFFICULTIES FOR LOCKE'S ACCOUNT OF SUBSTANCE

On the broader question of whether Locke's doctrine of substratum, as it actually stands, is philosophically tenable, what
should we say? It is widely assumed by Locke scholars that if
Locke's doctrine amounts to the view that substrata are so-called
'bare particulars', then indeed it is philosophically indefensible.
Some Locke scholars, indeed, seem to be so convinced of this that,
in the further conviction that Locke cannot have been so foolish as
to advocate what they regard as being a manifestly indefensible
position, they are determined to find in his writings an account of
substratum which cannot be construed as being committed to the
existence of bare particulars. I would only say that it seems to me a
dangerous procedure to adopt, in interpreting the views of great
philosophers of the past, to suppose them incapable of making
what we take to be philosophical blunders – not least because it is
arrogant to suppose that we have any better idea than they did as to
what genuinely constitutes a philosophical blunder. In any case,
there have been eminent metaphysicians in recent times who have
espoused the doctrine of bare particulars after very careful reflection on all the familiar objections to it, so we should not simply
assume without argument that this doctrine is philosophically
indefensible.

But *does* Locke's account of substratum in fact commit him to a
belief in the existence of bare particulars? A 'bare particular' would,
it seems, be something with an identity but no properties or nature
of its own, while at the same time being an inseparable constituent
of the object or thing of whose properties it would be the supposed
'bearer' or 'support'. Now, Locke says, to be sure, that a substratum
is something 'we know not what' and that it is indeed not just
unknown but unknowable to us. But at times he also intimates that
a substratum may have a 'nature', which might in principle be
knowable to other intelligences than ours – perhaps to angels and
presumably to God, as passages like the following suggest: 'Whatever therefore be the secret and abstract Nature of *Substance* in

general' (*Essay*, II, XXIII, 6) and '[B]ut what, and how clear [the idea of substance] is in the understanding of a seraphim . . . I cannot determine' (Locke 1823, p. 28). Against this, however, it is often objected that it would defeat the very purpose of invoking substrata to suppose them capable of possessing properties of their own, rather than of the things whose substrata they were. For if things with properties need substrata to support those properties and substrata are themselves things with properties, then it seems that they themselves will need yet other substrata to support their properties – and so on *ad infinitum*. On the other hand, it may be urged that substrata, if they existed, would at least need to possess the property of *being a bearer or support of properties* simply in order to fulfil their intended ontological role – so that they cannot be perfectly propertyless. This then seems to create an insoluble difficulty for substratum theory: substrata, it appears, must be both propertyless and propertied – and so cannot exist on pain of contradiction.

However, just how pressing this alleged difficulty really is may be disputed, since much turns on the question of what properties we are entitled to assume there are. Just because substrata are held to bear or support properties, it doesn't automatically follow that we must attribute to them the *property* of bearing or supporting properties – for we are certainly not entitled to assume that every meaningful predicate which is correctly applicable to some entity expresses a corresponding property possessed by that entity. On the other hand, if it can be argued that predicates are correctly applicable to entities only in virtue of properties that those entities possess, then it will still follow that a property-bearer must possess properties, even if it can't be assumed that there is any such property as that of being a bearer of properties. That being so, whether or not the difficulty now being canvassed really is a difficulty will turn on the question of whether it really would defeat the purpose of invoking substrata to suppose them capable of possessing properties of their own.

My own view about this last question is that the purpose of invoking substrata would not be defeated by supposing them capable of possessing properties of their own and, in particular, that this supposition need not run us into an infinite regress: but *only on the following condition* – that the substratum which 'supports' the properties of a given object, or in which those properties 'inhere', is identical with that very object itself. This, almost certainly, cannot be Locke's own view, not least because he says that substrata are completely unknown entities, whereas many of the property-possessing objects which – in his looser way of talking – he calls 'particular substances', such as trees and rocks, are far from being completely unknown to us: we know them, according to Locke, precisely inasmuch as we know some of their properties, such as their sensible qualities and their causal powers. It may, I concede, strike many philosophers as being entirely at odds with any doctrine of substratum to say that the substratum of a property-possessing object is that very object itself, but I disagree. Substrata are invoked, primarily, to play the role of something which is not itself a property, but upon which the properties of an object can depend for their existence and identity, on the assumption that properties themselves are not independent beings. But the very object which possesses the given properties is at least formally equipped to play this role, because it is not itself a property. Nor – I should say – is it a collection or bundle of properties. Why should the substratum of an object's properties have to be something which is not only a non-property but is also, in some mysterious way, a *constituent* of the object and thus distinct from it as well as from the properties that the substratum bears or supports?

As I have just indicated, I prefer an account according to which the substratum of an object's properties should be identified with that very object. On this account, substrata most assuredly are not 'bare particulars' and they are not, in general, 'something we know not what' – for we know at least something of them in knowing some of their properties. Hence, as I say, this view of substratum almost certainly cannot be attributed to Locke himself. But what we may be able to say is that it was open to Locke to adopt this view, consistently with many – even if not all – other important aspects of his philosophy. Remember that what, according to Locke, rationally compels us to posit the existence of substrata is our conviction that qualities cannot enjoy an independent existence – that they need to 'inhere' in something which is not itself a quality, but a self-subsistent entity. But why suppose that the subject of inherence is anything other than the very object whose qualities it 'supports'? And why, indeed, suppose that there is a genuine *relation* – one of 'support' – between substratum and quality? On the view that I am recommending, a quality is a quality 'of' its substratum, which is the qualitied object itself, not some peculiar *constituent* or *ingredient* of the object. But 'ofness' in this sense should not be thought to denote a special kind of relation in which two otherwise separable items can stand to one another – a mysterious kind of metaphysical bond or glue which holds them together. Apart from anything else, to introduce a relation here would be to initiate a vicious infinite regress (often referred to as 'Bradley's regress', after the British philosopher F. H. Bradley [1846–1924]). For if we say that substratum and quality need to be attached to one another by a special relation – call it 'ofness', or 'inherence', or what you will – then we shall need to explain how each *relatum* of that supposed relation is in turn 'attached' to the relation: instead of having just *two* items supposedly needing to be 'attached' to one another by means of the mysterious relation of 'inherence', we shall now have *three* – the original two plus the inherence relation itself. To avoid all such absurdity, we have to acknowledge that the dependency of a quality upon its bearer or substratum is absolutely necessary in character: that the quality cannot, of metaphysical necessity, exist save as a quality of that very object, because it is one of that object's *modes* – one of the ways that very object *is* – not an extraneous entity somehow 'attached' to it, nor yet something that somehow helps to 'compose' or 'constitute' it.

All of this Locke could perhaps have said. But then, I think, he would have been required to alter his account of the contents of sensory experience, for he could no longer have said at all comfortably that such experience only discloses to us the *qualities* of objects as opposed to the objects themselves. It must also be very questionable whether his empiricist account of concept-formation could deal adequately with the concept of metaphysical necessity which the present proposal involves. But then, to be fair, this is also a problem for present-day theories of concept-formation, to such an extent that many philosophers nowadays are thoroughly sceptical – I think excessively so – about the notion of metaphysical necessity. However, that is a subject for another time and place (for a defence of the notion, see Lowe 1998, ch. 1).

MARTIN'S INTERPRETATION OF LOCKEAN SUBSTRATUM

At this point, I want to say something about an alternative interpretation of Locke's account of substratum that has been advanced by C. B. Martin, for it is interesting in its own right and in some ways resembles my own 'revised' conception of substratum, while still differing from the latter in important respects. Whereas there is little real prospect of attributing my revised conception to Locke himself, for the reasons already given, Martin's account is rather more promising on this score. Martin, like some other commentators, does not want to saddle Locke with a crude version of the doctrine of bare particulars. He stresses a number of points about what he takes to be Locke's considered view. One is that, in his opinion, Locke does not regard substrata as *objects*, in the sense of 'object' in which this is interchangeable with the term 'particular substance' (see Martin 1980, pp. 3–4). Another is that Locke regards all properties or qualities of objects as being themselves *particular* entities, rather than 'universals', albeit not, of course, *objects* (see Martin 1980, p. 7). Rather, a property of an object is something *about* that object – a *way* it is. I agree entirely. This, indeed, is what it means to characterize properties as *modes*. There is a current term, coined by D. C. Williams, which serves pretty much the same purpose, namely, *trope* (see Williams 1966). Other philosophers have variously called such items individual accidents, particular qualities, or abstract particulars (see Campbell 1990). But I prefer the term 'mode', both on account of its antiquity and because Locke uses it extensively himself. Martin stresses – and again I agree with him entirely – that, for Locke, properties thus conceived are manifestly dependent beings, no collection of which can jointly *constitute* an object (see Martin 1980, pp. 7–8). To think that an object might simply be the sum of its properties is, as Martin says, to confuse the notion of a *property* with the notion of a *part*. The top half of an object is a part of it, but is itself an object which could exist even if the rest of the object were destroyed. By contrast, it doesn't make sense to think of the properties of an object, or any collection of those properties, as being capable of enjoying an independent existence.

So what, according to Martin, is a Lockean substratum? Here I should emphasize that Martin is not merely engaged in a project of expounding or elucidating what he takes to be Locke's views about substance: he is trying to 'refurbish' Locke's account as an independently worthy metaphysical doctrine, which we would do well to espouse ourselves. Consistent with this aim, we need not find it a fault in Martin's proposals that there may not be explicit textual evidence in Locke's writings for Locke's endorsement of every aspect of them. It should be enough that nothing in Locke's writings explicitly rules out Martin's interpretation and that it fits in with Locke's general framework of philosophical thought. With this qualification in view, Martin's suggestion is that a Lockean substratum is neither an object nor a property, but, rather, is what it is *about* an object that plays the role of bearing (or supporting) the object's properties: '[T]here must be something *about* the object that is the bearer of the properties . . . [a]nd *that* about the object is the substratum' (Martin 1980, pp. 7–8). This way of conceiving of substrata makes it clear that substrata are no more capable of an independent existence than are properties, thus meeting the objection that it is unclear why there should not be 'naked' substrata, which happen to support no properties. So, on Martin's account, both properties and substrata are, in different ways, items which are, as it were, *aspects* of objects – that is, of particular substances – and only the latter are self-subsistent, ontologically independent entities. But it would be wrong to think of an object's substratum as being a special kind of *property* of the object, for a property of any kind would still have to be a property *borne* rather than a property-*bearer*.

Martin endeavours, quite plausibly, to underscore the Lockean credentials of his account of substrata by emphasizing the importance for Locke of our capacity to engage in a 'partial consideration' of the objects which we encounter in experience — this capacity being, of course, at the root of the mental process of abstraction (see Martin 1980, pp. 5–6 and 9–10). Thus, when looking at some macroscopic object – Martin's favourite example is a passionfruit – we can selectively attend to its purple colour or its round shape: and each of these properties is something 'about' the object, rather than the object in its entirety. But, equally, Martin suggests, we can think of – even if we cannot literally *observe* – what it is 'about' the object that is a *bearer* of its various properties: what it is 'about' the object that is needed for us to have before us an *object*, rather than merely various compresent properties. This further item is not and, logically, *could not* be a property, but neither is it an object. The object is, as Martin puts it, 'the property-bearer–properties borne' (Martin 1980, p. 6), and thus a kind of complex or composite: but emphatically not a whole whose *parts* are the property-bearer or substratum and the various properties. For if an object has parts, its parts will themselves be objects which are likewise complexes of property-bearers and properties.

Do substrata, on Martin's account, have properties of their own? In one sense, the answer is, trivially, 'Yes': they have the properties of the object whose properties they bear, precisely in the sense that they are *bearers* of those properties (see Martin 1980, p. 6). But for Martin it would seem that these are what some philosophers would call *extrinsic*, as opposed to *intrinsic*, properties of substrata, although Martin himself does not use that terminology in this connection. He does imply, however, that a substratum has at least one intrinsic property, namely, the property of being a property-bearer (see Martin 1980, p. 6). This recalls our earlier discussion, where I pointed out that the mere fact that a substratum is, by definition, a bearer of properties does not of itself imply that a substratum must have the *property* of being a bearer of properties, because we have no right to assume that any such property must exist: not every meaningful predicate necessarily expresses a property. Perhaps, then, Martin too readily presumes that a substratum would at least have to have the property of being a property-bearer. Perhaps he should say that substrata have no intrinsic properties at all and in this sense, at least, have no properties 'of their own'. To this it might be objected that, even if there is no such property as the property of being a property-bearer, substrata would still need to have *some* intrinsic properties, or properties 'of their own', simply in order to *be* property-bearers. But that objection might be countered, on Martin's behalf, by urging that it is founded upon an illicit tendency to think of substrata as *objects* of a queer sort, when in reality they are something 'about' objects – their property-bearing aspect.

Martin's account, it seems to me, has much to recommend it, both as a metaphysical theory of substance and as an interpretation of what Locke is, albeit somewhat inchoately, driving at in his talk about substratum. It seems to escape the more obvious objections to crude conceptions of substrata as bare particulars. It provides a plausible basis on which to attack theories that hold objects to be mere collections or bundles of properties. And it seems to fit fairly comfortably with Locke's abstractionist empiricism. Even so, I have to say that I am not, finally, convinced that Martin's account is fully acceptable, either on its own terms or as an interpretation of the tendency in Locke's own thinking about substance.

Let us consider, first of all, the question of whether Martin's account correctly identifies the tendency of Locke's thought. One problem concerns the way in which we are supposed to arrive at our idea of substratum. For Locke, as we know, all of the materials of our understanding must ultimately arise from simple ideas of sensation and reflection. But experience, by Locke's account, can only discover to us the qualities of sensible things and the operations of our own minds. Now, the process of abstraction, which indeed involves 'partial consideration' or 'selective attention', enables us to think of some combinations of qualities without regard to other qualities which may happen to attend them in our experience. But no such process of 'partial consideration' can, it would seem, disclose to us any aspect of a sensible object which is not *qualitative* in character – not, at least, on Locke's empiricist principles. Rather, as Locke himself tries to explain, our idea of substratum must be constructed by the mind, using indeed the materials supplied by simple ideas of sensation and reflection, but in answer to a demand of *reason* that there be *something* – we know not what – which enables qualities to subsist, these not being self-subsistent entities themselves. Thus, it seems that for Locke substrata must be what present-day philosophers of science would call *theoretical* entities. If Locke had held that *objects* – that is, particular substances – rather than merely their *qualities* were experienced by us, then indeed he might have been able to say that by a 'partial consideration' of an object *qua* object, prescinding from its qualities, we can come by the idea of substratum, as that aspect of an object which serves its property-bearing role. But that is not how Locke regards the contents of experience.

A symptom, it seems to me, of this apparent mismatch between Martin's account and Locke's epistemology is that Martin has little scope to explain Locke's repeated insistence upon our *ignorance* of substratum, a fact which surfaces in Martin's somewhat odd remark that 'Our general idea of a substratum . . . is no more obscure or unknowable than the abstract general notion of "property" itself as Locke, at least, was able to see' (Martin 1980, p. 6). That might be so on Martin's account, but for that very reason, it seems to me, it cannot be supposed to be *Locke's* account, for Locke only too frequently emphasizes the *obscurity* of our idea of substratum.

Furthermore, but relatedly, it is not clear to me that Martin's account correctly identifies what Locke's idea of substratum is supposed to be an idea *of*. Martin insists that, for Locke, substrata are definitely not *objects*, that is, self-subsistent entities, but are something 'about' objects and as such dependent beings, quite as much as qualities are. But, to the extent that Locke says anything on this matter at all, it seems to me that he implies the very opposite of this, in a passage from the first Letter to Stillingfleet which is quoted by Martin himself. In this passage Locke remarks, concerning the notion of substance or substratum:

> But this is the best I can hitherto find, either in my own thoughts, or in the books of logicians: for their account or idea of it is, that it is 'Ens' or 'res per se subsistens, et substans accidentibus' . . . in short . . . something which supports accidents, or other . . . modes, and is not supported itself as a mode or an accident.
>
> (Locke 1823, p. 8)

The key phrase here is 'res per se subsistens' (literally, 'thing subsisting by itself'). For Martin contends, as I see it incompatibly with this passage, that 'Locke's use of the term "substance" . . . in which it may be interchanged with the term "substratum" . . . is very distinct from the use which means roughly "that which can subsist by itself"'' (Martin 1980, p. 3). I would acknowledge that the notion of something that can 'subsist by itself' is ambiguous, meaning either something that can exist separately from other entities or something that is the ground of its own existence – and that Locke, since he presumably does not think that there could be 'naked' substrata, does not think that a substratum can 'subsist by itself' in the first of these two senses. However, Martin seems committed to the view that Lockean substrata cannot 'subsist by themselves' in either sense, because for Martin a substratum is just as much something 'about' an object as any of its qualities are.

So, ingenious though Martin's proposal is, I do not think that it is fully consistent with Locke's tendency of thought, either as regards what substrata are or as regards the way in which we arrive at our idea of substratum. That is not to say that Martin's account of substratum may not be a good one in its own right, as an independent contribution to metaphysics. As I have already indicated, I agree with many of the reasons that motivate Martin's account. But, on balance, I prefer in the end a somewhat different account, according to which the substratum of an object's properties is to be identified with that very object. On this account, of course, substrata most certainly *are* objects and 'self-subsistent' entities. However, although I have framed this account as an alternative both to Locke's and to Martin's, I should mention that on occasion Martin seems to edge towards it himself, notably at the end of his discussion, where he says: 'The passionfruit under this partial consideration [that is, considered merely as a bearer of properties] . . . is indeed the substance or substratum' (Martin 1980, p. 10). Quite so. But then I don't think that it is open to Martin to say, as he does also say, that the substratum is something *about* the object, or an *ingredient* of the object (Martin 1980, p. 7), and that substrata are *not* themselves objects.

SUBSTANCE AND REAL ESSENCE

No discussion of Locke's views about substance would be complete without some mention of how those views relate to his conception of 'real essence' and his distinction between this and 'nominal essence'. At one point, Locke remarks:

> [W]e come to have the *Ideas of particular sorts of Substances*, by collecting such Combinations of simple *Ideas*, as are by Experience

... taken notice of to exist together, and are therefore supposed to flow from the particular internal Constitution, or unknown Essence of that Substance.

(*Essay*, II, XXIII, 3)

We have already noted how, according to Locke, the idea of a *sort* of substance is an abstract general idea which collects together the simple ideas of certain qualities which we find by experience regularly to accompany one another. For Locke, this abstract general idea constitutes what he calls the 'nominal essence' of any particular substance of that sort. But in the passage just quoted, he uses the term 'essence' in a different sense, to refer to the 'particular internal Constitution' of a substance – and this is what he means by its 'real essence'. In the case of material substances, he assumes that this 'internal constitution' will be a particular atomic structure, in accordance with the atomistic conception of matter favoured by the leading empirical scientists of his day, such as Robert Boyle. Of course, at that time atomism was only a speculative hypothesis, which is why Locke speaks of the real essences of material substances as being 'unknown'.

Some commentators have been tempted to suppose that Locke takes the substratum of any particular material substance actually to *be* its real essence. After all, real essence is like substratum in being unknown, at least to us. Moreover, as the passage just quoted indicates, Locke thinks that the observable qualities of a particular material substance are *dependent* upon its real essence – they supposedly 'flow' from it. And this sounds rather like the supposed dependence of those qualities upon the substratum. However, at least two considerations render this postulated identity of substratum with real essence highly implausible. The first is that, as I contended earlier, the dependence of qualities upon a Lockean substratum cannot plausibly be taken to be genuinely *causal* in character, even if Locke does on occasion use causal vocabulary in this connection. The second is that individual atoms are themselves particular material substances – indeed, for Locke they are so in a stricter sense, as we have seen, than that in which complex macroscopic material objects typically are. But these atomic substances, too, will have their particular qualities of shape, solidity and so forth – that is, various Lockean 'primary' qualities. So if there is a problem as to how qualities can be united together as the qualities of a single object, it is a problem that arises quite as much for the qualities of individual material atoms as it does for those of macroscopic objects possessing an 'internal constitution' in the form of a complex atomic structure. And, of course, atoms themselves are not supposed to have any 'internal constitution' in this sense. (Note here that we should not confuse Locke's hypothetical 'atoms' with what present-day physicists call 'atoms'. The latter are indeed taken to possess a complex internal structure of protons, neutrons and electrons. The nearest present-day equivalent to a Lockean atom would be a so-called 'fundamental particle', such as an electron or a quark.) That Locke himself was fully conscious of this point is indicated by the following passage:

> If anyone should be asked, what is the subject wherein Colour or Weight inheres, he would have nothing to say, but the solid extended parts: And if he were demanded, what is it, that that Solidity and Extension inhere in, [he would have to reply] something, he knew not what.
>
> (*Essay*, II, XXIII, 2)

For Lockean atoms, as I have just remarked, are certainly supposed to possess qualities such as solidity and extension.

Let me now briefly return to Locke's notion of *nominal* essence. According to Locke, the only way in which particular substances can be classified into sorts or kinds is by reference to their nominal essences, that is, by reference to the abstract general ideas which, in his view, our names for such sorts or kinds signify:

> Things are ranked under Names into sorts or *Species*, only as they
> agree to certain abstract *Ideas*, to which we have annexed those
> Names.
>
> (*Essay*, III, III, 15)

Of course, this is not to say that we have an entirely free hand as to
what simple ideas we may collect together to form the abstract
general idea of a really existing sort of substance, for we should
only include simple ideas of qualities that we find by experience
regularly to accompany one another. None the less, the implication is that, for Locke, nature contains no sorts or species of
substances independently of our practices of abstraction and
classification, at least so far as complex macroscopic substances
in Locke's looser sense are concerned. This is made clear in the
following passage:

> [T]he ranking of Things into *Species* . . . is done by us, according to
> the *Ideas* that we have of them . . . [I]f we suppose it to be done by
> their real internal Constitutions, and that Things existing are
> distinguished by Nature into Species, by real Essences, according
> as we distinguish them into *Species* by Names, we shall be liable to
> great Mistakes.
>
> (*Essay*, III, VI, 13)

Locke is, then, a 'nominalist' or anti-realist concerning the sorts or
species of naturally occurring macroscopic substances. Nature supplies us only with a multiplicity of particular substances which
resemble and differ from each other in various ways: it is we who
group them into species and name them accordingly. As Locke
vividly puts it at one point:

> *General and Universal*, belong not to the real existence of Things;
> but *are the Inventions and Creatures of the Understanding*.
>
> (Essay, III, III, 11)

LOCKE ON THE IDEAS OF NUMBER AND UNITY

As I mentioned in the previous chapter, in distinguishing between the primary and secondary qualities of bodies in the *Essay*, Locke notoriously included number amongst the first:

> The *Qualities* then that are in *Bodies* rightly considered, are of *Three Sorts*. *First*, the *Bulk, Figure, Number, Situation*, and *Motion, or Rest* of their solid Parts . . . These I call *primary Qualities*.
>
> (*Essay*, II, VIII, 23)

Later in the *Essay*, in the chapter entitled 'Of Number', he goes on to say:

> Amongst all the *Ideas* we have, as there is none suggested to the Mind by more ways, so there is none more simple, than that *of Unity*, or One: . . . every Thought of our Minds brings this *Idea* along with it . . . For Number applies it self to Men, Angels, Actions, Thoughts, every thing that either doth exist, or can be imagined.
>
> (*Essay*, II, XVI, 1)

Almost as well-known as Locke's view of number and unity is Berkeley's peremptory repudiation of that view, both in his *Principles of Human Knowledge* and in his earlier work, *An Essay towards a New Theory of Vision*. Thus, for example, in section 109 of the latter Berkeley roundly asserts that

> [N]umber . . . is entirely the creature of the mind . . . According as the mind variously combines its ideas the unit varies: and as the unit, so the number, which is only a collection of units, doth also vary. We call a window one, a chimney one, and yet a house in which there are many windows and many chimneys hath an equal right to be called one, and many houses go to the making of one city.
>
> (Berkeley 1975, p. 40)

This passage is quoted, with apparent approval, by the famous German philosopher of mathematics Gottlob Frege in his highly influential book, *The Foundations of Arithmetic* (Frege 1953). Indeed, such has been Frege's influence on present-day philosophy of language and mathematics that his view of number and unity has now almost completely prevailed over that advanced by Locke. I should stress, however, that Frege himself should not be taken to concur with Berkeley's suggestion that number is somehow subjective, or 'entirely a creature of the mind'. His agreement with Berkeley extends only as far as the latter's rejection of the view that, as Frege puts it, 'Number is a property of external things' (Frege 1953, p. 27). Frege's own view is that '[T]he content of a statement of number is an assertion about a concept' – and to illustrate what he means by this he remarks, 'If I say "the King's carriage is drawn by four horses", then I assign the number four to the concept "horse that draws the King's carriage" ' (Frege 1953, p. 59).

Frege himself appeals, on several occasions, to the sort of consideration that Berkeley adduces for rejecting Locke's view of number. For example, at one point he remarks that

> The Number 1 . . . or 100 or any other Number, cannot be said to belong to [a] pile of playing cards in its own right, but at most to belong to it in view of the way in which we have chosen to regard it.
>
> (Frege 1953, p. 29)

Here the suggestion seems to be that what is, from one point of view, one pack of cards is, from another point of view, fifty-two cards, while from yet another it is four suits, and so on. Even so, there is every indication that Frege is ambivalent about endorsing Berkeley in quite these terms – and not just on account of Berkeley's subjectivism concerning number. Rather, the problem is that it is not hard to discern a latent incoherence in this way of putting things. The incoherence is very near the surface in another passage of Frege's book, where he says: 'While looking at one and the same external phenomenon, I can say with equal truth "It is a copse" and "It is five trees" ' (Frege 1953, p. 59). For how can Frege say that *one and the same* 'external phenomenon' is both one copse and five trees? What is this 'it' that is somehow both a single copse and five different trees? Frege is clearly aware of the difficulty, for in first presenting the example of the pack of cards he remarks:

> [I]f I place a pile of playing cards in [someone's] hands with the words: Find the number of these, this does not tell him whether I wish to know the number of cards, or of complete packs of cards, or even say of honour cards at skat. To have given him the pile in his hands is not yet to have given him completely the object he is to investigate; I must add some further word – cards, or packs, or honours.
>
> (Frege 1953, pp. 28–9)

Clearly, Frege does not really want to say, *on his own account*, that one and the same thing can literally be both one and more than one. This is why he admits, later, that 'Several examples given earlier gave the false impression that different numbers may belong to the same thing' (Frege 1953, p. 61). It would seem, in fact, that Frege's use of the Berkeleian examples is supposed to contribute towards a *reductio ad absurdum* of the view that numbers are properties of objects. The idea seems to be that if we suppose that numbers are properties of objects, then we shall have to say that different numbers may, with equal legitimacy, be assigned to the same object or objects: that, for example, the same thing may be regarded as one pack of cards or as fifty-two cards. However, the trouble is that, far from creating a difficulty for philosophers like Locke, the argument, thus understood, rebounds against Frege himself. Berkeley, it should be noted, used the contentious examples to try to show that number is not a 'primary quality' of objects, which they possess independently of the mind: it was no part of his purpose to argue that number is not in any sense a property of objects. But Frege clearly recognizes the incoherence of saying that *anything* could be at once one thing and more than one thing and that this incoherence does not go away simply by supposing that number is somehow mind-dependent, or a matter of how we 'view' or 'regard' whatever it is to which we are assigning a number. If this is incoherent, however, then it cannot be something to which any philosopher is committed simply in virtue of supposing that number is a property of objects or things. Rather, the philosopher who takes this view must clearly just insist that, for example, one pack of cards cannot be identified with fifty-two different cards, even though it may, of course, be said to consist of fifty-two different cards. And, as we shall see when we look at Locke's account of the idea of identity, this is precisely the sort of thing that he himself would in any case want to say.

Frege has related remarks about the idea of unity which are equally unsatisfactory. Here again he follows Berkeley – who expresses contempt for Locke's suggestion that the idea of unity accompanies every other idea, saying that he can find no such idea in his own mind. Part of what Locke is suggesting, clearly, is that everything whatever that exists or could exist is 'one' or a 'unit': that simply in virtue of being itself and distinct from anything else, each and every thing has 'unity'. But Frege is just as contemptuous as Berkeley about this suggestion. Sarcastically, he comments:

> It must strike us immediately as remarkable that every single thing should possess this property [of being 'one']. The content of a concept diminishes as its extension increases; if its extension becomes all-embracing, its content must vanish altogether.
>
> (Frege 1953, p. 40)

But this argument, too, backfires on Frege. It is a poor argument against a putative concept that those who profess to deploy it suppose it to apply to everything whatever. Indeed, Frege himself, along with most other philosophers, would accept that the concept of self-identity applies to everything whatever, but cannot be convicted on that account of evacuating the concept of all content.

Now, if we are to take seriously Locke's suggestion that number is a property of things, then, clearly, the only number that can be assigned to a single thing – Berkeley's objection having been repudiated – is *one*. But this means, of course, that numbers other than one can only be assigned to *more than one* thing – that is, to *pluralities* of things. We say, for example, and quite properly, that the planets are nine in number, as are the muses of Greek mythology. In the sentence 'The planets are nine', the subject term, 'the planets', refers plurally to Mercury, Venus, Earth, Mars, Jupiter, Saturn, Uranus, Neptune and Pluto, and the predicate attributes the property of being nine *to that plurality*. We should not be misled here by the fact that the expression 'that plurality' is grammatically singular in form. It does not signify that there is some further *thing*, the 'plurality of the planets', in addition to the planets themselves. But notice now that since pluralities exist and are not themselves single things, Frege's objection to the concept of 'being one' – that its extension would have to be 'all-embracing' – is not only misguided, but rests on a false assumption. For the concept does not apply to, for example, the planets or the muses. Rather, the concept of *being nine* applies to these.

I have been concerned in this section to defend the Lockean view that numbers are properties of objects against Frege's objections. But so far I have not mentioned one consideration which seems to have weighed particularly heavily with Frege. This is the apparent problem confronted by the Lockean view in the case of the number *nought*, or *zero*. As Frege remarks, 'If I say "Venus has 0 moons", there simply does not exist any moon or agglomeration of moons for anything to be asserted of' (Frege 1953, p. 59). In other words, even if we can maintain that the property of being one is a property that an object can – and indeed *must* – possess and that numbers greater than one can be possessed by pluralities of objects, it seems that there plainly can't be any object that possesses the property of being zero. By contrast, the concept *moon of Venus* clearly can have assigned to it the property of 'including nothing under it', which is how Frege recommends us to understand the assertion 'Venus has 0 moons'. How can an adherent of Locke's view of number respond to this objection? Well, it may be pointed out that, although it comes very naturally to a mathematician like Frege to think of 'zero' as denoting a number, most ordinary folk would consider it at best a bad joke to be told, say, that there is a number of pound notes in a sealed envelope that has just been given to them, when in fact the envelope is empty. The response 'Well, I did say *a number* of pound notes – and nought is a number' would do nothing to pacify the irate recipient. The introduction of the zero symbol was undoubtedly an important landmark in the history of mathematics, but we should not assume that its utility in calculation is dependent upon its really denoting anything. In particular, we should not uncritically accept the currently standard view that 'zero' denotes *the empty set*, because it is far from clear that the notion of such a set really makes sense. All that we are ever informed about the empty set is that (1) it is a set, (2) it has no members and (3) it is unique amongst sets in having no members. However, there are very many things that 'have no members', in the set-theoretical sense – namely, all the things that are not sets. It is perfectly clear why these things have no members, for they are not sets. What is unclear is how there can be, uniquely amongst sets, a *set* that has no members. We cannot conjure such an entity into existence by mere stipulation – although this, it seems to me, is what many philosophers of mathematics, including Frege himself, effectively try to do. So, my reply to Frege on Locke's behalf to the objection that has just been raised is that the reason why the property of being zero cannot be possessed by any object or plurality of objects is that there is no such number as zero and consequently no such property as the property of being zero.

LOCKE ON IDENTITY AND PERSONAL IDENTITY

I have included the foregoing discussion of Locke's views concerning number and unity partly because, quite unjustly, they tend nowadays either to be entirely neglected or else to be dismissed as obviously mistaken. But I have also done so because it helps to prepare us for his even more important views about identity. These views, it must be said, have been very extensively discussed by other commentators and critics. Partly for that reason, I shall be relatively selective in what I have to say about them here, focusing in good measure on some less familiar points, while still making sure that the core features of Locke's doctrine are plainly to be seen. More, perhaps, has been written about Locke on personal identity than on any other single Lockean theme and it is a subject over which Locke scholars are particularly prone to disagree. Only a book-length treatment of the topic could possibly do full justice either to it or to the enormous secondary literature dealing with it. The most that I can hope to do here is to give the reader a taste of – and for – some of the important issues that it raises.

I remarked earlier, in connection with Frege's example of the pack of cards, that Locke himself would be entirely happy to agree that one pack of cards cannot be identified with fifty-two different cards, even though it may, of course, be said to consist of fifty-two different cards. This is an implication of Locke's greatest insight concerning the idea of identity, encapsulated in his observation that '[S]uch as is the Idea belonging to [a] Name, such must be the Identity' (Essay, II, XXVII, 7). It is this insight that leads him subsequently to make the remark: 'This being premised to find wherein personal identity consists, we must consider what Person stands for' (Essay, II, XXVII, 9). Locke's basic point here is that what makes for identity or diversity in the case of things of one sort or kind need not do so in the case of things of another sort or kind. Each sortal term or name – recalling that the expression 'sortal' is of Locke's own coinage – carries with it, as part of its very meaning, implications concerning the conditions under which particular things answering to that name are or are not capable of being identified with one another.

We can call such conditions the identity conditions of particular things belonging to the sort or kind named by the sortal term in question (although 'identity conditions' is not in fact a phrase that Locke himself uses). And, as I say, Locke's great insight is that the identity conditions of things of one sort need not be the same as the identity conditions of things of another sort. Locke, indeed, famously argues that the identity conditions of *persons* differ from those of animals and other living organisms, which in turn differ from those of mere material bodies. Returning to Frege's example of the pack of cards, we may likewise say that the identity conditions of the individual cards in a pack differ from those of the pack itself. Thus, for example, if I exchange one card in a pack for a new one – say, if I replace the old ten of clubs by a new ten of clubs – then, strictly speaking, I have in my hand a different pack of cards. A pack of cards, we may say, *depends for its identity* upon the fifty-two individual cards that belong to it, so that if any one of them is replaced, even by another exactly similar card, I am left with a different pack of cards. By contrast, I could replace a small part of the paper making up any individual card – if, for instance, it had become slightly damaged in some way – without thereby coming into possession of a different card. An individual card, we may say, does *not* depend for its identity upon the paper that happens to make it up at any given time, because at least some of that paper can be replaced by new and different paper without this affecting the identity of the card in question.

One of the first applications by Locke of his important insight is in drawing the distinction that he does between the identity conditions of what he calls 'bodies' or 'masses', on the one hand, and living organisms on the other. An example of a Lockean body or mass would, it seems, be something like a *lump of gold* or a *piece of chalk* – abstracting away, perhaps, from the fact that gold and chalk are different kinds of stuff, since Locke might allow that the very same body or mass could, in principle, change from being gold at one time to being chalk at another. Locke, in deference to the atomic theory of matter favoured by the great English scientists of his day, assumes that all masses are ultimately composed of indivisible material atoms. And with regard to the identity conditions of bodies or masses, his proposal is that

> [W]hilst [a number of atoms] exist united together, the Mass, consisting of the same Atoms, must be the same Mass, let the parts be never so differently jumbled: But if one of these Atoms be taken away, or one new one added, it is no longer the same Mass or the same Body.
>
> (*Essay*, II, XXVII, 3)

In other words, Locke holds that the identity of a body or mass depends on the identities of the atoms composing it: changing one of those atoms changes the identity of the mass – just as changing one card in a pack of cards changes the identity of the pack. By contrast, Locke has this to say concerning the identity conditions of living organisms:

> In the state of living Creatures, their Identity depends not on a Mass of the same Particles; but on something else. For in them the variation of great parcels of Matter alters not the Identity.
>
> (*Essay*, II, XXVII, 3)

Locke's point is that a living organism – such as, to use one of his own examples, an oak tree – constantly loses and gains material particles through processes of growth, metabolism and decay, without our being in the least inclined to say, on this account, that we have strictly and literally *different oak trees* before and after such a gain or loss, in the way we *do* say just the equivalent in the case of lumps of gold or pieces of chalk. So what, then, *does* make for sameness and difference in the case of something like an oak tree? Locke's answer is as follows:

> [W]herein an Oak differs from a Mass of Matter . . . seems to me to be in this; that the one is only the Cohesion of Particles of Matter any how united, the other such a disposition of them as constitutes the parts of an Oak; and such an organization of those parts, as is fit to receive, and distribute nourishment, so as to continue, and frame the Wood, Bark, and Leaves, *etc.* of an Oak, in which consists the vegetable Life.
>
> (*Essay*, II, XXVII, 4)

In short, we continue to have the same oak tree just in case, despite any change of material particles, the particles involved at any given time continue to sustain the same life. Thus, if an oak tree were to die and many years later, by chance, the material particles composing it at the time of its death once again came to compose an oak tree, this would not be the *same* oak tree, because the life-process on which the identity of the first tree depended would have been terminated and a new life-process begun with the second tree.

We are now in a position to consider Locke's account of *personal* identity, which begins with the remark quoted earlier, that 'This being premised to find wherein *personal identity* consists, we must consider what *Person* stands for' (*Essay*, II, XXVII, 9). Locke answers the question posed here by saying that he considers a person to be

> a thinking intelligent Being, that has reason and reflection, and can consider it self as it self, the same thinking thing in different times and places; which it does only by that consciousness, which is inseparable from thinking, and as it seems to me essential to it.
>
> (*Essay*, II, XXVII, 9)

Thus the defining characteristics of persons, for Locke, are rationality and consciousness, including *self*-consciousness. In the light of this answer, he then proposes that

> [S]ince consciousness always accompanies thinking, and 'tis that, that makes every one to be, what he calls *self*; and thereby distinguishes himself from all other thinking things, in this alone consists *personal Identity*, *i.e.* the sameness of a rational Being. And as far as this consciousness can be extended backwards to any past Action or Thought, so far reaches the Identity of that *Person*; it is the same *self* now as it was then; and 'tis by the same *self* with this present one that now reflects on it, that that Action was done.
>
> (*Essay*, II, XXVII, 9)

Locke is emphatic that the idea of a *person* and that of a *man*, or human animal, are quite different. This is the moral of the somewhat incredible story he tells of a certain 'rational parrot', which supposedly surprised a visitor by engaging in intelligent conversation (*Essay*, II, XXVII, 8). Such a creature would, by Locke's account, qualify as a person although obviously not as a *man*. Locke is adamant, consequently, that *personal* identity should not be confused with *animal* identity: that what makes for the sameness of a *person* differs from what makes for the sameness of any *animal*, including man – as the following passage makes clear:

> [T]he Identity of the same *Man* consists . . . in nothing but a participation of the same continued Life, by constantly fleeting Particles of Matter, in succession vitally united to the same organized Body.
>
> (*Essay*, II, XXVII, 6)

Even so, Locke does see a certain analogy between animal identity and personal identity, as another passage brings out:

> Different Substances, by the same consciousness (where they do partake in) [are] united into one Person; as well as different Bodies, by the same Life are united into one Animal, whose *Identity* is preserved, in that change of Substances, by the unity of one continued Life.
>
> (*Essay*, II, XXVII, 10)

Locke's thought here seems to be somewhat as follows. We have seen how he holds that animal identity consists in the participation of ever-changing material particles in the same continuing life-process. Now he seems to be suggesting that personal identity similarly consists in the participation of successive *spiritual substances* – that is, immaterial soul-like entities – in the same continuing process of consciousness. This is a good point at which to recall that, for Locke, the only things that are *strictly speaking* 'particular substances' are (1) individual material atoms and larger 'masses' of such atoms, (2) individual 'finite spirits' or souls and (3) God – supposedly an infinite immaterial substance. According to Locke, then, animals are not strictly speaking 'particular substances' because, although they are necessarily composed of material particles throughout their existence, they are not *identifiable* with masses of such particles, because animals and masses of matter have different identity conditions. Rather, they are 'modes'. Likewise, it seems, persons like ourselves are not, for Locke, strictly speaking 'particular substances', because they cannot be identified with the spiritual substances that are supposedly the bearers of the properties of consciousness and thought. We too, it seems, are really only *modes*. It is not hard to imagine how repugnant this suggestion must have been to the religious dogmatists of Locke's day. (To be fair, however, I should emphasize that this view of persons, which I am not alone in attributing to Locke, is at most only implicit in certain parts of the *Essay*, and is hard to discern or seemingly even contradicted in other parts — a fact that is hardly surprising in view of the *Essay*'s lengthy period of gestation and frequent revisions.)

It is worth remarking here that Locke does famously speculate at one point that God, in his omnipotence, could have 'superadded' a power of thought or consciousness to matter (*Essay*, IV, III, 6) — a suggestion still more repugnant to Locke's theological opponents. Even so, Locke clearly thinks it much more likely that we do in fact have immaterial souls and that thought and consciousness are properties of such spiritual substances — in short, that it is my soul that thinks 'in' me. Yet he is insistent that our identity as persons does not depend, logically, upon the identity of our souls as spiritual substances. His point is that it is, he believes, perfectly conceivable that one and the same person should undergo a *change* of spiritual substance during the course of his or her existence — and equally conceivable that one and the same spiritual substance should successively serve as the soul of two distinct persons. According to Locke, all that is required for the first possibility is that my present soul should be *conscious* of — that is, remember — the thoughts and experiences of my past soul. Likewise, all that is required for the second possibility is that my soul should be *unconscious* of – that is, *fail* to remember – the thoughts and experiences that it had when it was the soul of a previous person. And Locke appeals to certain imaginary examples to try to convince us of these possibilities.

But does Locke's account of persons and personal identity really make sense? It is hard to see how it can. For if we allow that there *are* souls which do the thinking 'in' us, we must surely allow that those souls are themselves *persons* in their own right, because they appear to satisfy Locke's definition of a person – they are thinking, self-conscious beings. And yet by Locke's account, it seems, my soul cannot be the *same* person as I am, because I could supposedly acquire a new soul and it could supposedly become the soul of someone else. My soul and I are, by Locke's account, things of two quite different kinds, with different identity conditions – and of the two of us, I alone supposedly have the identity conditions of a *person*, even though my soul also qualifies as a person by Locke's definition. The proper solution to these difficulties, I believe, is to repudiate Locke's distinction between persons and thinking substances. I think we should say that, if anything, persons *are* thinking substances. But we need not therefore suppose that they are 'immaterial souls'. If the notion of an immaterial soul lays itself open to sceptical doubts as to whether my soul has changed overnight, or is perhaps identical with the soul of some ancient Greek – as in one of Locke's imaginary examples – then so much the worse for *that* conception of a 'thinking substance'. The best conception that we can frame of a thinking substance, I suggest, is precisely the conception of a *person*, with *ourselves* providing paradigm examples of this category of being.

Another apparent problem with Locke's account of personal identity is that it commits him to saying that if I genuinely cannot recollect the past thoughts and deeds of some person, then I simply cannot be the same person as the one who had those thoughts and did those deeds. This is partly connected with Locke's conviction – which is perfectly sensible in itself – that 'person' is 'a Forensick

Term appropriating Actions and their Merit' (*Essay*, II, XXVII, 26):
in other words, that it is a legal-cum-moral term, closely connected
with our practices of attributing responsibility and distributing
rewards and punishments. Locke strongly believes that a person
should not be held responsible and punished for deeds which he or
she genuinely has no recollection of performing. But one could, of
course, agree with Locke that persons should not be penalised for –
and so in this sense should not be 'held responsible for' – misdeeds
which they genuinely do not recollect having done, without agreeing with him that such persons should never be regarded as
being the *authors* of those misdeeds and in *that* sense not be 'held
responsible for' them.

Some recent authors, such as Derek Parfit, have attempted to
resuscitate a broadly Lockean account of personal identity by modi-
fying the role that memory is supposed to play in that account – in
particular, by abandoning the seemingly problematic claim that I
can be identified with some person existing at a past time only if
I can remember having at least some of the experiences that were
had by that person at that time (see Parfit 1984). Instead, it is
suggested, all that is necessary is that there should be a single
'overlapping chain of memories' between me and that past person
– so that, for example, if I can remember the experiences that a
certain person had yesterday, and that person was able to remember the experiences that a certain person had the day before, then I
may be identified with the person who had those experiences the
day before yesterday, even though I cannot now remember any of
the latter experiences. This seems to get around a famous difficulty
raised against Locke's account of personal identity by the Scottish
philosopher Thomas Reid (1710–96), invoking the example of an
elderly general who could remember his exploits as a brave young
officer but not what he did as a child, even though the young
officer could remember his childhood experiences (see Reid
1975). The problem is that Locke's original account requires us to
identify the old general with the young officer and the young

officer with the child, but not to identify the old general with the young child, which appears to be contradictory. The proposed revision to Locke's account clearly does not suffer from this apparent difficulty.

However, it is certainly debatable whether Locke himself would have welcomed this revision. It is equally debatable whether he would have been very receptive to another famous objection raised by Joseph Butler (1692–1752), one-time Bishop of Durham, who urged that Locke's account of personal identity is circular, because memory itself presupposes personal identity and therefore cannot be used to explain it (see Butler 1975). His point is that it is a precondition of attributing to anyone a genuine memory of some past experience that the person to whom one is attributing the memory was indeed the person who had the experience – for it apparently makes no sense to say that one person could genuinely remember having another person's experiences. Neo-Lockean revisionists like Parfit seek to evade this apparent difficulty by invoking, instead of the ordinary notion of memory, the notion of what they call 'quasi-memory', which is supposed to be just like ordinary memory, but without the implication that it cannot in principle be attributed to one person in respect of experiences that were undergone by another. But, again, I doubt whether Locke himself would have welcomed the proposal. Locke was not a 'technical' philosopher, sympathetic to the use of complex revisionary definitions in order to overcome perceived objections to philosophical theories. I suspect that his own response to the objections of Butler and Reid would have been to 'bite the bullet' – that is, to stick to his original account and deny the force of the objections. Both Butler and Reid held human persons to be genuine substances in the strictest sense of the term and, given that assumption, their memory-based objections may well have some force. But, as I have tried to make clear, it seems that Locke himself did not share that assumption – and in its absence, it is not so clear that such objections are compelling. That is why I think that if one seeks to mount a challenge to Locke's account of personal identity, one had better aim it directly against the assumption in question, perhaps in the way that I attempted to do earlier.

All in all, Locke's account of persons and personal identity appears to be a failure, and certainly less than completely successful. But if so, it is a magnificent failure, not least because it was the first attempt to solve one of the deepest and most challenging problems in philosophy – a problem that unquestionably still remains unsolved.

SUMMARY

Locke's metaphysics, although in many ways unsympathetic to the metaphysics of his Scholastic predecessors, shares with it a commitment to an ontology of individual substances and their particular properties, or modes. His ontology of substance and mode stands, however, in some tension with his empiricist epistemology, because he seems to insist that our simple ideas of sensation can only be ideas of *qualities* – that is, of modes – of material substances, apparently leaving him inadequate resources with which to explain how we can acquire our idea of substance in general. But what individual substances are there in the world, according to Locke? Strictly speaking, it seems, he thinks that they include only individual material bodies – that is, material atoms and aggregates of such atoms – finite spirits or souls, and God. This apparently implies that, for Locke, neither living creatures nor human persons are, strictly speaking, substances, because he thinks that neither living creatures nor human persons have the identity conditions of either material bodies or finite spirits. According to Locke, the identity of a living creature depends on the continuity of the processes in which its life consists, while our identity as persons depends on the continuity of our consciousness. Life and consciousness are processes, not substances, and hence in Locke's ontology belong to the category of *modes*. This is not to suggest that, for Locke, I just *am* my consciousness, or the sum total of my conscious states throughout my existence, any more than it is to suggest that, for Locke, an animal or a plant just *is* its life-processes. None the less, the implication is that the place of human persons and living creatures in Locke's ontology is not amongst the substances, strictly so called, but alongside 'all other things [that are] but Modes or Relations ultimately terminated in substances' (*Essay*, II, XXVII, 2). Many of Locke's readers may not find this conception of what we are as human persons very congenial. Clearly, many of his historical critics did not, particularly those wedded to traditional theological views. But if we want to challenge it, we must challenge the assumption that lies at the heart of it: that only material bodies, finite spirits, and God can strictly speaking qualify as substances.

FURTHER READING

Alston, William & Bennett, Jonathan 1988: 'Locke on People and Substances', *Philosophical Review* 97, pp. 25–46.

Ayers, Michael 1975: 'The Ideas of Power and Substance in Locke's Philosophy', *Philosophical Quarterly* 25, pp. 1–27, reprinted in revised form in I. C. Tipton (ed.), *Locke on Human Understanding* (Oxford: Oxford University Press, 1977).

Ayers, Michael 1991: *Locke, Volume II: Ontology* (London and New York: Routledge)

Ayers, Michael 1994: 'The Foundations of Knowledge and the Logic of Substance: The Structure of Locke's General Philosophy', in G. A. J. Rogers (ed.), *Locke's Philosophy: Content and Context* (Oxford: Clarendon Press).

Bennett, Jonathan 1987: 'Substratum', *History of Philosophy Quarterly* 4, pp. 197–215.

Lowe, E. J. 1989: *Kinds of Being: A Study of Individuation, Identity and the Logic of Sortal Terms* (Oxford: Blackwell).

McCann, Edwin 1994: 'Locke's Philosophy of Body', in Vere Chappell (ed.), *The Cambridge Companion to Locke* (Cambridge: Cambridge University Press).

Noonan, Harold 2003: *Personal Identity*, 2nd edn (London & New York: Routledge).

Four

Language and Meaning

If there is one approach to language which almost all modern philosophers have been united in repudiating, often with ridicule, it is the *ideational* approach – with Locke's version of it being the most common target for attack. The fundamental principles of this view of language are as follows. First, that the primary purpose of language is the communication of thought. Second, that thought itself consists fundamentally in the entertaining of ideas in the mind. And third, that words serve to express thoughts by being made, through custom or convention, to signify ideas in the minds of those who entertain them. Much of the current philosophical opposition to this view stems ultimately from the hostility that Gottlob Frege and Ludwig Wittgenstein bore towards such a conception of language. Frege was vehemently opposed to 'psychologism' in semantics, logical theory and the philosophy of mathematics, because he saw in this a threat to the cherished objectivity of logical and mathematical truth. And Wittgenstein was rootedly sceptical about any attempt to explain linguistic behaviour by appealing to supposedly 'inner' or 'private' mental processes. But I think that seventeenth-century philosophers like Locke were not perhaps so absurdly and wildly mistaken in their accounts of language as present-day orthodoxy would have us believe. Modern objections to ideational accounts of linguistic signification are often directed at mere figures of straw, rather than at the accounts that philosophers like Locke actually advanced. One thing I hope to establish in this chapter is that Locke himself certainly supplies us with many valuable insights into the nature of thought, language and their interrelationship, even if he does not offer us anything like a comprehensive theory of linguistic meaning.

IDEATIONISM AND LOCKE'S ACCOUNT OF LANGUAGE

Before looking in some detail at what Locke himself says, I shall state briefly and in very general terms what I see as being the basic philosophical problem of language and how the ideational theory purports to solve it. The basic problem I take to be this. How is it that we can use words – which in themselves are merely arbitrary sounds or visible marks – to speak about things in the world? That is to say, how do words and sentences of language acquire *semantic* properties, such as reference, meaning and truth? In essence, the answer of the ideational theory is that words acquire such semantic properties in virtue of being used by speakers to express and communicate their thoughts about things in the world. That is to say, words come to be 'about' things in the world by being made, through custom and convention, to represent or stand for our thoughts about those things. But if such an answer is not to be either vacuous or circular, it must surely be denied that thought itself is essentially linguistic. And this is precisely what the ideationist does deny. The ideationist may perhaps concede that thought is *sometimes* linguistic – that on occasion we may indeed 'think in words' – but nonetheless insists that there is a fundamental level of thought at which it is not linguistic but *imaginative* in character. At this level, according to the ideationist, we 'think in ideas'.

The great advantage of the ideational view of thought is that there is – or, at least, appears to be – no particular problem or mystery as to how processes of imagination can be 'about' things in the world, in a way that there clearly is as to how *words* can. This is because such processes are clearly akin to – and in respect of their form and content ultimately derivative from – processes of *sense perception*. And processes of sense perception are quite *naturally* 'about' things in the world, because evolution has shaped them for that purpose. This stands in sharp contrast with the way in which linguistic utterances are only *conventionally* 'about' such things. It would be wrong, of course, to suppose that there is no problem at all as to how processes of imagination can be 'about' things in the world. We might call this the problem of the *intentionality of imagination* – 'intentionality' being the term that philosophers currently favour to describe the property of 'aboutness' that sentences, thoughts and other modes of representation have characteristically in common. The point, however, is that the prospects for a solution to this problem from an ideationist viewpoint are much more promising than are the prospects for a solution to the problem of how *words* can be 'about' things in the world from a viewpoint that opposes ideationism. And this has to do with the fact just alluded to, that the connection between imagination and its worldly objects is natural rather than conventional in character. A slightly cryptic way of putting the point would be to say that the things that we are primarily equipped by nature to think about are things which – however they may be 'in themselves' – are *for us* essentially possible objects of perception. Consequently, these things are also essentially *imaginable* for us and so *thinkable* for us, according to the ideationist's view of thought. Another way of putting the point is to say that our ability to *conceive* of physical objects of various sorts is intimately tied to our knowledge of how such objects *appear* to one or more of our sense modalities – for example, how they look, sound or feel – so that in thinking of such objects we necessarily draw upon recognitional capacities whose primary sphere of application lies in processes of sense perception.

In order to understand the ideational theory of language properly, however, it is important not to confuse two quite distinct but interrelated levels on which it operates. Only on one of these levels should it be seen as offering an account of linguistic *meaning* – a semantic theory – in anything like the modern sense. By a 'semantic theory' I mean a theory of those *word-to-world* relations which confer upon linguistic entities such properties as reference and truth.

Historically, proponents of the ideational approach like Locke did not in fact busy themselves much with this level, because they were much more concerned to present an account of linguistic *expression* – that is, a theory of those *word-to-thought* relations which confer upon linguistic entities a power to convey one speaker's thoughts to another. Clearly, though, a theory of word-to-thought relations can be combined with a theory of *thought-to-world* relations – a theory of *cognition* – to produce a theory of word-to-world relations. And that this is the correct route to semantic theory is implicit in the ideational approach, even if its historical proponents were not much concerned to chart that route in detail themselves. But, it seems to me, many modern critics of the ideational approach criticize its account of *linguistic expression* as though it were intended to be an account of *linguistic meaning*, with the result that the ideational approach is represented in so ridiculous a guise that it is hard to see how eminent philosophers like Locke, and before him Thomas Hobbes, could have entertained it at all.

It is vital to appreciate that the ideational theory of language does not maintain, absurdly, that the words or sentences that we utter *refer to* or are made *true or false by* the thoughts we use them to express. That is to say, the theory is not offering a subjective – indeed, almost solipsistic – theory of *meaning*. The explanation for this common misinterpretation, I suspect, is that it arises precisely from the disparity of interests between the historical proponents of ideationism and their modern critics. The critics, being primarily interested in semantic theory themselves, assume that when the ideationists speak at such length about words 'signifying' ideas they, too, must be advancing a semantic thesis. And they find confirmation for this assumption in the fact that little else in the way of explicit semantic theory appears in the writings which they criticize – not realizing that this absence is due to the ideationists' relative lack of interest in semantic theory altogether.

It is time now that we began to examine Locke's own account of language, especially as he presents it in the first two chapters of

Book III of the *Essay Concerning Human Understanding*. Chapter I opens with these words:

> God having designed Man for a sociable Creature, made him not
> only with an inclination, and under a necessity to have fellowship
> with those of his own kind; but furnished him also with Language,
> which was to be the great Instrument, and common Tye of society.
> *Man* therefore had by Nature his Organs so fashioned, as to be *fit to
> frame articulate Sounds*, which we call Words. But this was not
> enough to produce Language; for Parrots, and several other Birds,
> will be taught to make articulate Sounds distinct enough, which yet,
> by no means, are capable of Language.
>
> > (*Essay*, III, I, 1)

We may question, of course, the allegedly divine origin of our linguistic ability, as we may also question the teleological explanation offered by Locke for our ability to produce articulate sounds. We may suppose that creatures capable of language will just employ whatever species of physical signs or symbols they find most convenient, which in the case of human beings happen to be vocal. However, parrots, as Locke points out, can also make these same sounds: so what do parrots lack that renders them incapable of speech? Locke answers as follows:

> Besides articulate Sounds . . . it was farther necessary, that [Man]
> should be *able to use these Sounds, as Signs of internal
> Conceptions*; and to make them stand as marks for the *Ideas* within
> his own Mind, whereby they might be known to others, and the
> Thoughts of Men's Minds be conveyed from one to another.
>
> > (*Essay*, III, I, 2)

So what parrots lack is thought. They cannot speak because they have no thoughts to convey by speech. Or, at least, their utterances are certainly not used by them to *express* thoughts, even if they have any – and this is why their utterances do not constitute speech. (Let us set aside, now, Locke's tale of the 'rational parrot', discussed in the previous chapter.) Plainly, though, Locke's assumption here is that human thought itself is not essentially linguistic, but on the contrary *imaginative* – it consists of 'ideas'. If thought itself were conceived of as essentially involving speech – whether overtly or covertly, in the form of 'silent soliloquy' – then, as I have already emphasized, a theory such as Locke's would just be vacuous. For if, as Locke wants to say, what makes an utterance speech as opposed to mere babble is that it is expressive of *thought* and yet thought itself essentially involved the use of words, then we should need some further criterion to distinguish between words that are used 'thoughtfully' and those that are not.

Now, the suggestion that at the most fundamental level we 'think in ideas' can easily be made to seem preposterous by unsympathetic critics: for instance, by misrepresenting 'ideas' as being mental *images* – ghostly pictures floating before the mind's eye. However, as we saw in Chapter 3, it is open to question whether even Locke himself subscribed to this naive conception of ideas – and, certainly, it is a conception that is in no way essential to an ideationist theory of thought. I shall return to this issue in a moment, but first of all I want to stress again the close kinship between imagination and *perception*. It might almost be said that imagination is a kind of surrogate for perception – that to exercise one's imagination is to rehearse or anticipate actual or possible episodes of perceptual experience, although with a degree of voluntary control that is characteristically absent from perception itself. (In perception one can direct one's attention at will, but has very little voluntary control over *what* is perceived once one's attention has been fixed.) Imagination, like perception, may be classified by reference to its sensory modes – and thus we have visual, auditory and tactile imagination, just as we have these forms of perception. Unsurprisingly, there is neuropsychological and neurophysiological evidence that many of the same areas of the brain are typically engaged in imagination as are engaged in perception. A great deal more can no doubt be said about imagination and its relation to perception, but these observations should suffice to emphasize the intimacy of that relation.

What is particularly important for our present purposes is the fact that very often one may understand a situation simply in perceiving it – and that this kind of non-discursive or intuitive understanding carries across to processes of imagination. For example, in observing a road accident one may register in a holistic fashion what is happening before one's eyes. One's understanding of the situation isn't the product of a sequential articulation of the scene in thought. And it certainly isn't a matter of describing to oneself in words, sotto voce, what is happening. But then, in very much the same way, one may imagine just such a road accident – and here again the kind of understanding involved is intuitive or non-discursive. What one is then doing is precisely 'thinking in ideas' rather than in words. But such thought is certainly not a matter of being confronted with anything that one could helpfully call mental 'images'. Images or pictures, after all, require interpretation in order to be understood, whereas what I am saying about imaginative thought is that the understanding involved in it is integral to the imaginative process itself and not superimposed upon it by a further act of thinking. Obviously, in view of this it is somewhat unfortunate that we call imagination what we do, since it does not literally involve the presentation of 'images' for scrutiny by an 'inner eye'. The term is, no doubt, partly the product of a mistaken conception of the nature of the process in question – and that is why I prefer sometimes to call it 'ideation' instead, because this is a technical term which carries little baggage in the way of misleading connotations.

A LOCKEAN RESPONSE TO THE PREJUDICES OF LITERACY

I suspect that one reason why many modern philosophers tend to underrate the scope and versatility of imaginative thought is that they succumb to the prejudices of literacy, which lead them to exaggerate the importance of discursive thinking. Illiterate and inarticulate people often complain that they understand some matter perfectly clearly but are unable to express this understanding adequately in speech – they can't, they claim, put what they think 'into words'. Linguistic philosophers have tended to dismiss such claims with the argument that the only satisfactory test of whether or not people really do understand a certain matter is precisely whether or not they can clearly *state* what they mean in language. If they can't, it is assumed that they were only under the illusion of understanding clearly. Here we see the prejudices of literacy at work. Because philosophers are usually highly articulate themselves, they find that lack of clarity in their own thought is generally reflected in unclear linguistic expression – and by extension they tend to regard the rest of humanity in the same light. But the argument that I have just referred to – that clarity of expression is the only satisfactory criterion of clarity of thought – is plainly mistaken. For clear thought and understanding may surely be manifested in non-verbal behaviour, quite as well as in speech and writing.

Those philosophers who are sceptical regarding the possibilities of thought without language might do well to reflect on a famous passage (only a small part of which I quote here) in William James's *Principles of Psychology*, in which the remarkable childhood reminiscences of a deaf-mute are recorded:

> Some two or three years before my initiation into the rudiments of written language . . . I began to ask myself the question: *How came the world into being?* When this question occurred to my mind, I set myself to thinking it over a long time. My curiosity was awakened as to what was the origin of human life in its first appearance upon the earth . . . and also the cause of the existence of the earth, sun, moon, and stars.
>
> (James 1890, Volume I, pp. 266ff.)

If they are to be trusted, these memories are testimony to a capacity for non-discursive thinking even about matters of a fairly abstruse character, quite far removed from the concrete circumstances of everyday experience. This child, it seems, was perfectly capable of thinking non-verbally about the abstract and the general as well as about the concrete and the particular.

Locke himself has the beginnings of an answer to those who suppose language to be an inherently superior vehicle for abstract and general thought, when he remarks that

> [T]hose [Words], which are made use of to stand for Actions and Notions quite removed from sense, *have their rise from thence, and from obvious sensible* Ideas *are transferred to more abstruse significations*, and made to stand for *Ideas* that come not under the cognizance of our senses; *v.g.* to *Imagine, Apprehend, Comprehend, Adhere, Conceive, Instil, Disgust, Disturbance, Tranquillity*, etc. are all Words taken from the Operations of sensible Things.
>
> (*Essay*, III, I, 5)

What Locke is suggesting here is that etymology betrays the fact that the language that we use to discuss more 'abstruse' subjects has largely developed through the use of metaphors and similes grounded in our intuitive understanding of concrete, perceptible things. (Recall his – not entirely successful – application of this line of thought to our talk about substratum, discussed in the last chapter.) But if the scope of language can be extended in this way, so too can that of imaginative thought itself – indeed, according to an idea-tionist like Locke, the two developments almost inevitably go hand in hand. We should never underestimate the importance of imaginative models and metaphors in our understanding of even the most abstract and sophisticated subjects. Consider, for instance, the heuristic value of graphs and diagrams in mathematics and logic, or the historical role of visual and even physical models in the development of scientific theories of atomic and molecular structure.

Of course, it must be acknowledged that in an area like that of mathematical thinking, most of us depend very largely upon a painfully acquired ability to manipulate symbols according to formal rules. But it need not be claimed on behalf of the ideational theory that *whatever* can be thought in language can equally be thought 'in ideas'. One may readily concede, for instance, that a creature altogether lacking language could never entertain the thought that *tomorrow is Tuesday* – because we have no way of distinguishing between days of the week other than in terms of their names and the way in which those names are ordered in our calendrical system. It is quite enough that the ideational theory can rebut the charge that imaginative thought is, by its very nature, limited to the concrete and the particular, or to the here and now. At the same time, however, we shouldn't allow ourselves to be deceived by the familiarity of words and the facility with which we can use them into overestimating the extent to which ordinary language provides a vehicle for clear and determinate thought. Locke and his contemporaries were much more acutely aware than many modern philosophers seem to be of the deficiencies and abuses of words. The thoughts that language clothes are often much less splendid than their attire.

Quite commonly, the ideational theory of language is characterized by its detractors as maintaining that speakers and auditors are constantly engaged in processes of *translation* from ideas into words and from words into ideas – and is often criticized by them precisely on this account. But this characterization is a distortion, because it imposes a quasi-linguistic model upon the ideational theory of thought – as though 'ideas' occupied a wordlike role in a so-called 'language of thought'. Many modern philosophers of mind have in fact quite explicitly adopted the 'language of thought' hypothesis (see Fodor 1975) and, along with it, a theory of natural language comprehension which represents speakers as translating into and out of this supposed language, sometimes referred to as 'Mentalese'. But, however appropriate such a translational model might be for such a theory, it is clearly inappropriate to invoke it for the purposes of an ideational theory like Locke's. 'Mentalese', after all, is at least supposedly language-like in having, according to its advocates, quasi-lexical symbolic elements which combine to form sentence-like syntactical structures. But in describing ideational thinking as 'non-discursive', I am precisely implying that it fails to exhibit anything that could legitimately be called 'syntactical structure'. And, lacking any such structure, it cannot really be put into any relation of *translation* to linguistic utterances. 'Being a translation of' is a relation which holds between two language-like representations when they share the same *meaning* – that is, when they possess the same *semantic* properties. But, as we have already seen, according to the ideational approach it is vital not to confuse *semantic* (word-to-world) relations with *cognitive* (thought-to-world) relations. Consequently, it would be quite contrary to the precepts of ideationism to treat the *expressive* relation between thought and language as though it were a relation of *translation*. Indeed, the ideationist must regard the 'language of thought' hypothesis and its attendant account of natural language comprehension as being guilty of a serious confusion on precisely this score.

Another point which needs to be emphasized on behalf of ideationism is that its proponents can quite consistently allow that a good deal of our thinking, even when it concerns matters which *could* be thought about non-discursively, is done 'in words' – that is, in words of ordinary natural languages such as English and French. Such thinking often consists, in fact, in *imagined discourse* and thus still involves 'having ideas', albeit auditory ideas *of words*. But the ideationist will add that what makes such discursive thought thought about an *extralinguistic subject-matter*, rather than just thought about *words*, is that the person engaging in it has a capacity to use these words to express non-discursive, imaginative thoughts about that same subject-matter.

When we think purely 'in words' we are, as Berkeley would put it, 'regarding only the signs' – but what gives life to these signs, on the ideationist view, is precisely our capacity to use them at will to express our *ideas*. Hence, on this view, when speakers use words, whether overtly or in 'inner speech', without knowing what non-verbal ideas the words may serve to express, they use them insignificantly – unless, of course, the words (or symbols) are indispensable for thought about the subject-matter in question, as in mathematics. In this, as in many other respects, Berkeley's rather sophisticated version of the ideational theory – especially as developed in his mature work of 1732, *Alciphron* (Berkeley 1949) – represents a considerable advance on Locke's original rather sketchy and inchoate account. It should be added that Berkeley did not regard the ideational approach as appropriate to all aspects of language use. In particular, he saw its limited applicability to mathematical language and rightly emphasized the performative and emotive dimensions of our use of words – for example, to make promises, issue commands and raise passions – but the core of his theory is still clearly ideational in character.

To conclude this section, I want to repeat with emphasis my warning against a facile acceptance of those tiresome modern criticisms of the ideational theory that are directed at crude or grossly distorted versions of it (see, for example, Taylor 1970, pp. 132ff. and pp. 141ff.). The problem of negation provides an object lesson. Modern critics often laughingly dismiss the ideational theory as one which assigns a mental image of redness as the meaning of the word 'red', a mental image of a cat as the meaning of the word 'cat' – and so on. Then the supposedly devastating blow is dealt, with the question: What, then, according to ideationism, is the meaning of a word like 'not'? Is it somehow supposed to be a mental image of mere *absence* or *non-being*? But how could there be any such image – any more than there could be a picture or photograph of, quite literally, *nothing*? Or is the meaning of the word 'not' somehow supposed to be, rather, the *absence of a mental image* – in which case, *what* mental image must be absent, or doesn't it matter? For instance, does the ideationist propose that the meaning of a sentence such as 'The cat is not on the mat', which contains the word 'not', is a mental image of a mat with no cat on it? But how then does that differ from a mental image of a mat with, say, no dog on it? If the images are the same, the absurd implication would seem to be that 'The cat is not on the mat' and 'The dog is not on the mat' have the same meaning.

We already know how to counter crude gibes like this. The ideational theory is not committed to an imagistic view of ideas, nor does it represent ideas as being the meanings of words. Furthermore, it does not treat the relation between language and thought as one of translation, with individual words or phrases being paired off with individual ideas on a one-to-one basis. Consequently, the theory is simply not in the business of looking for some specific 'ingredient' or 'component' of thought which plays a role in thought exactly corresponding to that played by the word 'not' in language. At most the ideationist is committed to holding that, at least sometimes, a sentence containing a negative expression is used by a speaker to express a negative thought – and that thinkers are capable of imagining negative states of affairs. But the latter claim seems entirely uncontroversial, because it would be very hard to deny that creatures altogether lacking language can nonetheless perceive negative states of affairs – that, for instance, a dog can see that its dish is empty or that its master has gone. And if these states of affairs can be perceived, then they can also be imagined, at least by creatures like ourselves with a capacity for imagination. Moreover, any suggestion that human beings were simply incapable of entertaining negative thoughts before the inception of language is plainly quite incredible, for a creature so cognitively limited would surely be incapable of developing or learning language in the first place. If anything, then, the problem of negation, rather than being a problem for ideationism, is a problem for its opponents – particularly those who are wedded to a strong version of the doctrine that thought requires language.

I do not want to give the impression that Locke himself would have agreed exactly with the foregoing account of negation, except to the extent of denying that a word like 'not' stands for any specific idea in the mind of the person using it. Locke does in fact offer a brief account of the linguistic function of what he calls 'particles' – words like 'not' and 'but' – in the *Essay* (III, VII, 'Of Particles'). Here is what he says concerning them:

> Besides Words, which are names of *Ideas* in the Mind, there are a great many others that are made use of, to signify the *connexion* that the Mind gives to *Ideas, or Propositions, one with another*. The Mind, in communicating its thought to others, does not only need signs of the *Ideas* it has then before it, but others also, to shew or intimate some particular action of its own, at that time, relating to those *Ideas*. This it does several ways; as, *Is, Is not*, are the general marks of the Mind, affirming or denying.
>
> (*Essay*, III, VII, 1)

Locke's suggestion here is that the word 'not' is used by English speakers to indicate the mental act of *denial*, as opposed to affirmation. This has some plausibility, but faces certain difficulties if advanced as a comprehensive account of the use of the word. One problem is that the word 'not' may appear in the antecedent clause of a conditional sentence, such as 'If it does not rain, the match will be played'. A speaker who asserts this sentence is making an affirmation, albeit a conditional one. But such a speaker is not *denying* that it will rain: rather, he or she is leaving it open whether or not it will rain. Consequently, it appears that he or she cannot in this case be using the word 'not' to indicate the mental act of denial. Rather, what such a speaker seems to be doing is entertaining the *hypothesis* or *supposition* that it will not rain – and what that supposition concerns, it seems to me, is what I earlier called a *negative state of affairs*. However, although I cannot agree fully with what Locke himself has to say concerning the linguistic function of the word 'not', the important point is that he recognized that an ideational theory of thought and language need not, and should not, suppose that this word stands for any specific idea.

LOCKE AND THE PROBLEM OF PRIVACY

I come now to what many would regard as being the fatal difficulty of the ideational theory: the problem of *privacy*. In Chapter II of Book III of the *Essay*, Locke writes as follows:

> Man, though he have great variety of Thoughts, and such, from which others, as well as himself, might receive Profit and Delight; yet they are all within his own Breast, invisible, and hidden from others, nor can of themselves be made to appear. The Comfort, and Advantage of Society, not being to be had without Communication of Thoughts, it was necessary, that Man should find out some external sensible Signs, whereby those invisible *Ideas*, which his thoughts are made up of, might be made known to others . . . The use Men have of these Marks, being either to record their own Thoughts for the Assistance of their own Memory; or as it were, to bring out their *Ideas*, and lay them before the view of others: *Words, in their primary or immediate Signification, stand for nothing, but the* Ideas *in the Mind of him that uses them.*
>
> (*Essay*, III, II, 1–2)

Now, Locke would obviously see no absurdity in the notion of a *private* language – for instance, one used purely 'for the Assistance of [a person's] Memory'. But his insistence that words 'primarily' signify ideas 'in the Mind of him that uses them' lays him open to the charge that he makes *all* language irredeemably private – a charge which is scarcely undermined by his rather lamely remarking, a little later, that '[U]nless a Man's Words excite the same Ideas in the Hearer, which he makes them stand for in speaking, he does not speak intelligibly' (*Essay*, III, II, 8). On his view, it might seem, different speakers who have their *words* in common may, for all we know, assign them very different meanings, so that the same word in the mouths of two different speakers of English may effectively be related in the same way as homophones of two different languages – which is as much as to say that what we call 'English' is not in reality a single language at all. The problem, at root, is this:

how, by means of words, can one speaker, *A*, convey to another speaker, *B*, the ideas that are in *A*'s mind, if the only ideas that B can ever attach to those words are ideas that are in B's own mind?

At this point we need to appreciate that, although Locke's theory does indeed face a prima-facie difficulty here which requires some careful handling, the difficulty in question is not one which should be described in *semantic* terms. The question of whether or not two speakers speak the *same language* is a semantic question – a question of whether or not the words that they utter stand in the same word-to-world relations – whereas the difficulty which Locke's theory faces concerns, rather, the word-to-thought relations (the *expressive* relations) of different speakers. Indeed, Locke himself, by implication, rejects the suggestion that speakers who use the same words to express different ideas should for that reason alone be deemed to be speaking different languages, when he criticizes what he takes to be the common supposition that a speaker's words can be signs of ideas in another person's mind:

> [Men] *suppose their Words to be Marks of the* Ideas *in the Minds also of other Men, with whom they communicate*: For else [they suppose] they should talk in vain, and could not be understood, if the Sounds they applied to one *Idea*, were such, as by the Hearer, were applied to another, which [they suppose] is to speak two Languages. But in this, Men stand not usually to examine, whether the *Idea* they, and those they discourse with have in their Minds, be the same: But think it enough, that they use the Word, as they imagine, in the common Acceptation of that Language; in which case they suppose, that the *Idea*, they make it a Sign of, is precisely the same . . .
>
> [*Essay*, III, II, 4]

As I have acknowledged, Locke is still faced with a prima-facie difficulty here, albeit one concerning the expression and communication of thought by means of language rather than one concerning semantics, or the meanings of words in a common language. The problem is that we have – and apparently *can* have –

no interpersonal standard of comparison between the 'ideas' of different speakers, by which we can determine whether the ideas expressed by one speaker's use of certain words are the same as or different from those expressed by another's use of them, even when the speakers are indisputably talking the same language. One might be inclined to respond to this problem on Locke's behalf by urging that, since human beings are made in much the same mould, they will, in all probability, receive similar ideas of sense perception in similar perceptual situations, so that there will be conformity amongst their ideas in thinking too. Indeed, Locke himself surmises that this is so, remarking that 'I am . . . very apt to think, that the sensible *Ideas*, produced by any Object in different Men's Minds, are most commonly very near and undiscernibly alike' (*Essay*, II, XXXII, 15). But, quite apart from the fact that this response is purely speculative, it threatens to undermine the whole basis of Locke's account of language and thought by raising the suspicion that, in fact, it really *doesn't matter* what 'ideas', if any, speakers associate with words, nor whether there is any conformity or resemblance between the 'ideas' of different speakers.

The point can be made vivid by reference to the notorious 'inverted spectrum' problem: for all we know, it seems, A's idea of red might resemble B's idea of green and vice versa – and yet since this would not be reflected in any detectable difference between A's and B's uses of the terms 'red' and 'green' to describe things, their ability to communicate successfully with one another using colour terminology would not be in the least disrupted. If it is then urged that, in view of the physiological similarities between A's and B's visual systems, it is unlikely that their ideas of red really do differ in this way, it may be replied that since it apparently doesn't matter *whether or not* such a resemblance obtains, to propose that it does serves no useful purpose. And from this it seems but a short step to conclude that any appeal to 'ideas' in one's account of the communication of thought by language – and hence, by extension, in one's theory of thought itself – is idle and vacuous. However, as we shall see, this 'short step' is in fact nothing less than a giant leap – and a quite unwarranted one.

The first thing to note at this point is that Locke himself was fully aware of the inverted spectrum problem – indeed, it seems to have originated with him – and yet was not at all disconcerted by it. Here is what he says:

> Neither would it carry any Imputation of *Falshood* to our simple *Ideas, if* . . . it were so ordered, That *the same Object should produce in several Men's Minds different* Ideas at the same time; *v.g.* if the *Idea*, that a *Violet* produced in one Man's Mind by his Eyes, were the same as that a *Marigold* produced in another Man's, and *vice versa*. For since this could never be known . . . neither the *Ideas* . . . nor the Names, would be at all confounded.
>
> (*Essay*, II, XXXII, 15)

Clearly, Locke's verdict on the inverted spectrum problem is that it would indeed not hinder the communication of thought by language if such inversions occurred, but that this by no means implies that ideas are not the very stuff of human thinking. The conclusion must be that, charitably interpreted, Locke is *not* committed to the view that successful communication of thought by language requires the *replication* in the hearer's mind of ideas present in the speaker's mind. This is not to say that the ideas of speaker and hearer need bear *no particular relation at all* to one another in order for communication between them to be successful. As we shall see, their ideas *do* need to be appropriately related, but – and this is the crucial point – the relation in question is one which can plausibly be known to obtain without appeal to any sort of intersubjective comparison between those ideas themselves.

In order to begin to get a grip on the nature of the required relation, a simple example may help. Consider the case of two boys, Alf and Ben, who want to see a football match but cannot afford to pay for tickets to get into the stadium. They discover that if one of them stands on the other's shoulders he can see over the wall and describe the match to his friend – so they take it in turns to do this. Now suppose that Alf has the first turn to watch. He will experience certain 'ideas' of sense perception which he will then 'put into words'. Ben will hear these words and as a result enjoy certain 'ideas' of imagination as he envisages the scene taking place on the pitch. This seems to be the picture of linguistic communication that Locke is offering us, at a fairly primitive level – and it has a good deal of intuitive appeal. But now the question arises: what sort of ideas of imagination ought Ben to experience if Alf is to communicate satisfactorily to Ben his perceptions of what is going on inside the stadium?

At first one might suppose that what is required is that Ben's imaginings should somehow replicate Alf's first-hand experiences, so that Alf's description of the match enables Ben to visualize the match pretty much as Alf himself sees it. But this, as we are by now aware, is to impose a requirement of interpersonal similarity between ideas whose satisfaction is impossible to verify. It seems, however, that a much less stringent requirement will secure all that is needed for successful communication between Alf and Ben. This is that Ben's imaginings should sufficiently resemble, not *Alf's* first-hand experiences, but rather the first-hand experiences that *Ben himself* would have had if he had been in Alf's place. Success in meeting this requirement is easy enough to corroborate: all that Ben needs to do is to exchange places with Alf in order to confirm that the scene as he imagined it on the basis of Alf's description is consistent with what he now experiences at first hand.

We may draw from this example the following conclusion concerning the proper relationship between the ideas of speaker and hearer in a successful episode of linguistic communication, according to the ideational account. Rather than demand that a word used by the speaker, *A*, to signify a certain idea of imagination in his own mind should excite the *same* idea of imagination in the mind of the hearer, B – meaning by 'the same' idea in this context an *exactly resembling* idea – the ideationist ought to demand only that the word should excite what we may call a *corresponding* idea in B's mind. The criterion for such 'correspondence', we might say, is roughly speaking this: B's idea of imagination should resemble the *perceptual* idea that B would enjoy were he to confront an object that would excite in *A* a perceptual idea resembling the idea of imagination that *A*'s use of the word in question signifies. However, having made it clear that it is such a *correspondence* – rather than a relation of exact resemblance – that is required, the ideationist could legitimately go on to say that correspondence of this sort does in fact constitute a kind of 'sameness' between the ideas of different subjects. After all, even exact resemblance is not sameness in the strictest possible sense – that of numerical identity – and we often talk of numerically distinct items being 'the same' in various looser senses, of which the sense that implies an exact resemblance between those items is only one. It is indeed perfectly conceivable that it is a 'sameness' just in the sense of 'correspondence', as I have called it, that Locke himself really intends when he sometimes speaks, however incautiously, of speaker and hearer having the 'same' ideas in mind in a successful episode of linguistic communication. The vocabulary of sameness and difference is notoriously slippery and Locke's use of it is as prone to ambiguity and misinterpretation as any other philosopher's.

It is not difficult to see how a correspondence between the ideas which a word signifies in the minds of different speakers within the same speech community could be set up through the process of passing language on from adult to child. Consider the archetypal situation so often called upon by philosophers, in which an adult teacher draws a child's attention to various instances of some perceptible quality or feature – say, by pointing to them – and then utters the appropriate word: as it might be, 'red'. The ideationist story would then go as follows. In such a situation both teacher and learner enjoy certain ideas of sense perception and the learner, if she successfully identifies the perceptible feature pointed to by the teacher, comes to associate the word 'red' with the idea which she enjoys in perceiving that feature. When the learner subsequently attempts to use the word to describe a perceptible feature to the teacher, whether she is describing something that she currently perceives or something that she merely remembers or imagines, her implicit aim should be to excite in the mind of the teacher an idea of imagination resembling the perceptual idea that *the teacher* enjoyed in perceiving the perceptible feature which figured in the original learning situation. Success in this aim can be confirmed by the learner's pointing to another exemplar of the perceptible feature that she has in mind – one which is concurrently visible to the teacher – and seeing whether the teacher agrees with the description of it as 'red'.

At no stage during this process need either the teacher or the learner make any assumptions concerning intersubjective similarities or differences between their respective ideas. The success of the process would be in no way hindered if the idea that the learner associated with the word 'red' in fact resembled the idea that the teacher associated with the word 'green', and vice versa. At the same time, it is clear that the role of ideas in this account of the learning process is by no means an idle one. Thus an ideationist like Locke can rebut the charge that the inverted spectrum problem demonstrates the vacuity of the appeal to ideas in a theory of thought and language. By the same token, he can defeat the accusation that the fact that ideas are 'private' – meaning by this that no one can really know what another's ideas are like – makes them worthless in an account of the workings of a public language.

THE ESSENTIAL ROLE OF IDEAS IN THINKING

Critics of Locke's theory of language may concede, perhaps, that the strategy of the preceding section saves that theory from complete vacuity. But at the same time they may urge that the explanatory role which it confers upon 'ideas' is a superfluous one, in the sense that the phenomena which ideas are invoked to explain can be explained more economically without their aid. In the ideationist story of language learning briefly sketched above, it was suggested that the learner comes to associate the word 'red' with *the idea* that she enjoys in perceiving a certain perceptible quality or feature. But why, it may be asked, can't speakers learn to associate words *directly* with perceptible features, without the mediation of 'ideas'?

Well, in order to associate a word, such as 'red', with a certain perceptible feature, redness, one must be able to *think of both* in association with one another: the thought of one must call to mind the thought of the other. However, when I think of something I must think of it *in some way*. I might, for instance, think of it *in words*. But, it seems clear, if one could only ever think 'in words', it would be impossible, after all, ever to associate words with non-verbal features of the world, but at most only to associate words with other words. For in order to think of something 'in words', I must *already* have associated those words with the thing in question. So words cannot come to be associated with things unless there is some *other* way of thinking of things – this other way being, according to the ideationist, the 'way of ideas'. And notice that the problem that faces the theory that we only ever think 'in words' does *not* repeat itself for the theory that, at the most fundamental level, we think 'in ideas'. For we don't need to *associate* our ideas with perceptible features in order to be able to think of those features by entertaining those ideas. As I remarked earlier, the connection between imagination and its objects is natural, in sharp contrast with the conventional connection between word and object.

The following thought-experiment may help to drive home the foregoing conclusion. Suppose that there were – *per impossibile*, as I believe – a race of beings capable of our full range of sense perception but lacking all powers of imagination save an ability to call to mind various words and phrases, in the form of imagined sequences of spoken or written symbols. Then what would entitle us to say that their exercising this ability would ever constitute *thinking*, 'in words', about extralinguistic features of the world? Even if we allow, for the sake of argument, that these creatures could correctly apply words to name or describe perceptible features of the world *when they were actually confronted with those features*, in what sense could they be said to know what those words serve to name or describe when they were *not* confronted with the features in question? Lacking as the creatures supposedly do any *ideas* of these features, there is, I suggest, no sense at all in which they could be said to possess such knowledge. I suppose it might be urged against me that their knowledge would consist simply in a *disposition* to apply the words correctly in the presence of the features. But to this it may be replied that the creatures' possession of such a disposition would not provide them with any *actual* conception of the features in their absence and so, I submit, could not in fact constitute the sort of knowledge that we seek.

However, at this point someone might want to challenge my assumption that thought of something must always be, as I put it, thought of it *in some way* – whether 'in words' or 'in ideas'. Why, it may be asked, can't there be what we might call 'pure' thought of something? This is a deep and puzzling question, which I can only begin to get a grip on by asking what it is that a person *has in mind* when he or she thinks of something, such as the perceptible feature redness. In one sense, of course, what he or she has in mind is that very perceptible feature. But a perceptible feature can't *literally* be 'in one's mind'. When one has redness 'in mind', one's mind is not itself *red*! But, surely, one's mind must be modified in *some* way, such that it is in virtue of *that* modification that one has *redness* in mind as opposed, say, to *greenness*. Redness can only be 'in the mind' as a so-called *intentional* object – that is, as something *thought of*. But what makes my thought of redness a thought of *redness* as opposed to a thought of *greenness*? It is obviously no answer to say that what makes my thought a thought of redness is that it has redness as its 'intentional object' – for the very notion of an intentional object has been introduced as the notion of *something that is thought of* and so already presupposes an answer to the question of how a thought comes to be 'of' one thing rather than another. Now, the ideationist *does* have an answer to this question. The answer is that one may have *redness* 'in mind' by having an *idea* of redness, that is, by *imagining* something red. According to the ideationist, the mind is indeed modified in different ways in thinking of different things: and these modifications – which the ideationist takes to be modifications of *consciousness* – consist in its having different 'ideas'.

Some may be reminded at this point of a well-known remark of Wittgenstein's which seems to bear upon this issue. At one point in the *Philosophical Investigations*, Wittgenstein says:

> What makes my image of him into an image of *him*? Not its looking like him.
>
> (Wittgenstein 1958, p. 177)

Here the original German word *Vorstellung* has been translated as 'image' rather than as 'idea'. However, the full German version of Wittgenstein's remark is: '*Was macht meine Vorstellung von ihm zu einer Vorstellung von ihm? Nicht die Ähnlichkeit des Bildes*' – and the use here of the word *Bild* (= 'picture', 'image') seems to support this translation. But this, I think, is crucial if we are to see in this passage a genuine problem for the ideationist. That is to say, I think that the passage really only poses a problem for an *imagist* conception of ideas. For only on that view might one suppose that we can talk at all literally about a *resemblance* or lack of it between an idea and its worldly or extra-mental object – with all the difficulties that, as we saw in Chapter 2, attach to such a supposition. However, having an idea of red in mind isn't having in mind an idea that is itself *red*, as an imagist conception of ideas might suggest. Rather, it is just *imagining* something red – where 'imagining' is not, despite the etymology of the word, construed in terms of the mind's being confronted with images of any kind. And if it is now asked: 'What makes my imagining something red imagining something *red*?', we can answer by appealing once again to the kinship between *imagining* something red and *seeing* something red. That is to say, the relevant resemblance is between mental *acts*, not between a mental *object* and a non-mental object. And if it is then further asked: 'What makes my seeing something red seeing something *red*?', the obvious answer is, very roughly, that what makes it so is the fact that something red is the *cause* of my perceptual state and of similar perceptual states of mine in relevantly similar circumstances.

A RESPONSE TO SOME OBJECTIONS

Alexander Miller has criticized an earlier attempt of mine (Lowe 1995, pp. 143–53) to attribute to Locke, and defend on Locke's behalf, an ideational account of language and thought along the foregoing lines (see Miller 1995). It may help to clarify certain matters if I use this opportunity to reply to Miller's criticisms. Miller focuses especially on my analysis of and attempted solution to what I called earlier 'the problem of privacy'. But his broader aim is to demonstrate the 'inadequacy' of my proposal that Locke's ideational theory is primarily concerned with what I call *expressive* (word-to-thought) relations, rather than with *semantic* (word-to-world) relations. His main criticism is directed at my account of what I now call the 'correspondence' relation between ideas of different speakers. In my earlier account, I exploited a story much like the one sketched above involving the boys Alf and Ben. Miller comments:

> Two points have to be made about this. First of all, the role given to ideas in this story makes it clear that Locke is after all providing a theory of *meaning* here. Why does the fact that there is a regular connection between, e.g. [the idea that B associates with the word 'red'] and B's encounters with red things come into the story at all? Answer: because the fact that there is this relationship between the idea and instantiations of redness determines the *semantic relation* between the associated word – 'red' – and the instantiations of redness. To put it slightly differently: it is necessary for the idea associated with the word 'red' to stand in such a relationship to red things because that fact is what determines the semantic

properties of the word . . . Locke's theory about the expressive
relation between words and ideas is not *separate* from his theory
about how words refer to things in the way that Lowe envisages:
rather, his expressive theory is intended as *part* of his theory about
the semantic relation. It is, as Simon Blackburn might put it . . . a
'dog-legged theory of meaning'.

(Miller 1995, pp. 154–5)

However, it is not my intention to deny that Locke, as an ideationist,
has the resources to construct a theory of meaning in the semantic
sense. Such a theory will indeed be a 'dog-legged' one, for the
reason explained earlier: namely, because it will involve combining
a theory of *expressive* (word-to-thought) relations with a theory of
cognitive (thought-to-world) relations to produce a theory of *semantic*
(word-to-world) relations. And, of course, Locke himself does have
much to say about cognitive relations. My point is that, for a philosopher like Locke, the proper direction of explanation is *from*
expressive and cognitive relations *to* semantic relations, never the
reverse. For Locke, expressive and cognitive relations are of primary
interest and they can, moreover, be studied relatively independently
of each other, because in his view thought is relatively independent
of language. But, while Locke certainly has the resources for a theory of semantic relations, I also contend that he is not in fact much
concerned to frame such a theory himself – in which opinion I
concur with the verdict of Ian Hacking (see Hacking 1975, ch. 5).
And in defending Locke against certain modern critics, I want to
make it plain that they entirely miss their target to the extent that
they interpret what he has to say about expressive relations as
though it was meant to be about semantic relations.

But Miller has another and, in his view, more fundamental
criticism of the account that I offer of Locke's position:

Second, and more importantly, even on Lowe's new model, the
privacy of ideas *still* leaves an insurmountable problem for Locke.
On the new model, in order to know that his attempt at

communication has been successful, *A* does not have, *per impossibile*, to compare IDEA1 with IDEA2; but he does nevertheless have to know that IDEA2 is the idea which is regularly produced in *B*'s mind on his confrontations with red objects, since that fact is what constitutes the success of the attempt at communication. And how is he supposed to be able to know *that*, given the admittedly private nature of ideas? Even on the new model it is utterly impossible for *A* to know that his attempt at communication has been successful – the old problem of privacy remains, albeit in a slightly different guise.

(Miller 1995, p. 155)

The answer to this supposed difficulty has already been provided earlier, however, in my account of the hypothetical engagement between a teacher and a learner of the word 'red'. All that each party to the engagement is required implicitly to assume is that objects possessing a certain perceptible quality regularly produce certain perceptual ideas in the minds of those who perceive those objects and that any given user of the word 'red' associates with that word an idea of imagination resembling the perceptual idea that is regularly produced in that person's mind by objects possessing the quality in question. *A* does not have to know *what* idea is 'regularly produced in B's mind on his confrontations with red objects', only that *some* specific idea is so produced and that an idea of imagination resembling this idea is associated by B with the word 'red'. If *A* and B are simultaneously confronted by an object possessing the relevant quality, *A* will be able to recognize that the perceptual idea produced in his own mind by that object resembles the idea of imagination that he has learned to associate with the word 'red'. He will also be entitled to assume that this object produces in B's mind a perceptual idea which resembles an idea of imagination that B is capable of enjoying and which B may or may not associate with the word 'red'. In order to check whether or not B associates the idea in question with the word 'red', *A* can point to the object and ask 'Red?'. Since B will at that time be enjoying a perceptual idea produced in his mind by the presence of the given quality, B will know whether or not he associates any resembling idea of imagination with the word 'red'. If he does associate such an idea with the word 'red', he may respond to A's query with the affirmation 'Red'. In this fashion, A and B may confirm that they associate what I call 'corresponding' ideas with the word 'red' and thereby be justifiably confident that they can use that word to communicate successfully with each other, in accordance with the ideational model of successful communication that I have proposed on Locke's behalf. Of course, the story as I have just told it is a highly idealized and simplified one, but it suffices, I believe, to rebut Miller's charge that 'even on Lowe's new model . . . the old problem of privacy remains'.

SUMMARY

Locke, like many of his seventeenth-century contemporaries, adopts an ideationist view of thought and linguistic signification, whereby thought consists fundamentally in the entertaining of ideas of imagination and the basic purpose of language is to communicate one person's thoughts to another. Such a view may well seem hopeless to philosophers who assume that Locke adheres to an imagistic conception of ideas, but we have already seen that it is by no means necessary to ascribe such a conception to Locke. The view will also be misunderstood by philosophers who suppose that Locke, in offering his account of linguistic signification, is presenting a theory of *meaning* – a semantic theory – in anything like the present-day sense. He is in fact offering an account of the *expressive* capacities of language: that is, a theory of word-to-thought relations, not a theory of word-to-world relations. Furthermore, in answer to those philosophers who are apt to criticize an ideational theory of linguistic signification like Locke's on the grounds that the privacy of ideas makes it impossible, according to the theory, for speakers to know whether or not they are successfully communicating their thoughts by means of their words, we may respond that these critics are guilty of assuming an unduly simplistic view of what such communicative success is supposed to consist in. An idea is successfully communicated when a *corresponding* idea is evoked in the mind of the listener: it is quite unnecessary for an *exactly resembling* idea to be evoked, as Locke himself made perfectly clear in his discussion of the inverted spectrum problem. Finally, Locke is by no means committed, as some uncharitable critics may suppose, to the extreme doctrine that *every* word in a linguistic utterance should serve to signify a distinct idea in the mind of the speaker, even including such particles as the word 'not'. Properly understood, Locke's theory of thought and linguistic signification is not only free of the supposed difficulties commonly raised in criticism of it, but is also in many ways more promising and less counterintuitive than most of the theories advanced by present-day philosophers in preference to it. It is high time that the theory was accorded the respect and interest that it deserves.

FURTHER READING

Ashworth, E. J. 1981: ' "Do Words Signify Ideas or Things?" The Scholastic Sources of Locke's Theory of Language', *Journal of the History of Philosophy* 19, pp. 299–326.

Ashworth, E. J. 1984: 'Locke on Language', *Canadian Journal of Philosophy* 14, pp. 45–73.

Cromer, Richard F. 1991: *Language and Thought in Normal and Handicapped Children* (Oxford: Blackwell).

Guyer, Paul 1994: 'Locke's Philosophy of Language', in Vere Chappell (ed.), *The Cambridge Companion to Locke* (Cambridge: Cambridge University Press).

Kosslyn, Stephen M. 1990: 'Mental Imagery', in Daniel N. Osherson *et al.* (eds), *Visual Cognition and Action* (Cambridge, MA: MIT Press).

Kretzmann, Norman 1968: 'The Main Thesis of Locke's Semantic Theory', *Philosophical Review* 77, pp. 175–96.

Losonsky, Michael 1994: 'Locke on Meaning and Signification', in G. A. J. Rogers (ed.), *Locke's Philosophy: Content and Context* (Oxford: Clarendon Press).

Ott, Walter R. 2004: *Locke's Philosophy of Language* (Cambridge: Cambridge University Press).

Five

Agency and Will

Because my overall aim in this book is to discuss a representative sample of Locke's philosophical thought, concentrating on certain issues that I take to be of perennial interest and importance, there are good reasons to include some discussion of his philosophy of action. One is that Locke's account of agency has provoked strong reactions, many of them highly critical. Another is that, despite such criticism, Locke is widely acknowledged as having laid the foundations for all subsequent philosophical debate concerning the nature of voluntary action and the so-called problem of 'free will'. A third is that – again, despite such criticism – some modern philosophers of action, amongst whom I would include myself, believe that Locke's account of action and the will is fundamentally correct. Finally, a fourth reason is that a discussion of Locke's philosophy of action serves as a natural bridge between his metaphysics and epistemology, on the one hand, and his political philosophy on the other – which I shall discuss in the next chapter. For in political philosophy we are above all concerned with human beings in their capacity as *agents*. Moreover, for a political philosopher like Locke, who is especially concerned with the liberty of the citizen and government by consent, human freedom of action must obviously be something of paramount importance. For if, by our very nature as human beings, we lacked such freedom, there could be no sense in trying to base the legitimacy of civil government on the freely given consent of the governed, nor in making the protection of the liberty of citizens a distinguishing feature of just political authority.

LOCKE ON FREE ACTION AND 'FREEDOM OF THE WILL'

Towards the end of Chapter XXI of Book II of the *Essay Concerning Human Understanding* – entitled 'Of Power' – Locke remarks, with all the appearance of sincerity and genuine modesty, that

> Impartial deductions of reason in controverted points being so very rare, and exact ones in abstract notions not so very easy, especially if of any length . . . I should think my self not a little beholding to any one, who would upon these or any other grounds fairly clear this subject of *Liberty* from any difficulties that may yet remain.
>
> (*Essay*, II, XXI, 72)

This chapter was substantially revised by Locke for the second edition of the *Essay* and it seems clear from the foregoing remark, as well as from other expressions of hesitancy in the chapter, that Locke was never entirely happy with his treatment of the topic which is the chapter's dominant concern – free agency and the so-called problem of 'free will'. Locke himself notoriously regarded the expression 'freedom of the will' as a linguistic monstrosity because, as he puts it:

> the *Will* is nothing but one Power or Ability, and *Freedom* another Power or Ability: So that to ask, whether the *Will has Freedom*, is to ask, whether one Power has another Power, one Ability another Ability; a Question at first sight too grosly absurd to make a Dispute, or need an Answer.
>
> (*Essay*, II, XXI, 16)

But, fortunately for philosophical posterity, Locke did not leave the matter at that, recognizing that 'Philosophy . . . when it appears in publick, must have so much Complacency, as to be cloathed in the ordinary Fashion and Language of the Country, so far as it can consist with Truth and Perspicuity' (*Essay*, II, XXI, 20). Certainly, Locke recognized that there is a genuine philosophical issue that has, however misleadingly, been called 'the problem of free will', and he does his best to try to identify and solve it – though with how much success it is hard to judge, not only on account of the complexity and difficulty of the problem itself, but also because obscurities and apparent tensions in Locke's text have provoked a number of different interpretations of his views on the subject.

Many present-day commentators interpret Locke as being a so-called *compatibilist* in the matter of free will, although some of these acknowledge – wisely, I think – that the claim that Locke is a compatibilist is at least contestable (see, for example, Yaffe 2000, p. 142, n. 5). Here I take a 'compatibilist' to be someone who holds that freedom of the will is compatible with universal causal determinism – that is, who holds that even if the operations of the will are all causally necessitated by prior events, the products of those operations, in the form of our bodily and mental actions, may nonetheless be said to be 'free' in the fullest sense of the term and hence properly subject to moral appraisal as commendable or blameworthy. Even if such an interpretation can be defended, however, it seems clear that there is more to be said about what precisely it is, in Locke's view, that confers upon human agency a liberty 'worth the Name' (*Essay*, II, XXI, 50). In short, we still need to be given an account of what Gideon Yaffe has called 'the Elusive Something' (Yaffe 2000, p. 19): the crucial factor that distinguishes, for Locke, human action that is fully morally accountable from behaviour that is not.

Now, for all his heavy sarcasm about the phrase 'freedom of the will', Locke is in fact clear enough about what should be meant by freedom of *action*. According to Locke, one is free to act in a certain way – for instance, to raise one's arm – just in case *both* (1) if one were to will to raise one's arm, one's arm would rise as a consequence *and* (2) if one were to will to forbear to raise one's arm, one's arm would fail to rise as a consequence (see Lowe 1986, p. 154). As he himself puts it:

> [S]o far as a Man has a power to think, or not to think; to move, or not to move, according to the preference or direction of his mind, so

far is a Man *Free*. Where-ever any performance or forbearance are
not equally in a Man's power; where-ever doing or not doing, will
not equally follow upon the preference of his mind directing it, there
he is not *Free* . . . that Agent is under *Necessity*.

(*Essay*, II, XXI, 8)

To illustrate his conception of what it is for an agent to be acting
under necessity, Locke offers the famous example of a man asleep
in a locked room, who wakes to find a friend there with whom he
is happy to stay and talk. This man, Locke says, stays in the room not
freely but *under necessity*, because if he were to will to leave it he
would not succeed in doing so, the door being locked. The example
is supposed to support a further contention of Locke's, namely, that
'*Voluntary . . . is not opposed to Necessary*' (*Essay*, II, XXI, 11), on the
grounds that, while the man stays under necessity, his stay is nonetheless *voluntary* – though whether it really does support this contention is not in fact as clear as it might seem to be (see Lowe 1986 and
Lowe 1995, pp. 128–32). (Some readers may be tempted to see in
this contention of Locke's – that an action may be voluntary even
though it is done 'under necessity' – an implicit endorsement of
compatibilism, but I think that that would be mistaken: for at this
point Locke is not discussing freedom of will but only freedom of
action, and compatibilism is a doctrine concerning freedom of will.)

So far, we have only been considering what it is, according to
Locke, for an agent to be *free to act* in a certain way – for instance, to
stay in a certain room or to leave it. However, as Locke himself
acknowledges, after some preliminary beating about the bush, a
question which it seems natural to raise at this point is '*Whether a
Man be at liberty to will which of the two he pleases, Motion or Rest*' (*Essay*, II,
XXI, 25). It is natural to ask this precisely because willing, as Locke
himself seems to conceive of it, is itself a species of action, albeit a
mental action. For Locke, volition or willing is 'a thought or preference of the mind ordering, or as it were commanding the doing or
not doing such or such a particular action' (*Essay*, II, XXI, 5). But

Locke dismisses the question peremptorily as one that is manifestly absurd, on the grounds that

> to ask, whether a Man can *will*, what he *wills*; or be pleased with what he is pleased with [is a] Question, which, I think, needs no answer: and they, who can make a Question of it, must suppose one Will to determine the Acts of another, and another to determinate that; and so on *in infinitum*.
>
> (*Essay*, II, XXI, 25)

But this is surely just bluster on Locke's part. If willing is a kind of action – a question to which I shall return later – it should certainly make sense to ask whether one can will what one wills. And it should be possible, in principle, to give a positive answer to this question without committing oneself automatically to an infinite regress of willings. What is more to the point, though – and perhaps this is really all that Locke means to convey – if 'freedom of will' were merely a matter of our being free, at least sometimes, to 'will what we will', then this would not be a kind of freedom that we don't already possess in good measure in respect of other actions that we perform, such as raising our arms. Hence, freedom of will, so conceived, would not be what Yaffe calls 'the Elusive Something'. If there is a deeper or more significant species of 'freedom' to which we can and should aspire, beyond our Lockean freedom of action, we must seek it elsewhere than in a freedom to 'will what we will'.

Here it is worth considering Gideon Yaffe's own answer to the question of what it is that Locke identifies as 'the Elusive Something', for it is both interesting and novel. The key to this question, Yaffe thinks, lies in Locke's remarks concerning the kind of freedom possessed by God and other 'superiour Beings above us, who enjoy perfect Happiness' (*Essay*, II, XXI, 49). For, Locke says, if we reflect upon their condition,

> we shall have reason to judge that they are more steadily *determined in their choice of Good* than we; and yet we have no reason to think

they are less happy, or less free, than we are. And if it were fit for
such poor finite Creatures as we are, to pronounce what infinite
Wisdom and Goodness could do, I think, we might say, That God
himself cannot choose what is not good; the Freedom of the
Almighty hinders not his being determined by what is best.

(*Essay*, II, XXI, 49)

So for Locke, according to Yaffe, we are free in the deepest and most
significant sense just to the extent that our choices are 'determined
by what is best', that is, by the good. And 'determined' here means
necessitated. Of course, the kind of necessitation in question cannot
straightforwardly be *causal* necessitation, but it may still rest upon
causal necessitation: for if our choices are causally determined by
our desires and our desires are for the good, then there is a clear
sense in which our choices – and so our consequent actions – are
determined by the good. And Locke *does* seem to hold that our
choices – our volitions or exercises of the will – are causally determined by our desires or 'uneasinesses', for in answer to the 'Question, 'what is it determines the Will?' (*Essay*, II, XXI, 29) he replies
that the 'true and proper Answer is . . . always some *uneasiness*' (*Essay*,
II, XXI, 29). As for the implied identity of uneasiness with desire,
Locke himself remarks a little while later that 'This *Uneasiness* we may
call . . . *Desire*; which is an *uneasiness* of the Mind for want of some
absent good' (*Essay*, II, XXI, 31).

The Locke that emerges from this analysis is a sophisticated
compatibilist, who holds that our actions are all causally necessitated and yet may be 'free', in a deeper sense than that which
attaches to them merely in virtue of their being dependent upon
our will or choice, in so far as they are determined by the good,
which they may be precisely to the extent that the desires that
causally determine our choices are desires for the good. If our
choices are so caused, we are no less free than God and the angels,
whose choices are also determined by the good and who are, as a
consequence, in a constant state of perfect happiness. It would

be madness to hanker after some sort of rationally undetermined 'freedom' instead:

> Is it worth the Name of *Freedom* to be at liberty to play the Fool, and draw Shame and Misery upon a Man's self? If to break loose from the conduct of Reason, and to want that restraint of Examination and Judgment, which keeps us from chusing or doing the worse, be *Liberty*, true Liberty, mad Men and Fools are the only Freemen.
>
> (*Essay*, II, XXI, 49)

But how are we supposed to get ourselves into a condition in which our choices are determined by the good, given that our psychology is not divine or angelic in nature? This, I think, is where both Locke and Yaffe's interpretation of Locke meet a certain difficulty. Locke makes at one point the following crucial remarks:

> There being in us a great many *uneasinesses* always solliciting, and ready to determine the *will*, it is natural . . . that the greatest, and most pressing should determine the *will* to the next action; and so it does for the most part, but not always. For the mind having in most cases, as is evident in Experience, a power to *suspend* the execution and satisfaction of any of its desires, and so all, one after another, is at liberty to consider the objects of them; examine them on all sides, and weigh them with others . . . This seems to me the source of all liberty; in this seems to consist that, which is (as I think improperly) call'd *Free will*. For during this *suspension* of any desire, before the *will* be determined to action . . . we have opportunity to examine, view, and judge, of the good or evil of what we are going to do.
>
> (*Essay*, II, XXI, 47)

The difficulty for Locke, now, is this. Clearly, 'suspending' the satisfaction of some present desire, whatever else it may be, must surely qualify as an action of some kind and, presumably, one that we can engage in voluntarily. But if it is, thus, an action which is determined by the will, the question arises as to what determines the will when, by an act of will, we 'suspend' the satisfaction of some present desire. Locke has just said that 'it is natural . . . that the greatest, and most pressing [uneasiness or desire] should determine the will to the next action; and so it does for the most part, but not always'. So what is the case when, by an act of will, we 'suspend' the satisfaction of a present desire? A dilemma seems to loom for Locke. Either he must say that, in such a case, what happens is what happens 'for the most part', namely, that our most pressing desire determines our will: but this seems to imply the absurdity that our most pressing desire may determine the 'suspension' of its own satisfaction. Or else he must say that, in such a case, what happens is what happens 'not always', namely, that we exercise our power to 'suspend' the satisfaction of our most pressing desire. But then we seem to be setting off upon a regress, of precisely the sort that Locke wished to avoid, for now we have invoked our power of 'suspension' in order to explain how an exercise of that power is not determined, on a given occasion, by our most pressing desire. It seems to me, in fact, that Locke, in appealing to our alleged power of 'suspension', is ultimately falling back on a *libertarian* conception of 'free will' which is intuitively appealing but completely at odds with his official doctrine, at least as this is interpreted by Yaffe and other commentators who see Locke as straightforwardly being a compatibilist. (By a 'libertarian' conception of free will, I mean one that holds that genuine free will exists but is not compatible with universal causal determinism, because free choices and the actions that follow from them are not causally necessitated by prior events. It is worth mentioning, incidentally, that Locke's discussion of the 'suspension' of desire was a later addition to Chapter XXI, a fact which may help to explain some of the tensions that commentators find in this part of the *Essay*.)

There is one feature of Locke's position, rightly emphasized by Yaffe, which I have not so far mentioned. This is Locke's contention that the mere recognition of some future happiness, whether in this life or the next, as being a good for oneself is not enough, by itself, to supplant the force of present pleasures or pains as determinants of one's will. Deliberation, for Locke, is not a merely intellectual activity, but plays also the vital motivating role of making contemplated future pleasures or pains sufficiently vivid that they can come to weigh in the balance against present pleasures and pains and, at least in some cases, outweigh them and thereby determine one's will in one's own best interest:

> And thus, by a due consideration and examining any good proposed, it is in our power, to raise our desires, in a due proportion to the value of that good, whereby in its turn, and place, it may come to work upon the *will*, and be pursued.
>
> (*Essay*, II, XXI, 46)

However, interesting and important though this element in Locke's position undoubtedly is, it does nothing to resolve the difficulty that he faces in explaining how it is that one can 'suspend' the satisfaction of present desires in order to enable deliberation (or 'examination') to have the effect on one's will that he describes.

LOCKE ON CAUSATION, VOLITION AND VOLUNTARY ACTION

It is worth recalling that Locke's discussion of human action occurs in a chapter entitled 'Of Power'. Locke sees the notions of agency, causation and power as being intimately related to one another, as indeed they plausibly are. Causation is clearly involved in many, if not all, instances of human action, as well as in processes taking place in the realm of wholly inanimate things. However, when we ask what exactly causation is, we are apt to find ourselves perplexed. Present-day philosophers tend to assume that causation is, fundamentally, a relation between *events* – and some of our ways of talking about causation seem to support this view, as when we say, for example, that the explosion of a bomb caused the collapse of a bridge: for explosions and collapses are clearly species of events.

But other ways of talking about causation suggest a rather different view, as when we say that *the bomb* caused the collapse of the bridge – for a bomb is an object, or individual 'substance', rather than an event. And it is to things like bombs that we attribute causal *powers*, such as the power to destroy things like bridges. According to this way of thinking about causation, it is, in the final analysis, *substances* that cause effects of various kinds, which they do by exercising or manifesting various of their causal powers. Moreover, if one adopts this view of the matter, it is natural to think of human agency along the same lines, conceiving human agents as being substance-causes – or, more specifically, as so-called 'agent-causes' – of various effects, brought about by the exercise of a distinctive kind of power.

Because present-day philosophers tend to think of causation exclusively as a relation between events, some of them are prone to assume that Locke himself is no advocate of substance-causation and so, *a fortiori*, no advocate of agent-causation – not wishing, perhaps, to foist upon Locke an approach to causation and agency which they deem to be philosophically untenable. This tendency seems to me at once somewhat anachronistic and philosophically less well motivated than its representatives appear to think. It is a tendency that is exhibited, for example, by Gideon Yaffe, who expressly represents Locke as being a thoroughgoing event-causalist. I suspect, however, that commentators like Yaffe, in declining to interpret Locke as a substance-causalist, have an inappropriate conception of substance-causation in mind. A substance-causalist holds that causation is primarily a relation between individual things or substances – the bearers of properties – and only in a derivative sense, at best, a relation between events. This is a natural position to hold for a philosopher who, like Locke, puts causal powers and liabilities at the heart of his doctrine of causation: for such powers and liabilities belong primarily to individual substances rather than to events. By exercising their causal powers and manifesting their causal liabilities, individual substances act on, and are acted upon by, other individual substances. Seen in this light, the canonical form of a singular causal statement should be taken to be something like this: 'Substance S_1, by Fing, caused substance S_2 to G' – for instance, 'The sun, by radiating heat, caused the lump of wax to melt', or 'The bomb, by exploding, caused the bridge to collapse'. And, indeed, Locke himself speaks very much in these terms when he talks about voluntary human action, as when he defines what is meant by 'will', 'volition' and 'voluntary':

> [W]e find in our selves a *Power* to begin or forbear, continue or end several actions of our minds, and motions of our Bodies, barely by a thought or preference of the mind ordering, or as it were commanding the doing or not doing such or such a particular action. This *Power* . . . we call the *Will*. The actual exercise of that power . . . we call *Volition* or *Willing*. The forbearance or performance of that action, consequent to such order or command of the mind, is called *Voluntary*. And whatsoever action is performed without such a thought of the mind, is called *Involuntary*.
>
> (*Essay*, II, XXI, 5)

For here the implication is that in an episode of voluntary human action, the agent, by willing – that is, by exercising his or her will – causes, for example, motion or rest in some part of the agent's body. I set aside, for the time being, the complication that, for Locke, human persons are not in the most fundamental sense *substances*, but will return to this matter later.

Now, it is true enough that Locke also uses the language of event-causation, even in the context of talking about voluntary human action. For instance, he remarks at one point, in Book IV, that

> all our voluntary Motions . . . are produced in us only by the free Action or Thought of our own Minds . . . For example: My right Hand writes, whilst my left Hand is still: What causes rest in one, and motion in the other? Nothing but my Will, a Thought of my Mind: my

Thought only changing, the right Hand rests, and the left Hand
moves.

(*Essay*, IV, X, 19)

Here Locke is saying that a volition or act of will is a cause of a
motion in one of my hands – and volitions and motions plausibly
belong to the category of *events*. However, it is perfectly consistent
for a substance-causalist to speak in event-causation terms, since
the substance-causalist's thesis is not – or should not be – that there
is no such thing as event-causation, but only that the notion of substance-causation is prior to that of event-causation and that the
latter notion is derivable from the former. For instance, it may be
held that to say that one event, c, is a cause of another event, e, is just
to say that there is some substance, S_1, and some substance, S_2, such
that, for some manner of acting, Fing, and some other manner of
acting, Ging, c consisted in S_1's Fing and e consisted in S_2's Ging, and
S_1, by Fing, caused S_2 to G (see Lowe 2002, ch. 11). Thus, for
example, to say that a certain volition caused a certain motion is, by
this account, just to say that a certain agent, by willing, caused some
body-part to move in a certain way. In other words, a substance-
causalist may happily resort to event-causation talk simply as a kind
of shorthand, without compromising his thesis that substances,
rather than events, are the primary relata of causal relations.

However, some of the recent literature on 'agent-causation'
clearly encourages the thought that any substance-causalist is
committed to the improbable thesis that, in an episode of substance-causation, a substance causes an event to occur without itself
doing anything whatever to cause that event. It seems to be this
conception of substance-causation that Yaffe, for example, has in
mind when he mentions, only to dismiss, a certain line of thought
which, as he puts it,

> pushes toward a substance-causal reading of Locke's account of
> action: A motion is begun by a substance just in case the motion, or
> the modification of the substance by virtue of which the motion is

caused, is caused by the substance itself and not by any
modification of the substance.

(Yaffe 2000, p. 81)

However, Yaffe seems to be assuming here that we have only two
mutually exclusive alternatives to choose from: (1) to follow the
event-causalist and say that a modification of the substance – the
substance's being F, or its Fing – is directly or indirectly the cause
of a certain motion, or else (2) to adopt what Yaffe apparently takes
the substance-causalist's position to be and say that 'the substance
itself' and not any modification of it is directly or indirectly the
cause of the motion. But, as I hope my earlier remarks make clear,
this is a false antithesis, for a sensible substance-causalist can say
that the way in which 'the substance itself' causes the motion is
precisely by Fing, that is, by acting or becoming 'modified' in some
specific way – and that for this very reason we can also say, albeit
only in a derivative sense, that the modification is a 'cause' of the
motion.

I have dwelt upon this issue at some length only because commentators like Yaffe seem so keen to interpret Locke in event-
causation terms to the exclusion of any substance-causal reading of
him, almost as if this were necessary in order to make Locke's
position at all acceptable to the present-day philosophical reader.
Yaffe himself acknowledges, in fact, that 'Locke did not distinguish
explicitly between event causation and substance causation' (Yaffe
2000, p. 154, n. 16), but then adds, rather revealingly, 'I believe
(somewhat controversially, I know) that an appeal to substance
causation should be avoided for philosophical reasons, and hence
the account . . . that I offer here invokes only event causation' (Yaffe
2000, pp. 154–5, n. 16). I would only say that this illustrates the
dangers of interpreting the great philosophers of the past in the
light of present-day perceptions of what constitutes a philosophically tenable thesis on some subject. One such danger is that we do
not learn as much as we might from the texts of such authors,

whose perennial value consists not least in their ability to prompt us to challenge some of the most deep-seated philosophical prejudices of our own time.

LOCKE AND THE PROBLEM OF 'DEVIANT CAUSAL CHAINS'

An important issue that arises in attempting to understand Locke's theory of voluntary action is the question of whether, for Locke, it is *both necessary and sufficient* for an action's being voluntary that the event concerned should have been caused by a volition of the agent to perform such an action – or, to put the same point in substance-causation terms, that the agent should have caused the event concerned by willing to perform such an action. That Locke held this to be a *necessary* condition for voluntariness seems to be borne out by, for example, the passage from Book IV of the *Essay* quoted a little earlier. But an important consideration that might make one hesitate to say that Locke also thought this to be a *sufficient* condition for voluntariness is that this would apparently render Locke's account vulnerable to counter-examples involving so-called 'deviant causal chains', of the kind supplied by Donald Davidson's famous case of the nervous climber (see Davidson 1980). I shall describe this case in a moment, but first I want to declare an interest in the issue at stake here. In earlier work (Lowe 1986, p. 150), I maintained that the following schema captures the essence of Locke's conception of what it is for an agent S to act in a manner A voluntarily:

> *S A*s voluntarily if and only if an *A*-result is caused by a volition of
> *S*'s to *A*.

Here, as I say, S is an agent and A is a manner of acting, such as, for example, raising one's arm. I shall explain the notion of an 'action-result' more fully later, but in this instance it would be an event of one's arm's rising. So, in this particular instance, my contention was that, according to Locke, S raises his arm voluntarily if and only if an event of S's arm's rising is caused by a volition of S to raise his arm. In saying this, I committed myself to the view that, for Locke, causation by a volition of the agent is both necessary *and sufficient* for voluntary action – in short, that Locke espoused both of two claims, which we may call, respectively, *the necessity claim* and *the sufficiency claim*. In his recent book, Gideon Yaffe agrees with me about the necessity claim, but not about the sufficiency claim, remarking:

> The account of voluntary action that Lowe attributes to Locke is not philosophically sound, because causation by volition simply isn't sufficient for voluntariness. The account runs into difficulties, in particular, from cases involving deviant causal chains.
>
> (Yaffe 2000, p. 104)

In my earlier work, I acknowledged the possibility that the account might suffer from this difficulty, but commented that 'I propose to waive such issues precisely because Locke was not addressing them' (Lowe 1986, p. 161, n. 3). That still seems to me to be a perfectly reasonable comment. However, since Yaffe himself has raised the matter, I shall now address it and argue that, in fact, it is not as clear as Yaffe supposes that 'causation by volition simply isn't sufficient for voluntariness', when one takes every relevant consideration into account. But first let us return to Davidson.

In Davidson's famous example, a climber is desperately holding on to a rope supporting his companion, strongly desiring to let go of it and believing that if he does so his companion will fall to his death – but this desire and belief so unnerve him that they actually cause him to let his companion fall. The problem is that, according to a causal theory of intentional action like Davidson's, it would seem that the climber must be said to have let his companion fall *intentionally* – because his action of letting go was apparently caused by an appropriate combination of belief and desire – and yet our intuition is to say that this agent in fact acted unintentionally. Now, Davidson himself is no volitionist and his example is meant to illustrate something about the concept of intentional, rather than voluntary, action. But Yaffe adapts it to his own purpose thus:

If I have a volition to let go, and reflection on the fact that I had such
a volition causes me to become so nervous that I let go, then my
volition caused my letting go, despite the fact that I did not do so
voluntarily.

(Yaffe 2000, p. 104)

As with regard to the distinction between event-causation and
substance-causation, Yaffe acknowledges that nothing in Locke's
text suggests that he was alive to this issue and hence that the
problem of deviant causal chains doesn't really constitute evidence
against the thesis that, for Locke, causation by volition is sufficient
for voluntariness. Yaffe thinks, as we shall see, that there is, none the
less, textual evidence of another sort against the thesis. But why
even mention the problem of deviant causal chains, in that case?
The thought seems to be that Locke's supposed grounds for denying the sufficiency claim can, in fact, be brought to bear on the
problem of deviant causal chains and help in its solution, thereby
demonstrating the strength of his account, as interpreted by Yaffe.
However, I am rather doubtful whether the problem of deviant
causal chains really does beset the sufficiency claim in any case:
Yaffe is too ready, on the basis of a very sketchily drawn example, to
suppose that it does. A careful volitionist will take pains to specify
very precisely the intentional content of the volition that is causally
implicated in any instance of voluntary action. In the case of a
climber who voluntarily lets go of the rope bearing his companion,
what he wills to do is to cause his grip to loosen *now*, directly by this
very act of will – so that the intentional content of the volition or
act of will has a self-referential aspect (see Lowe 1996, pp. 149ff.).
But such a description does not fit the case of the nervous climber,
who may plausibly be conceived to possess a general *desire* to let go
sometime soon and be so upset by the thought of having such a
desire that he unintentionally lets go now, but who cannot coher-
ently be conceived to *will* to let go now, directly by means of this
very act of will, and yet let go *in the way that he willed to* only as an

unintended consequence of reflecting on the fact that he had such a volition. For if such a volition does not *immediately* give rise to a letting go, but only indirectly via an episode of reflection and consequent state of anxiety, then it does not cause what its own intentional content requires it to cause in order for the ensuing action to qualify as voluntary.

But what more is required, according to Yaffe's interpretation of Locke's position, for an act to be voluntary than causation by volition? Yaffe begins by distinguishing between 'a volition causing an action, and an action satisfying the content of a volition' (Yaffe 2000, p. 108). Then he says that, for an action *A* to satisfy the content of an agent's volition to *A*,

> the agent's *A*-ing must have come about as a result of the [agent's] . . . volition. Further, the agent's conception of her volition as the exertion of a power that is, usually, an active power to *A* must be confirmed by the occurrence of the action. The action's occurrence will not confirm the agent's conception of her volition unless the volition causes her action in a particular way, in the way that the agent expects her volition to cause her action.
> (Yaffe 2000, pp. 108–9)

Finally, Yaffe proposes that, for Locke, an action *A* of an agent *S* is voluntary if and only if *A* 'satisfies a volition to *A* on the part of *S*' (Yaffe 2000, p. 109). This account of voluntary action, Yaffe maintains, is not vulnerable to counter-examples involving deviant causal chains. For instance, in the nervous climber case, 'the letting go was not caused by the volition in the appropriate way' (Yaffe 2000, p. 110), because 'if my letting go is accounted for in part by appeal to the fact that I got nervous, then the aspect of myself that explains why I got nervous . . . is also involved in accounting for the occurrence of my letting go' (Yaffe 2000, p. 110). However, it may by now seem that Yaffe's proposed solution to the problem of deviant causal chains boils down, in effect, to something very much like my own earlier proposal for dealing with this supposed problem: in both cases, it may seem, the key lies in exploiting an essential feature of the intentional *content* of a volition, namely, that it is always a volition to cause an occurrence 'in a particular way, in the way that the agent expects her volition to cause [the occurrence]', to use Yaffe's own phrase. This phrase might seem designed to capture once more the self-referential aspect of volitional content. But then my point would be that when such a constraint on volitional content is acknowledged, it may be argued, as I argued earlier, that the sufficiency claim is not, after all, vulnerable to counter-examples invoking deviant causal chains.

However, on closer inspection, it is clear that the two proposals are in fact significantly different. Yaffe's proposal does not appeal to a constraint on what we might call first-order *volitional* content, but rather to a condition on the agent's 'conception' of the causal role of his or her volition and thereby to a constraint on the content of a second-order mental state that is distinct from the volition itself. This connects with another peculiar feature of Yaffe's understanding of Lockean volitions, namely, his contention that volitions, for Locke, are not *intrinsically* volitional in nature. As Yaffe puts it:

> It is a necessary condition for a particular act of my mind to count as a volition that I conceive of it in a particular way: namely, as an exercise of my ability to control my body (or some other part of myself) . . . So, an act of the mind does not count as a volition simply by virtue of its intrinsic, nonrelational properties. That is, we could demote a mental act from its status as a volition . . . merely by changing the surrounding psychological facts.
>
> (Yaffe 2000, pp. 89–90)

Yaffe calls this condition 'the Conception Condition on volition', and in support of Locke's adherence to it he cites, for example, the following passage from the *Essay*:

> *Volition*, 'tis plain, is an Act of the Mind knowingly exerting that
> Dominion it takes it self to have over any part of the Man, by
> imploying it in, or witholding it from any particular Action.
>
> (*Essay*, II, XXI, 15)

However, there is a difficulty for Yaffe's view that seems quite serious. This is that Locke takes a volition to be a species of thought – 'a thought or preference of the mind ordering, or as it were commanding the doing or not doing such or such a particular action' (*Essay*, II, XXI, 5) – and he also notoriously holds that all thought is self-conscious in character:

> [C]onsciousness . . . is inseparable from thinking, and as it seems to
> me essential to it: It being impossible for any one to perceive,
> without perceiving, that he does perceive.
>
> (*Essay*, II, XXVII, 9)

How, then, could Locke contemplate the possibility of one's engaging in an act of mind which falls short of counting as a volition only because one does not think of this act of mind as an exercising of one's ability to control part of one's body – that is, which in every other way but this qualifies as a volition? For it could only qualify as a volition at all if it were a thought 'ordering, or as it were commanding the doing or not doing such or such a particular action' – it would have to be a thought with that sort of intentional content – and yet, at the same time, one would have to 'perceive' it (that is, think of it) as being just such a thought, because, according to Locke, all thought is conscious in this sense.

Returning to my own earlier proposal for dealing with the problem of deviant causal chains, I readily concede that there is no clear evidence that Locke himself thought that volitional content is 'self-referential' in the way that I suggest, although there is nothing in his position inimical to this idea. If the problem of deviant causal chains had occurred to him, he could certainly have adopted this sort of solution and thereby have defended the sufficiency claim. As for the question of whether there is clear evidence that Locke espoused the sufficiency claim – which Yaffe, of course, denies – I shall discuss that in the next section. Certainly, I think that there is no clear evidence that he rejected it. What I do maintain, though, is that the package that Yaffe offers on Locke's behalf – a rejection of the sufficiency claim together with an acceptance of the Conception Condition – is not one that sits at all comfortably with some central tenets of Locke's philosophy of mind and action.

INVOLUNTARINESS AND THE SUFFICIENCY CLAIM

I now want to address the main objection that Yaffe raises against attributing the sufficiency claim to Locke. But I should advise readers that this section of the present chapter unavoidably involves some very detailed exegesis and argumentation and can safely be omitted by those who are concerned only to understand in broad terms the character of Locke's theory of voluntary agency. I have included the section because I think that the issues at stake are important for the philosophy of action and I hope that this discussion of them will provide a useful example of the way in which close engagement with a famous historical text can help to illuminate and enrich present-day philosophical concerns.

Yaffe's main objection arises out of Locke's remark that '[W]hatsoever action is performed without [a volition], is called *Involuntary*' (*Essay*, II, XXI, 5). Yaffe initially canvasses two possible interpretations of this remark, both of which he intends to reject. According to what he calls the 'First Interpretation', the remark may be interpreted as merely making the claim that 'absence of an appropriate volition is sufficient for the involuntariness of an action' (Yaffe 2000, pp. 104–5). Call this claim *claim* (1). The first thing I want to point out is that Yaffe is wrong to assert as he does that claim (1) 'is the contrapositive of the claim that causation by [an appropriate] volition is necessary for voluntary action' (Yaffe 2000, p. 105). Call the latter claim *claim* (2). Claim (2) is, of course, what I earlier called *the necessity claim* and it is a claim that both Yaffe and I want to attribute to Locke. The reason why claim (1) cannot be the 'contra-positive' of claim (2) is that the contrapositive of a claim is logically equivalent to it and yet claim (1), unlike claim (2), makes no mention of causation.

A few words of explanation are called for here. One normally speaks of the 'contrapositive' of a *conditional* statement. The contra-positive of a conditional statement of the form 'If p, then q' is another conditional statement, of the form 'If not q, then not p' – and two such statements are standardly taken to be logically equiva-lent. When such a pair of statements is true, we may say that p is sufficient for q and q is necessary for p, or, equivalently, that not q is sufficient for not p and not p is necessary for not q. By extension, then, one might say that the statement that p is sufficient for q is the 'contrapositive' of the statement that not q is sufficient for not p and hence also of the equivalent statement that not p is necessary for not q. Now, claim (1) states that absence of an appropriate volition is sufficient for the involuntariness of an action and it will be seen that this is the contrapositive of the statement that non-absence of an appropriate volition is necessary for the non-involuntariness of an action – or, in other words, that *presence* of an appropriate volition is necessary for the *voluntariness* of an action. Claim (2), however, states instead that *causation* by an appropriate volition is necessary for the voluntariness of an action. So Yaffe is mistaken in asserting that claim (1) is the contrapositive of claim (2).

But let us move on. Yaffe urges next that the First Interpretation of Locke's remark is unsatisfactory, on what seem to me to be the untenable grounds that 'it means that Locke never (as far as I know) explicitly offered necessity conditions for *involuntary* action (that is, sufficiency conditions for *voluntary* action) . . . [and so] means that Locke left an important lacuna in his philosophy of action' (Yaffe 2000, p. 105). As I shall make clear shortly, Locke undoubtedly did explicitly offer sufficiency conditions for voluntary action, quite independently of the remark now under discussion – and, oddly enough, Yaffe himself later acknowledges as much. Be that as it may, Yaffe now considers a Second Interpretation of Locke's remark, according to which it is to be taken as meaning that absence of an appropriate volition is not only sufficient but also *necessary* for the involuntariness of an action. This Second Interpretation, he maintains, conflicts with my view that the *sufficiency claim*, as I call it, is attributable to Locke:

> If the Second Interpretation captures Locke's meaning, then he cannot have consistently held the view that Lowe attributes to him. He cannot, that is, have held that causation by [an appropriate] volition is sufficient for voluntariness.
>
> (Yaffe 2000, p. 105)

Yaffe's point seems to be that if *absence* of an appropriate volition is *necessary* for the *involuntariness* of an action, then it follows that *presence* of an appropriate volition is *sufficient* for the *non-involuntariness* – in other words, for the voluntariness – of an action, even if that volition plays no causal role in the production of the action. As Yaffe puts it, 'Under the Second Interpretation, actions that are preceded by volitions that are not causally responsible for them are . . . voluntary' (Yaffe 2000, pp. 105–6). However, this does not in fact conflict with the *sufficiency* claim but only with what I have been calling the *necessity* claim, which Yaffe himself is happy to attribute to Locke. This is easier to see if we formulate these claims as conditional statements. In this form, the sufficiency claim states that if an action is preceded by a volition that is causally responsible for it, then it is voluntary. But this is perfectly consistent with its also being the case that if an action is preceded by a volition that is *not* causally responsible for it, then it is voluntary. What the latter is *not* consistent with is the necessity claim, which states that if an action is voluntary, then it is preceded by a volition that is causally responsible for it. For from 'If an action is preceded by a volition that is *not* causally responsible for it, then it is voluntary' and 'If an action is voluntary, then it is preceded by a volition that is causally responsible for it' we may infer the absurd conclusion 'If an action is preceded by a volition that is *not* causally responsible for it, then it is preceded by a volition that is causally responsible for it'.

We see, thus, that the Second Interpretation only creates a difficulty for an aspect of my account of Locke's position with which Yaffe himself is in full agreement. It creates no more difficulty for me than it does for Yaffe and he is obliged to reject it for exactly the same reason that I am. As it turns out, Yaffe in fact rejects both of the canvassed Interpretations of Locke's remark and favours a third, based on the proposal that I examined in the previous section. He surmises, however, that 'Lowe would probably want to avoid the inconsistency between the Second Interpretation and his claim that, for Locke, causation by [an appropriate] volition is sufficient for voluntariness by returning to the First Interpretation' (Yaffe 2000, p. 107). As we have just seen, in reality there is no such inconsistency for me to have to avoid, only an inconsistency between the Second Interpretation and the claim that both Yaffe and I want to make that, for Locke, causation by an appropriate volition is *necessary* for voluntariness. But to avoid this inconsistency I do not, in point of fact, favour Yaffe's First Interpretation. Rather, I prefer to see in Locke's remark an implicit affirmation of the claim that absence of *causation* by an appropriate volition is sufficient for the involuntariness of an action. Call this claim *claim* (3). Claim (3), by the way, really is the 'contrapositive' of the claim that causation by an appropriate volition is necessary for the voluntariness of an action – claim (2) above, or the *necessity* claim, as I have been calling it – and so is merely equivalent to that.

To see why I favour this interpretation of Locke's remark that '[W]hatsoever action is performed without [a volition], is called *Involuntary*', note that this remark immediately follows Locke's assertion that 'The. . . performance of [any] Action, consequent to [a volition], is called *Voluntary*' (*Essay*, II, XXI, 5). Now, as I argued in the paper that Yaffe is criticizing, 'consequent to' here cannot plausibly be interpreted in a purely non-causal sense, implying mere temporal succession (see Lowe 1986, p. 150). Indeed, I see in this

assertion of Locke's the clearest evidence we have that he subscribed to what I have been calling *the sufficiency claim* – the claim that
causation by an appropriate volition is sufficient for the voluntariness of an action. But, by the same token, when Locke speaks, in the
immediately following remark, about an action's being performed
'without' a volition, this too is not plausibly to be read in a purely
non-causal sense – a fact, incidentally, that Yaffe himself later
acknowledges, if somewhat obliquely (see Yaffe 2000, p. 111).
Plausibly, what Locke has in mind here is an action which is not
brought about by means of the agent's will. For just as performing an
action 'with' a volition is naturally construed as performing it *by*
exercising one's will, so an action's being performed 'without' a
volition is naturally construed as its *not* being performed by exercising one's will. At the very least, it should be acknowledged that this
reading of Locke's remark is quite as natural as one which inter-
prets it as asserting merely that absence of an appropriate volition is
sufficient for the involuntariness of an action – claim (1) above. It
should be noted, though, that claim (1) is *implied* by the reading of
Locke's remark that I favour. On my reading of Locke's remark, it
makes claim (3), that absence of causation by an appropriate volition is sufficient for involuntariness. But absence of an appropriate
volition is obviously sufficient for absence of causation by an
appropriate volition and so, given that the latter is sufficient for
involuntariness, so too is absence of an appropriate volition sufficient for involuntariness. For if *p* is sufficient for *q* and *q* is sufficient for *r*, then *p* is sufficient for *r*.

I now come to the crucial question of whether Yaffe's denial that
Locke espoused – or, at least, was committed to – the sufficiency
claim can be rendered consistent with the text of the *Essay*. I believe
that it cannot, with any plausibility. Yaffe seems, however, to be
confused about one vitally important matter here. He too notes that
Locke's remark that '[W]hatsoever action is performed without [a
volition], is called *Involuntary*' is immediately preceded by Locke's
assertion that 'The. . . performance of [any] Action, consequent to

[a volition], is called *Voluntary*'. But, without actually quoting this preceding sentence at this point – although he does so earlier (see Yaffe 2000, p. 99) – Yaffe describes it here as the 'claim made in the preceding sentence (*namely, that causation by volition is necessary for voluntariness*)' (Yaffe 2000, p. 105, my emphasis). And, indeed, Yaffe offers as a further reason for rejecting the First Interpretation of Locke's subsequent remark concerning involuntary action that, on this interpretation, that remark would be 'just a reiteration of [the] claim made in the preceding sentence' (Yaffe 2000, p. 105). But this cannot be correct. The preceding sentence, as we have just seen, is 'The . . . performance of [any] Action, consequent to [a volition], is called *Voluntary*' – and this cannot be construed merely as a *necessity* claim concerning voluntariness. For it clearly implies that *if the performance of an action is consequent to a volition, then it is voluntary* and thus that an action's being performed consequent to a volition is *sufficient* for its being voluntary. This still leaves it open that it may be intended to imply necessity *as well as* sufficiency and also leaves open whether 'consequent to' should be construed in a causal or in a merely temporal sense – or perhaps in some third sense. But that it constitutes a sufficiency claim concerning voluntariness cannot be in doubt.

Now, if 'consequent to' should be construed in either a causal or a merely temporal sense, Yaffe clearly cannot maintain that Locke is not committed to what I have been calling 'the sufficiency claim' – that is, the claim that causation by an appropriate volition is sufficient for the voluntariness of an action. For we have just seen that Locke is undoubtedly committed to *a* sufficiency claim concerning voluntary action, namely, that being 'consequent to' an appropriate volition is sufficient for the voluntariness of an action. But precisely because the temporal sense of 'consequent to' is *weaker* than the causal sense, Locke is committed to what I have been calling 'the sufficiency claim' *whichever sense* is attributed to 'consequent to'. The point is once again a simple one concerning the logic of sufficient conditions. Being *caused by* an appropriate volition is a sufficient condition for being *preceded* by an appropriate volition, because any cause necessarily precedes its effect. Hence, if Locke means that being *preceded* by an appropriate volition is sufficient for the voluntariness of an action – in accordance with the merely temporal interpretation of 'consequent to' – then he is committed also to holding that being *caused* by an appropriate volition is sufficient for the voluntariness of an action.

Clearly, then, Yaffe must deny that Locke understands 'consequent to' in either the causal or the merely temporal sense. And that is precisely what he does do, in the following passage:

> [Locke] says that the voluntary actions are those that are performed 'consequent to' . . . a volition. This is a peculiar phrase and suggests that he wanted to avoid using the language of causation when offering his sufficiency condition for voluntary action. The remark is, of course, inconclusive, but I think that it suggests that things are more complicated than Lowe allows.
>
> (Yaffe 2000, p. 109)

Notice that Yaffe here contradicts his earlier mistaken supposition that the sentence containing 'consequent to' merely states a *necessary* condition for voluntariness and at the same time undercuts the main reason he offered for rejecting the so-called 'First Interpretation' of Locke's remark about involuntariness. I would only add that Yaffe's attempt to construe Locke's phrase 'consequent to' as having neither a causal nor a merely temporal sense seems to me speculative in the extreme. If Locke really did have a special meaning in mind, would he not have taken pains to spell it out carefully, given the evident importance of the issue at stake? Yaffe's own construal of 'consequent to' is, of course, intimately bound up with his proposed new account of Locke's conception of voluntary action, discussed in the previous section, and so stands or falls with that proposal. And I have already explained why I think that the proposal is untenable. That leaves us, I think, with no good reason to deny that Locke either espoused or was at the very least committed to the sufficiency claim.

I have considered it worthwhile to go into this matter in such detail for two reasons, in addition to those mentioned at the beginning of the section. The first is that it really is very important to get as clear as we can about how Locke understood the relationship between volition and action, not least because this has an intimate bearing on how we understand his views about freedom of action and freedom of will. The second is that, as will no doubt have become evident, it is very easy to get confused in discussions concerning necessary and sufficient conditions. Moreover, since Locke himself does not explicitly use the terminology of necessary and sufficient conditions, great care needs to be taken in attributing to him claims made in those terms. I hope that the discussion in this section has provided, at the very least, an object lesson in the perils attending philosophical debate about such conditions.

PERSONHOOD, PERSONAL IDENTITY AND FREE AGENCY

As we saw in Chapter 3, much is often made of Locke's views concerning the relationship between the identity of persons and their capacity to remember episodes in their past lives. Rather less tends to be said, however, concerning links between his conception of personal identity and his views about free agency. But such links are certainly very well worth exploring. Locke, we should recall, denies that personal identity consists in the identity of substance of any kind, material or spiritual, making the notoriously obscure and controversial claim that it consists instead in 'consciousness. . . as far as this consciousness can be extended backwards to any past Action or Thought' (Essay, II, XXVII, 9). However, although Locke's discussion of personal identity explicitly concentrates on 'backward-looking' consciousness, of the sort that characterizes memory, it is clear that 'future-directed' consciousness of the sort that is involved in action is implicitly quite as central to Locke's overall conception of personhood and personal identity. Moreover, it is important that Locke's denial that personal identity consists in the identity of substance of any kind should be understood in context. As we saw in Chapter 3, his point is that human persons are not persons in virtue of their purely material or biological characteristics, nor in virtue of any purely spiritual characteristics that they may have, but rather in virtue of their psychological characteristics. But this is not best taken to imply that, for Locke, human persons just *are*, or are 'reducible to', certain 'bundles' of psychological states, or temporally extended sequences of such 'bundles': they may still qualify as 'substantial' beings and indeed as physical beings, even though their persistence over time does not rest upon the persistence of any particular material or spiritual substance. Here we should beware, once more, of the danger of interpreting Locke anachronistically, this time in the light of conceptions of personhood and persistence that have really been advanced explicitly only in recent years. I do not, for example, think that it is very helpful, in trying to explain Locke's conception of personal identity, to talk in terms of 'consciousness between person-stages', in the way that some modern commentators tend to do (see, for instance, Yaffe 2000, p. 120).

In one of the relatively few recent discussions of the connections between Locke's conception of personal identity and his views about human agency, Gideon Yaffe interestingly raises what he calls the 'Where's the Agent Problem' (Yaffe 2000, p. 121), which he thinks afflicts all causal theories of agency. The problem is supposed to be something like this. A causal theory of agency represents actions as being caused by antecedent mental episodes of a suitable kind – in the case of volitionist theories, volitions or willings. But these mental causes of actions, it is said, are not themselves actions and have in turn other non-actions as causes, in an unbroken chain of event-causation which stretches back indefinitely far in time. Hence, an agent's actions appear to be nothing more than elements in the ongoing stream of event-causation and the 'agent' seems thereby to be denied any genuine role as the author of his or her actions. Yaffe himself seems to think that the Conception Condition which he attributes to Locke helps with this problem, because the fact that, according to this view, a volition must be the object of self-conscious awareness to count as a volition makes it somehow especially internal to the person whose volition it is and thereby provides a robust sense in which an action caused by such a volition has that person as its agent and author.

I think it is wrong to suppose that all causal theories of agency, or even all volitional theories, have the structure that Yaffe describes. First of all, many causal theorists would deny, in my view rightly, that bodily actions – such as the action of raising one's arm – have mental episodes, such as volitions, as their *causes*. Such theorists would distinguish between the action of raising one's arm – that is, causing one's arm to rise – and the event of arm-rising that is an essential ingredient or part of that action. To distinguish the two, the arm-raising may be called the action proper and the arm-rising the 'action-result'. Yaffe himself always talks in terms of actions and their causes, never in terms of action-results, because he thinks that Locke himself never used the distinction between actions and action-results (Yaffe 2000, p. 157, n. 24). However, although Locke does not explicitly make the distinction, it would be surprising if it were not implicitly present in his writing, since it is built into the very semantics of natural language – for instance, in terms of the distinction between transitive and intransitive senses of the verb 'move' (see Hornsby 1980, pp. 2–3). To move$_T$ an object O is to cause O to move$_I$, where 'move$_T$' and 'move$_I$' are, respectively, the transitive and intransitive forms of the verb 'move'. Recall again the passage from the *Essay* quoted earlier, where Locke says that

> all our voluntary Motions . . . are produced in us only by the free Action or Thought of our own Minds . . . For example: My right Hand writes, whilst my left Hand is still: What causes rest in one, and motion in the other? Nothing but my Will, a Thought of my Mind.
>
> (*Essay*, IV, X, 19)

Here Locke is saying that a movement$_I$ in my hand is caused by a volition of mine. It is true that he speaks of this motion or movement$_I$ in my hand as being 'voluntary', but that doesn't necessarily imply that he takes my *action* in this case to be the movement$_I$ in my hand, as opposed to my moving$_T$ my hand by an act of will. In any case, whatever Locke's own view may or may not be, I would urge that the proper view for a volitionist to take in this matter is that my *action* in this case is my moving$_T$ my hand by willing to move$_T$ it in a certain way and that what is caused by my so willing is not my action but the *action-result* of my hand's moving$_I$ in the appropriate way. The upshot is that, on this view of the matter, actions such as hand-movings$_T$ are *not*, after all, mere elements in the ongoing stream of event-causation, because they are not events but *causings* of events, and do not have events – not even volitions – as their causes (see Lowe 2002, ch. 12).

To this it may be responded that still, on this view, action-results and the volitions that are their causes are mere elements in the ongoing stream of event-causation, so that the real difficulty has not been allayed. But here I would question another assumption that Yaffe makes on behalf of causal theorists of agency, namely, that the mental causes which they invoke in their theories are not in any special sense *actions*, but mere 'happenings': 'causal theorists of agency build doings out of happenings and causal relations' (Yaffe 2000, p. 121). Well, that may be true of some causal theorists, such as Donald Davidson, but it is certainly not true of all volitionists, many of whom certainly qualify as causal theorists. A volitionist may contend that although willing is not causing, in the way that arm-raising is causing one's arm to rise, it is nonetheless a kind of action, not a mere happening or event. Carl Ginet is an example of such a volitionist, though one may not find altogether felicitous his description of volitions as having an 'actish phenomenal quality' (see Ginet 1990, pp. 11ff.). I would rather make the point myself by assimilating willing to *trying* or *endeavouring* (without wishing to identify the two notions exactly), for trying incontrovertibly falls within the sphere of genuine action (see Lowe 1996, pp. 157ff.). The upshot is that there is plenty of scope for a causal theorist of agency to reject the idea which Yaffe thinks gives rise to the 'Where's the Agent Problem', namely, that all doings are built out of happenings and causal relations – especially if one takes into account the considerations raised earlier in favour of the primacy of substance-causation.

Despite all of the problems undoubtedly besetting Locke's account of personhood and personal identity, some of which we examined in Chapter 3, my own opinion is that his views concerning human agency strengthen rather than weaken that account, and do so precisely because those views are most naturally construed as belonging to the substance-causation tradition. Locke's conception of the person as agent is, to my mind, considerably more compelling than his conception of the person as a repository of memories, even though the latter is typically given much more prominence by present-day commentators on Locke's work.

SUMMARY

Locke is a volitionist: he holds that voluntary action consists in the causation of certain bodily or mental events by volitions or acts of will, that is, by exercises of a special mental power or capacity, the will. He is also, I believe, a substance-causalist, holding that it is substances, rather than events, that are in the most fundamental sense causes of anything. For Locke, then, voluntary human action is a special case of substance-causation. An agent is *free to act* in a certain way, according to Locke, just in case whether or not he acts in that way depends on whether or not he wills to act in that way. On the other hand, *freedom of the will*, he is inclined to say, is at best a misnomer: but he agrees that there must be more to human freedom in the fullest sense of the term than is simply involved in our being free to act in various ways. What this 'more' exactly is, according to Locke, is hard to pin down, although it is clear that he thinks that it has something to do with our ability, at least sometimes, to 'suspend' the satisfaction of our most pressing desires. Whether Locke is properly to be regarded as a compatibilist or, perhaps, as an implicit libertarian is also very hard to determine. What is very clear, however, is that Locke thought that our capacity for free agency is absolutely central to our status as persons, quite as much as our capacities for reason, reflection and memory. The chapter 'Of Power' in the *Essay* resists easy interpretation, because Locke himself revised it extensively and was never entirely satisfied with it. But it is also one of the most philosophically rewarding chapters of that work and repays constant re-reading.

FURTHER READING

Chappell, Vere 1994: 'Locke on the Freedom of the Will', in G. A. J. Rogers (ed.), *Locke's Philosophy: Content and Context* (Oxford: Clarendon Press).

Clarke, Randolph 2003: *Libertarian Accounts of Free Will* (New York: Oxford University Press).

Magri, Tito 2000: 'Locke, Suspension of Desire, and the Remote Good', *British Journal for the Philosophy of History* 8, pp. 55–70, reprinted in Udo Thiel (ed.), *Locke: Epistemology and Metaphysics* (Aldershot: Dartmouth, 2002).

Six

Liberty and Toleration

Our main source for Locke's political philosophy is his *Two Treatises of Government*, published anonymously late in 1689. Locke never openly acknowledged the work as his own during his lifetime, although his authorship of it is beyond question and is implied by a codicil to his will. It seems that it was largely composed in the early 1680s, prior to Locke's departure to Holland in 1683 following the disclosure of the Rye House plot (see Chapter 1 above). The target of the *First Treatise* is Sir Robert Filmer's ultra-royalist tract, *Patriarcha* (Filmer 1991), published in 1680 – almost thirty years after its author's death – as a piece of propaganda on the part of the Tory supporters of Charles II and the right of his Roman Catholic brother James to succeed to the throne. The *Second Treatise* offers a positive account of the basis of legitimate government in counterbalance to the negative thrust of the *First Treatise*, the latter being designed to undermine Filmer's biblically based arguments in favour of absolute royal power. The *Two Treatises* could not, of course, have been published while Charles II was still on the throne, in view of their implicitly seditious character. Indeed, Algernon Sidney (or Sydney), one of the Rye House conspirators, had been tried and executed for treason, partly on the evidence of a manuscript work attacking Filmer, his *Discourses Concerning Government* (Sidney 1996). Locke's very possession of the manuscript of the *Two Treatises* at that time put him in danger of his life. But why did he choose to publish them six years later, in 1689, after English politics had taken a turn very much to his liking? Partly, no doubt, as a vindication of the course of events leading to the Glorious Revolution of 1688 and the replacement of James II by William of Orange and his wife Mary – as Locke's Preface to the *Two Treatises* implies. Partly too, perhaps, because Locke was anxious that the tendency of political developments following the installation of William and Mary was not as radical as he had hoped and there was some danger of a reversion to more authoritarian rule (see Ashcraft 1986, pp. 590–601). Certainly, Locke could not be sure of political stability at such a time and this may partly explain his continuing determination not to reveal his authorship of the work.

One thing that does seem relatively clear is that the *Two Treatises* were neither explicitly nor even implicitly intended by Locke to constitute a refutation of the greatest intellectual supporter of absolutist government of the age, Thomas Hobbes (1588–1679), whose *Leviathan* (Hobbes 1996) had appeared in 1651. Hobbes's arguments in favour of absolutism were quite different from Filmer's and, unlike Filmer's, had no currency amongst the Tory politicians of the day who did support the king. Even so, from a present-day perspective, comparisons and contrasts between Hobbes's and Locke's political philosophies are extremely interesting and instructive. It would be pointless to avoid them simply because Locke's immediate concern was not to refute Hobbes. Locke was, of course, perfectly aware of Hobbes's doctrines and consequently of the differences between Hobbes's views and his own. Such was Hobbes's fame – or perhaps we should say notoriety – at the time, that Locke could not avoid writing in the shadow of his illustrious predecessor. In this chapter, therefore, I shall not hesitate to compare and contrast Locke's views with those of Hobbes, which they do both resemble and differ from in very interesting ways. However, I shall not examine Locke's arguments against Filmer in the *First Treatise* because, important though Filmer's writings were in Locke's day, they are now mainly of historical interest.

Before leaving Filmer and Locke's response to him, I should say just a little about the nature of their differences. Filmer's central thesis was that God had granted absolute dominion over the earth and all of its inhabitants to Adam, the first man, and that this divine right to rule had been passed on, over the generations, to first-born sons, so that the rightful dominion of a king over his people was effectively that of a father over his children, wife and servants. At a time when biblical authority was scarcely questioned, such a doctrine must have appeared entirely compelling to many people – and Locke's attempted refutation of it correspondingly provocative. But to a modern reader, the bulk of this dispute may seem at best quaint and at worst hardly comprehensible. Much of interest and value can in fact be learned from it and we should not, of course, suppose that seventeenth-century authors wrote any less intelligently about issues which rested on assumptions now generally dismissed as false than they did about issues which still seem important to us. But, unfortunately, limitations of space prevent me from delving further here into this aspect of Locke's political thought and I shall pass on directly to his positive doctrine. At the end of the chapter, I shall move on from discussing Locke's *Second Treatise* to say something about his views on religious toleration, as set out in his *Letter Concerning Toleration* of 1689.

THE STATE OF NATURE AND THE NATURE OF MAN

Locke, like Thomas Hobbes before him and Jean-Jacques Rousseau after him, was a *social contract theorist* – as indeed were many other political theorists in the seventeenth and eighteenth centuries. Although these three philosophers ultimately endorse very different ideals of government – roughly speaking: Hobbes absolute monarchy, Locke parliamentary democracy and constitutional monarchy, Rousseau extreme democracy on something like the Greek city-state model – they have in common an aim to ground political obligation on *consent*. That is to say, all of them consider that legitimate government is fundamentally government by the consent of the governed. Moreover, this consent is understood by all three of them in *contractual* terms – that is, by reference to an actual or hypothetical *contractual agreement* between people, freely entered into by the parties concerned, which imposes upon them certain obligations in return for certain anticipated benefits. (Hobbes actually uses the word 'contract' in this context – and also the word 'covenant' – whereas Locke prefers the term 'compact'. It is Rousseau who uses the phrase *contrat social*, or 'social contract', but this has now become so widespread that it is not really misleading to speak of Hobbes and Locke as being 'social contract theorists'.)

Different social contract theorists operate with significantly different conceptions of the sort of 'consent' that is involved here and I shall examine Locke's particular conception in some detail in a later section. But despite such differences, at the root of all social contract theories is the idea that there is a fundamental distinction to be drawn between civil society and a supposedly apolitical human condition, traditionally described as the 'state of nature'. Civil society is taken to be characterized by the presence of political authority and the rule of law, backed by an effective monopoly of coercive power. The social contract theorist then attempts to explain how people either do, or at least *could*, make a transition from the state of nature to civil society, without any violation of their natural rights and through their own 'consent' or willing participation, simply by entering freely into a mutual agreement or 'contract'.

By no means all social contract theorists of Locke's time held the state of nature to be an *actual* historical condition, once universal amongst human beings. However, some did consider it to be a condition still existing amongst 'primitive' peoples in certain parts of the world. And all regarded it as one that automatically obtains between different sovereign powers. Thus Hobbes remarks in Chapter 13 of *Leviathan* that he 'believe[s] it was never generally so, over all the world', but adds that 'there are many places, where they live so now . . . in . . . *America*' and that 'in all times Kings, and persons of Soveraigne authority' are in a state of nature – or 'war', as he describes it – with respect to one another (Hobbes 1996, pp. 89–90). Locke explicitly concurs with Hobbes on this last point, asserting that 'all Princes and Rulers of Independent Governments all through the World, are in a State of Nature' (Second Treatise, 14). However, there is also another way to think of the state of nature that we can find in writers of the time. This is to think of it primarily as a possible condition into which civil society is perpetually in danger of degenerating, as when Hobbes comments that 'it may be perceived what manner of life there would be, where there were no common Power to feare' (Hobbes 1996, pp. 89–90). This in turn is not so very different from thinking of the state of nature as a merely hypothetical condition, or even just as a way of describing human communities which abstracts away from their political relationships and institutions. It is in something like this guise that the theoretical role of the state of nature has been revived in modern contractarian political thought, most notably in John Rawls's notion of 'the original position' (see Rawls 1972, pp. 11–22). In any case, it certainly need be no decisive objection to a social contract theory that no state of nature ever really existed, or that the people living in an existing civil society may never individually have made a transition from a state of nature to their current situation – a point that I shall address in a later section with specific reference to Locke's theory.

However, what might well be objected to – particularly by those 'collectivist' or 'organicist' political philosophers who regard human individuality itself as a product of civil society – is the very idea that human beings can be meaningfully characterized independently of their political relationships. In short, it may be urged that man is essentially a 'political animal', in Aristotle's famous phrase. Against this, all social contract theorists are committed – albeit in varying degrees – to an individualistic conception of civil society, according to which the individual is ontologically prior to, or more fundamental than, any civil society to which he or she belongs. Of course, such theorists can perfectly well concede that civil society creates opportunities for individuals which would be impossible for them without it. However, this concession falls far short of what their opponents insist upon – that there would simply *be* no human 'individuals' but for civil society. The question as to which side in this long-standing debate has the better arguments is too large a one for me to enter into here. Suffice it to say that any social contract theory, including Locke's, rests on what I have just called an individualistic conception of civil society and that such a conception is certainly open to challenge.

Precisely how a social contract theory characterizes the state of nature will depend in other ways upon the conception of human nature that is associated with it – for there is plenty of room for disagreement about this even amongst theorists who share an individualistic outlook. Thus, in Hobbes's theory, his radically egocentric view of human psychology evidently plays a large part in leading him so famously to characterize the state of nature as that of 'a warre . . . of every man, against every man' in which 'the life of man [is] solitary, poore, nasty, brutish, and short' (Hobbes 1996, pp. 88–9). Hobbes's egocentricism is reflected in his assertion that 'of the voluntary acts of every man, the object is some *Good to himselfe*' (Hobbes 1996, p. 93). But it should be stressed that even Hobbes, while he identifies the state of nature with a state of *war*, does not regard such a state as one of perpetual violence – only as one in which there is a perpetual threat of it. As he puts it, '[T]he nature of War, consisteth not in actuall fighting; but in the known disposition thereto' (Hobbes 1996, pp. 88–9). As to the causes of this state of war, where all political authority is absent, Hobbes contends that there are 'three principall causes of quarrell . . . [f]irst, Competition; Secondly, Diffidence; Thirdly, Glory' (Hobbes 1996, p. 88). In other words, Hobbes blames our supposedly hostile disposition towards one another on what he takes to be our natural psychological propensities for rivalry, fear and pride. Of course, another and less purely theoretical reason why Hobbes may have represented the state of nature as so appalling is that he wrote at the time of the English Civil War and could observe all too vividly in that conflict the dire consequences of the removal of effective political authority. However, Locke also lived through this tumultuous period of English history and yet when we turn to his conception of the state of nature, we see a much more peaceful picture. Locke seems to have envisaged that state as typically comprising a population of self-sufficient yeoman farmers, each looking after his own immediate family members and living in relative harmony with his neighbours. It seems fair to say, then, that one of the crucial differences between Locke and Hobbes lies in the relative optimism of the former and pessimism of the latter concerning human nature. They differ fundamentally regarding the desire and capacity of ordinary folk to get on with their own lives without unduly interfering with the lives of other people. Certainly, Locke is emphatic in denying Hobbes's identification of the state of nature with a state of war and this seems largely to be a consequence of his very different assessment of human motivation.

But there is another important respect in which Hobbes and Locke are in agreement about the basic human condition. They do at least agree that all human beings – or, at any rate, all adult men – are *naturally equal* in the state of nature and that, whether rightly or wrongly, only civil society creates significant inequalities. Thus, Hobbes remarks that

> Nature hath made men so equall, in the faculties of body, and mind . . . that . . . the difference between man, and man, is not so considerable, as that one man can thereupon claim to himselfe any benefit, to which another may not pretend, as well as he.
>
> (Hobbes 1996, pp. 86–7)

Locke concurs that the state of nature is 'A *State* also of *Equality*' (*Second Treatise*, 4) – and it is clear that by this he means not just a *moral* equality, but an equality of power. This assumption of natural equality is indeed essential to the workings of any social contract theory, because only beings who are at least roughly equal in their physical and intellectual powers could derive any benefit from freely entering into a mutual agreement of the kind that such a theory envisages.

What rights and obligations, if any, may be presumed to exist in the state of nature? Clearly, no political rights or obligations, since these are what the social contract is supposed to generate. But what about moral ones? And if these may be presumed to exist, what could be the source of their authority? God? Or Reason? Or do these sources coincide, because God is necessarily supremely rational and has created us as rational beings in his own image? Hobbes was regarded by his contemporaries as a thinly veiled atheist, although how fairly is a matter for dispute. Locke, however, not only sincerely adhered to the Christian faith but even believed that God's existence was capable of rational demonstration or proof – along with the central principles of morality. He also held, as we saw in Chapter 2, that although we have no innate knowledge we do have a natural capacity for reason, which is divine in origin.

Significant differences between Hobbes and Locke regarding the questions just raised are readily apparent in the texts. Hobbes, for instance, speaks of the *right of nature* which, he says, is 'the Liberty each man hath, to use his own power, as he will himselfe, for the preservation of his own Nature' (Hobbes 1996, p. 91). And he contends that in the state of nature 'every man has a Right to everything; even to one anothers body' (Hobbes 1996, p. 91). He does indeed formulate certain 'Laws of Nature', as he calls them, but regards these as prudential maxims which reason instructs us to endeavour to follow in order to secure our own self-preservation and well-being. As he puts it:

> A Law of Nature . . . is a Precept, or generall Rule, found out by Reason, by which a man is forbidden to do, that, which is destructive of his life, or taketh away the means of preserving the same; and to omit, that, by which he thinketh it may be best preserved.
>
> (Hobbes 1996, p. 91)

However, whether these 'laws' are supposed by Hobbes to have any moral authority in the usual sense is very debatable. He draws a distinction between obeying a law merely *in foro interno* – in intention, as we might say – and obeying it *in foro externo*, or in action, remarking:

> The Lawes of Nature oblige *in foro interno*; that is to say, they bind to a desire they should take place: but *in foro externo*; that is, to the putting them in act, not alwayes.
>
> (Hobbes 1996, p. 110)

Hobbes is clear, in fact, that in the state of nature, where there is no political power to enforce the laws of nature by the threat of effective punishment, reason can at most constrain us only to obey these laws *in foro interno*. For Hobbes, the first or 'Fundamentall Law of Nature . . . is, *to seek Peace, and follow it*' (Hobbes 1996, p. 92) – but he stresses that it would be irrational simply to lay down one's arms with no guarantee that others will do likewise.

Locke, in contrast, does not accept this apparently amoral view of the state of nature. According to Locke,

> [T]hough [the state of nature] be a *State of Liberty*, yet it is *not a State of Licence* . . . The *State of nature* has a Law of Nature to govern it, which obliges every one: And Reason, which is that Law, teaches all Mankind . . . that . . . no one ought to harm another in his Life, Health, Liberty, or Possessions.
>
> (*Second Treatise*, 6)

Indeed, Locke considers that in the state of nature it is every man's right to punish offenders against the law of nature, to a degree sufficient to deter them from committing further offences against it. Compare all of this with Hobbes's much starker view that in the state of nature 'nothing can be Unjust' because 'Where there is no common Power, there is no Law: where no Law, no Injustice' (Hobbes 1996, p. 90). By 'law' in this context Hobbes means, of course, politically authorized law, backed by effective coercive power. Indeed, Hobbes goes even further and says that in the state of nature there is 'no Propriety [i.e. property], no Dominion, no Mine and Thine distinct' (Hobbes 1996, p. 90), whereas Locke is perfectly clear that property may very well exist in the state of nature, along with rights of acquisition and transfer – as we shall see more fully in a later section. However, we have now seen enough of how Hobbes's and Locke's views of the state of nature both resemble and differ from each other and it is time to look at their respective conceptions of the foundation of civil society.

SOCIAL CONTRACT AND GOVERNMENT BY CONSENT

As I remarked earlier, both Hobbes and Locke – along with many other seventeenth- and eighteenth-century political theorists – invoke the idea that political obligation rests fundamentally upon the consent of the governed. But their conceptions of the nature of that consent and its exact role in legitimating governmental authority differ considerably. For although their conceptions have in common an appeal to the quasi-legal notion of a 'contract' or 'covenant', their understandings of the rationale and terms of such an agreement – whether it be construed as quasi-historical or as merely hypothetical in character – are significantly at variance with one another, as close attention to their respective texts reveals. According to Hobbes,

> The only way to erect such a Common Power, as may be able to defend [men] . . . and . . . secure them in such sort, as that . . . they may nourish themselves and live contentedly; is, to conferre all their power and strength upon one Man, or upon one Assembly of men, that may reduce all their Wills . . . unto one Will . . . This is more than Consent, or Concord; it is reall Unitie of them all, in one and the same Person, made by Covenant of every man with every man . . . This done, the Multitude so united in one Person, is called a COMMON-WEALTH . . . And he that carryeth this Person, is called SOVERAIGNE.
>
> (Hobbes 1996, pp. 120–1)

On the face of it, Locke seems to be saying something very similar to this when he asserts that 'The only way whereby any one devests himself of his Natural Liberty, and puts on the bonds of Civil Society is by agreeing with other Men to joyn and unite into a Community' (*Second Treatise*, 95). However, there are fundamental differences between Hobbes and Locke concerning the nature of the sovereign power that is created by the contract – these differences arising out of the form and purpose of the contract itself, as Locke and Hobbes respectively conceive of it.

Most importantly, Hobbes believes that the person (or persons) in whom sovereign power is invested by the parties to the contract can commit no injustice, for the following reason:

> The Right of bearing the Person of . . . all [the contractors], is given to him they make Soveraigne, by Covenant onely of one to another, and not of him to any of them . . . [Hence] there can happen no breach of Covenant on the part of the Soveraigne . . . [and so] whatsoever [the sovereign] doth, it can be no injury to any of his Subjects . . . It is true that they that have Soveraigne power, may commit Iniquity; but not Injustice.
>
> (Hobbes 1996, pp. 122–4)

For Hobbes, then, the sovereign is above the laws of the state because he is not himself a party to the contract. But Locke entirely disagrees with this conception of legitimate sovereign power, holding that an absolute monarch of the sort that Hobbes envisages 'is as much in the state of Nature, with all under his Dominion, as he is with the rest of Mankind' (*Second Treatise*, 91) and that 'No Man in Civil Society can be exempted from the Laws of it' (*Second Treatise*, 94). According to Locke, any individual or group of individuals in whom authority to rule is invested by the parties to the contract must be parties to the contract themselves and must thus be just as much subject to the laws of civil society as everyone else. It makes no sense to Locke to suppose, with Hobbes, that the contractors should confer sovereign power upon someone who was not himself a party to the contract. For such a person would subsequently remain quite as much in a 'state of nature' with respect to them as he was beforehand. They, therefore, would remain just as vulnerable to his predations as they were before, whereas he, having been invested with sovereign power over them, would now be subject to no similar danger from them. For Locke, this is simply a recipe for tyranny and social disaster.

Hobbes, on the other hand, clearly believes that the 'war of all against all' – the state of nature as he conceives it – is so dire a condition that it is better for all of the contractors to submit themselves to the absolute authority of a single powerful person or group of people, rather than to dissolve civil society altogether. For it can, he supposes, hardly be in the interest of this person or group of people to render the contractors as miserable as he thinks that they would inevitably be in the state of nature. Moreover, such is Hobbes's pessimism regarding human nature that he does not believe that the contractors can achieve any more desirable but equally stable condition by investing political authority in any of their own number, whether by election or by other means. A crucial consequence of this difference of opinion between Hobbes and Locke is that according to Hobbes there is, for the citizen, no court of appeal higher than that of the sovereign power itself – whereas Locke believes that at least sometimes an 'appeal to heaven', in the form of a rebellion against the sovereign power, is legitimate. I shall return to this historically important aspect of Locke's political doctrine in a later section.

Another superficial similarity between Hobbes's and Locke's views is that both of them consider that the transition from the state of nature to civil society entails the relinquishing or curtailment of certain individual rights or liberties. But, once again, they differ considerably over the details. Hobbes, recall, has a particularly pessimistic view of personal relationships in the state of nature, which he identifies as a condition of 'war of every man against every man'. He thinks that reason, embodied in the laws of nature, instructs all men, even in the state of nature, that their individual interests are best served by establishing peace – which, he believes, can be achieved only if each gives up his natural right to everything on condition that all the rest do likewise. Indeed, his second law of nature enjoins

> That a man be willing, when others are so too, as farre-forth, as for Peace, and defence of himselfe he shall think it necessary, to lay down his right to all things; and be contented with so much liberty against other men, as he would allow other men against himselfe.
>
> (Hobbes 1996, p. 92)

But, Hobbes urges, such a peace agreement must be subject to effective enforcement, since 'Covenants, without the Sword, are but Words, and of no strength to secure a man at all' (Hobbes 1996, p. 117). The contractors must therefore agree to the sovereign power's possessing an absolute monopoly of force to enable it to police the agreement.

However, as is frequently pointed out by critics of Hobbes, there seems to be a 'chicken and egg' problem here – or, more precisely, what modern decision theorists would call a 'co-ordination problem'. The problem, apparently, is that if only *enforceable* agreements or 'covenants' are effective, an agreement designed to *set up* an enforcement agency already presupposes the existence of what it is supposed to create. More specifically, it seems that although Hobbes's warring individuals would do best to lay down their arms in favour of a central enforcement agency, no one can trust the rest to do likewise in the absence of such an agency, since others could then take advantage of him. Each Hobbesian individual in the state of nature can foresee four possible outcomes of any collective attempt to achieve peace by a mutual agreement to lay down one's arms – and will rank these outcomes in the following order of preference, from his own point of view. (1) Others comply with the agreement, but I do not. (2) Everyone complies with the agreement. (3) No one complies with the agreement. (4) I comply with the agreement, but others do not. A Hobbesian individual ranks outcome (1) above the rest because of his egocentric psychology, which leads him to prefer his own advantage to that of anyone else. But the trouble is that because all Hobbesian individuals are alike in this respect, all will secretly intend not to comply with the agreement, with the consequence that outcome (3) will result – despite the fact that every individual would prefer outcome (2) to outcome (3). Whether or not Hobbes himself really saw or had a solution to this problem is a matter for debate which I cannot go into here. But the problem, such as it is, does seem to be peculiar to Hobbes's own version of the social contract approach, largely turning once again on his highly pessimistic conception of human nature and of the condition that the contract is supposed to deliver us from.

Locke's version of the social contract theory is not, it seems, subject to anything like this difficulty. Lockean individuals in the state of nature are not presumed to be entirely selfish and amoral. They can accordingly trust one another to keep their promises to a sufficient extent to make the contract workable in the absence of an antecedently existing power to enforce it. The rights and liberties that a Lockean individual relinquishes upon entering civil society are correspondingly fewer or less in extent than those that a Hobbesian individual is required to give up. We shall see this more fully later. Even so, Locke's theory does suffer from a prima-facie difficulty which seems quite as troublesome as that affecting Hobbes's. This is that he needs to explain how it is that individuals born *after* the institution of civil society may incur a duty to obey its laws, given that they were not consenting parties to the original agreement or contract. For Locke is emphatic that consent is indeed a necessary condition of any individual's political obligation – children, of course, being excluded from consideration on account of their youth and supposedly immature powers of reason: 'Men being . . . by Nature all free, equal and independent, no one can be put out of this Estate, and subjected to the Political Power of another, without his own *Consent*' (*Second Treatise*, 95). Moreover,

Locke is insistent that political obligation is not transferable from one person to another – say, from father to son: '[W]hatever Engagements or Promises any one has made for himself, he is under the Obligation of them, but *cannot* by any *Compact* whatsoever, bind *his Children* or Posterity' (*Second Treatise*, 116).

However, what may indeed be heritable is *property* – and, as Locke points out, states commonly make allegiance to them a condition of inheritance: 'Commonwealths not permitting any part of their Dominions to be dismembered, nor to be enjoyed by any but those of their Community, the Son cannot ordinarily enjoy the Possessions of his Father, but under the same terms his Father did, by becoming a Member of the Society' (*Second Treatise*, 117). And one may, Locke suggests, forgo one's inheritance if one so wishes. One does not have an inalienable right to transfer property to or receive it from someone else, subject only to the mutual agreement of the parties to the transaction. Such a right is, according to Locke, alienated or relinquished upon joining civil society, since it is necessary that the rightful ownership of property be subject to the laws of the state. For the state's primary purpose, in Locke's eyes, is the protection of persons and their property – and this requires that titles to property be subject to the state's jurisdiction. Even so, the question still remains as to how, or in what sense, an individual coming of age and choosing to inherit property – or indeed simply choosing to continue to live in the territory governed by a particular state – may be said to owe a political obligation to obey the laws of that civil society in virtue of his *consent* to be ruled by the government that enacted them.

Locke's answer to this crucial question invokes a distinction between *express* and *tacit* consent. Express consent to membership of a civil society – through, say, the deliverance of an oath – creates, according to Locke, a perpetual obligation to obey its laws. This obligation cannot be renounced or set aside save by the dissolution of the state – as a consequence of war, for example – or by the legal expulsion of that member. But tacit consent, Locke thinks, is implied by an individual's mere decision to enjoy the protection of the state and its conveniences:

> [E]very Man, that hath any Possession, or Enjoyment, of any part of the Dominions of any Government, doth thereby give his *tacit Consent*, and is as far forth obliged to Obedience to the Laws of that Government . . . and in Effect, it reaches as far as the very being of any one within the Territories of that Government.
>
> (*Second Treatise*, 119)

And tacit consent, according to Locke, only creates political obligation while the conditions making for that consent prevail – so that anyone who has not given express consent to the government of the state in which he is living is free at any time to depart and join another state or set up a new one in virgin territory.

However, it may be objected, with some justice, that Locke's so-called tacit consent scarcely deserves the name 'consent' and that, in any case, it is doubtfully either needed for or capable of creating the sort of political obligation that he wants it to. For one thing, why say that a person who chooses to enjoy the conveniences of a civil society owes it a duty to obey its laws in virtue of his consent to the political regime of that society, rather than simply in virtue of his very choice to enjoy the benefits in question? Is not the notion of 'consent' here an idle wheel, invoked only to support Locke's general thesis that legitimate government is always and only government by the consent of the governed? There is indeed a school of thought according to which, in certain circumstances, the voluntary enjoyment of benefits does in itself create obligations. Thus, H. L. A. Hart has urged as a general principle that

> [W]hen a number of persons conduct any joint enterprise according to rules and thus restrict their liberty, those who have submitted to these restrictions when required have right to a similar submission from those who have benefited by their submission.
>
> (Hart 1984, p. 85)

In line with such thinking, it is frequently maintained, for example, that those who benefit from trade union activities – for instance, by receiving wage increases and improved working conditions – ought to pay union dues, so that 'free riders' may justly be denounced and even penalized for accepting the benefits while avoiding the associated costs. Hart himself criticizes social contract theorists precisely for conflating sources of obligation of this kind with those involving mutual agreement or consent:

> The social contract theorists rightly fastened on the fact that the obligation to obey the law is . . . something which arises between members of a particular political society out of their mutual relationship. Their mistake was to identify *this* right-creating situation of mutual restrictions with the paradigm case of promising.
>
> (Hart 1984, p. 86)

Much earlier, David Hume, in his essay 'Of the Original Contract', went even further in criticizing social contract theorists – and Locke in particular – when he asked:

> What necessity, therefore, is there to found the duty of *allegiance* to magistrates, on that of *fidelity*, or a regard to promises, and to suppose that it is the consent of each individual which subjects him to government, when it appears that both allegiance and fidelity stand precisely on the same foundation, and are both submitted to by mankind, on account of the apparent interests and necessities of human society?
>
> (Hume 1985)

Hume's contention is that the obligation to keep a promise itself arises from the fact that 'the commerce and intercourse of mankind, which are of such mighty advantage, can have no security where men pay no regard to their engagements' (Hume 1985), so that it cannot provide an independent source of obligation to obey the laws of civil society. We may perhaps judge that Hume goes too far here and agree with Hart that the very act of promising can in itself create an obligation. Even so, we may be inclined to concur with both Hart and Hume in thinking that political obligation typically does not rest so much upon consent, whether express or tacit, as on mutually advantageous co-operative relationships between the members of a community.

Even setting aside such fundamental doubts, however, other and more specific criticisms may be levelled at Locke's doctrine of tacit consent. For instance, one might ask how realistic or fair it is to say to someone who is born into a given civil society and is brought up within its territory that he may emigrate and start life elsewhere if he does not like the laws that he finds in operation, or the system of government that is in place. As Hume remarks:

> Can we seriously say, that a poor peasant or artisan has a free choice to leave his country, when he knows no foreign language or manners, and lives, from day to day, by the small wages which he acquires? We may as well assert that a man, by remaining in a vessel, freely consents to the dominion of the master.
>
> (Hume 1985)

The position of a foreigner choosing to settle in or just travel through a country is significantly different, since in either case he has a genuine choice beforehand and in the latter case he typically has relatively little to lose by forgoing his visit. But, as Hume points out, although '[t]he truest *tacit* consent of this kind that is ever observed, is when a foreigner settles in any country . . . yet is his allegiance, though more voluntary, much less expected or depended on, than that of a natural born subject' (Hume 1985).

A related question that we may raise is this. Why should it be assumed that the tacit consent supposedly implied by a person's voluntary enjoyment of certain of a state's conveniences creates a blanket obligation to respect *all* of its laws and institutions? But if it doesn't create such an overall obligation, who is to say precisely how far the obligation does extend in any given case? Does someone who enjoys more benefits somehow tacitly consent to obey more laws? If not, then is someone who scarcely benefits at all under as far-reaching an obligation as someone who benefits enormously? That scarcely seems fair. It may be replied that if this is a difficulty for Locke, then it is also – and more immediately – a difficulty for Hume and Hart, since they contend that political obligation rests directly upon social relationships of mutual advantage. However, our primary concern is with Locke's theory of express and tacit consent and it does seem that, all in all, it provides a somewhat tenuous basis for a general account of political obligation.

It is important to observe in this connection that Locke does not invoke the right to vote as a condition of 'consent' and hence of political obligation. There is no implication in his theory that government by the consent of the governed necessarily involves the right of the governed themselves to participate in government, nor even to help to decide the composition of the government through electoral processes. Here, however, we should be conscious of both the historical context of Locke's account and his own political allegiances. Locke was writing at a time at which only male property-owners of a certain standing could vote in parliamentary elections and he had no obvious wish to challenge that arrangement (but for another view see Ashcraft 1986, pp. 556ff., and Waldron 2002, pp. 115–19). If we dig beneath the surface of Locke's democratic language, we shall perhaps find rather more conservative assumptions in place. Modern readers may suspect that his liberal-sounding pronouncements concerning the need for legitimate government to rest upon the 'consent' of the governed have less real substance than initially meets the eye. However, Locke's libertarianism was genuine and bold for its day, even if it now appears in some respects unduly timid and restrictive – as it may to those of us who have the good fortune to live in the sort of democratic state that Locke's political philosophy has helped to bring about. Locke's courageous and principled defence of political liberty has earned him a place in the history of English political thought second only to Hobbes – and a permanent place in the hearts of all true friends of liberal democracy.

LOCKE'S THEORY OF PROPERTY AND PROPERTY RIGHTS

If what makes government legitimate for Locke is the consent of the governed, what makes it both desirable and beneficial is the protection that it provides for individual property and property rights. Whether or not one agrees with his judgement about this, it must be acknowledged that Locke's account of property is interesting in its own right and has influenced later political theorists even up to the present day. However, it is important to appreciate from the outset that Locke uses the term 'property' not only in a narrow sense, to include such things as material possessions and land, but also in a wide sense, in which it includes an individual's own person and labour:

> [E]very man has a *Property* in his own *Person*. This no Body has any Right to but himself. The *Labour* of his Body, and the *Work* of his Hands, we may say, are properly his.
>
> (*Second Treatise*, 27)

As we shall shortly see, for Locke there is an important linkage between the two notions of property, because he holds that property in material possessions and land ultimately arises out of property in one's own person and labour. But it should in any case be emphasized in this context that the term 'property' as it was generally used in seventeenth-century England had rather different connotations from those associated with its present-day use (see Tully 1980).

It is important to recall here that Locke's Two Treatises were explicitly written in opposition to the views of Sir Robert Filmer who, in his Patriarcha, was defending absolute monarchy and the divine right of kings. In the chapter on property in the Second Treatise,

Locke is not least concerned to counter Filmer's contention that monarchical property rights arise through primogeniture – the supposed right of a first-born son to inherit his father's wealth and possessions – from God's original 'gift' of the earth and its fruits to Adam and his descendants in perpetuity. More particularly, Locke wishes to show how, even though – as he contends – the earth was given to mankind 'in common', individual exclusive property rights in goods and land can have arisen without any violation of natural law and, moreover, without the need for any universal consent or 'compact'. The significance of this latter qualification is that Locke was also concerned to combat certain rival views advanced at the time – by Hobbes amongst others – according to which all property rights necessarily arise only subsequent to the formation of civil society and even then only through appropriate forms of political authorization. However, this should not be allowed to obscure the fact, mentioned earlier, that Locke himself emphasizes that property rights in civil society are a matter for civil jurisdiction and 'positive law'. He is only concerned to show that individual property rights *can* perfectly well arise in the state of nature.

As I have just indicated, Locke maintains, against Filmer, that God originally gave the earth and its fruits to mankind *in common* – the implication being that in the beginning there were no exclusive individual property rights, such as those supposedly granted to Adam and his heirs. For this Locke appeals not only to the evidence of scripture, but also to 'natural *Reason*, which tells us, that [all] Men . . . have a right to their Preservation, and consequently to . . . such . . . things, as Nature affords for their Subsistence' (*Second Treatise*, 25). He then goes on to argue, however, that the subsequent creation of private property rights in goods and land is perfectly compatible with this original commonality of all natural resources. The argument appeals to his contention that each person has a natural property right in his own body and labour. From this he concludes that

Whatsoever . . . [a man] removes out of the State that Nature hath
provided, and left it in, he hath mixed his *Labour* with, and joyned to
it something that is his own, and thereby makes it his *Property* . . .
[N]o Man but he can have a right to what [his labour] is once joyned
to, at least where there is enough, and as good left in common for
others.

(*Second Treatise*, 27)

Locke's argument here is that by 'mixing' one's labour with natural
resources which are not yet the exclusive property of any other
individual – for instance, by gathering fruit from trees in the wild
or by tilling virgin land and sowing it with corn – one thereby
comes to have an exclusive property right in the products of that
labour.

Locke's argument may sound odd to the extent that it treats
'labour' almost as though it were a kind of substance or stuff,
capable of being 'mixed' with material substances such as earth
and metal, but perhaps that is just a quaint feature of his choice of
words and incidental to the reasoning involved. More worryingly,
though, as Robert Nozick has pointed out, it is not immediately
obvious why mixing one's labour with unowned natural resources
shouldn't be a way of *losing* or *wasting* one's labour, rather than a
way of *acquiring* whatever it is that is thereby produced (see Nozick
1974, pp. 174–5). And if the point is supposed to be that by
mixing one's labour with something one thereby typically adds
value to it, then, as Nozick also points out, it isn't obvious why
one should be entitled to anything more than the added value that
one has created. In any case, complications evidently arise in circumstances in which more than one person's labour is expended
in producing certain goods or improving a piece of land, especially when one or more people work for another person, as his or
her employees. Locke seems to take it for granted – perhaps
because he was a member of the minor gentry himself and thus
accustomed from childhood to being surrounded by servants –

that included in 'my' labour is any labour that I may have hired or purchased:

> [T]he Grass my Horse has bit; the Turfs my Servant has cut; and the Ore I have digg'd in any place where I have a right to them in common with others, become my *Property*, without the assignation or consent of any body. The *Labour* that was mine, removing them out of that common state they were in, hath *fixed* my *Property* in them.
>
> (*Second Treatise*, 28)

But if I have paid my servant the full value of the labour that he expends for me, how can there be any surplus value created by him that accrues solely to me? If there can't be, then, it may seem, I can benefit by employing a servant only if I unjustly underpay him. This is an issue that I shall return to later.

Still, Locke certainly makes a compelling point when he says that it is labour that creates by far the larger part of the value of any commodity and that 'Nature and the Earth furnished only the almost worthless Materials, as in themselves' (Second Treatise, 43), so that 'though the things of Nature are given in common, yet Man (by being Master of himself, and Proprietor of his own Person, and the Actions or Labour of it) had still in himself the great Foundation of Property' (Second Treatise, 44). We might be tempted to see in Locke's account here the rudiments of what was later to become the much-disputed 'labour theory of value', famously put to radical use by communists like Karl Marx in the nineteenth century. But Locke himself, it must be emphasized, had no communist leanings whatsoever – indeed, quite the reverse, as we have just seen. His intention was to justify the existence of private property, both in the state of nature and in civil society.

Locke imposes two important limitations on the right to appropriate goods or land through mixing one's labour with natural resources 'given in common'. And here it is worth stressing that Locke does believe that land itself can become private property by this means:

As much Land as a Man Tills, Plants, Improves, Cultivates, and can use the Product of, so much is his *Property.* He by his Labour does, as it were, inclose it from the Common.

(Second Treatise, 32)

The two limitations are, first, the proviso that any such appropriation should leave 'enough, and as good . . . for others' (*Second Treatise*, 27) and, second, the 'spoilage' limitation:

As much as any one can make use of to any advantage of life before it spoils; so much he may by his labour fix a Property in. Whatever is beyond this, is more than his share, and belongs to others. Nothing was made by God for Man to spoil or destroy.

(Second Treatise, 31)

Much debate has gone on about both of these limitations and their relationship to one another. Some commentators hold that the spoilage limitation has no real force independently of the proviso about leaving 'enough, and as good . . . for others' – which I shall henceforth simply call, as is customary, the Lockean proviso, or just the proviso. We shall see, though, that even if there is such a dependency between the two limitations, the spoilage limitation does play an important role in Locke's attempt to explain how large differences in personal wealth may justifiably arise once money has been introduced into an economy.

Turning now to the Lockean proviso, clearly, much depends on precisely how the phrase 'enough, and as good left in common for others' (*Second Treatise*, 27) is to be interpreted. Some commentators have taken it to mean that others must have left to them the opportunity of making similar appropriations from natural resources 'given in common'. However, this creates a difficulty pointed out by Robert Nozick, namely, that it threatens to prohibit even the first such appropriation (see Nozick 1974, p. 176). For if the nth person who wishes to appropriate is prohibited from doing so by the proviso, because such an appropriation would not leave 'enough, and . . . as good for others', then so is the $(n-1)$th person, because his appropriation would lead to the prohibition of the nth person. So it appears that the prohibition 'zips back', as Nozick puts it, to the very first person who wishes to appropriate. Nozick himself accordingly suggests – and, indeed, endorses – a weaker version of the proviso, according to which leaving 'enough, and . . . as good for others' merely means not worsening their situation. And it might appear that Locke himself understands the proviso in pretty much these terms, since he makes a number of remarks to the effect that anyone who appropriates and cultivates land actually *benefits* the rest of mankind by doing so, as when he says:

> [H]e who appropriates land to himself by his labour, does not lessen but increases the common stock of mankind . . . [H]e, that incloses Land and has a greater plenty of the conveniencys of life from ten acres, than he could have from an hundred left to Nature, may truly be said, to give ninety acres to Mankind.
>
> (*Second Treatise*, 37)

Moreover, Locke is anxious to argue that even in 'civilized' parts of the world where all of the land has been appropriated, no natural injustice is done to those without land because their circumstances of life are greatly improved by these arrangements, in comparison with what they would have been without them. He remarks that, indeed, 'a King of a large and fruitful Territory [in America] feeds, lodges, and is clad worse than a day Labourer in *England*' (*Second Treatise*, 41).

More particularly, as we shall shortly see more fully, Locke links this state of affairs – that is, the complete appropriation of all available land – to the introduction of *money*. This, he implies, leads to the legitimate suspension of the original 'rule of propriety':

> [T]he same *Rule of Propriety*, (*viz.*) that every Man should have as much as he could make use of, would hold still in the World, without straitning any body, since there is Land enough in the World to

suffice double the Inhabitants had not the *Invention of Money*, and the tacit Agreement of Men to put a value on it, introduced (by Consent) larger Possessions, and a Right to them.

(*Second Treatise*, 36)

All of this suggests that Locke believed that the proviso did indeed originally imply that enough and as good to appropriate should be left to others, but that once money has been introduced and the market economy emerges, the proviso becomes transmuted into a requirement that no one else be disadvantaged by any further appropriations from natural resources. Here we should recall that Locke's 'rule of propriety' is, after all, only a derived rule – derived, that is, from the fundamental right to preserve one's life. It may thus be argued that if this right is better supported in a civil society in which all land has been appropriated than in the state of nature, then the 'rule of propriety' may in such circumstances justly be set aside.

It is widely held that one of Locke's chief concerns in Chapter 5 of the *Second Treatise* is to explain how, in his view, considerable inequalities in personal wealth may arise without any violation of natural law and independently of any political arrangements arrived at by general agreement or mutual consent – and hence how such inequalities can still be equitable even within existing civil society, provided that no political agreement has established contrary rules for the distribution of property as a matter of 'positive law' (but for another perspective, see Tully 1980). For Locke, the key to this possibility lies in the introduction of money – which, he considers, depends essentially only upon the tacit consent of the people concerned to use it as such. Here, then, it is important to appreciate that Locke does not consider that the existence of civil society and political authority is a necessary condition for the emergence of a monetary system, even though it might be a somewhat primitive system in their absence. Money, for Locke, is in essence just a durable article which people agree to use as a medium of exchange – 'some lasting thing that Men might keep without spoiling, and that by mutual consent, Men would take in exchange for the truly useful, but perishable Supports of Life' (*Second Treatise*, 47). The durability of money enables men to build up wealth – that is, purchasing power – without violation of the spoilage limitation. Locke is clear that it is indeed *money* that permits large-scale inequalities in personal wealth to arise – that 'this *Invention of Money* gave [men] an opportunity to . . . enlarge [their possessions]' (*Second Treatise*, 48) – although he acknowledges that barter can also result in such inequalities, albeit only on a much smaller scale. This is despite the fact that, as we saw earlier, Locke held *labour* to be by far the greatest source of all wealth.

The problem is to reconcile these two opinions: for if it is assumed that each man is entitled only to the wealth that has been generated by his own labour, then it is not at all clear how one man could ever amass vastly more wealth than another, since different men's labour power is not markedly different. At least part of the answer lies in the ambiguity of the phrase 'his own labour' – which, for a theorist like Locke, might either be taken to mean 'the labour of his own body' or else to mean 'the labour owned by him'. For if it is allowed – as Locke certainly does allow – that the labour of a man's body is an alienable commodity that may be purchased by another man, whose property it then becomes, one man may in principle own the labour of many men's bodies. Thus, while the introduction of money cannot as such enable a man to enclose and cultivate vastly more land than he can plough and sow himself, it does enable him to do this if he is also permitted to purchase with his monetary savings the labour of many other men's bodies. And why should Locke *not* allow that the labour of a man's body is alienable? It might be complained that the great landowner unfairly appropriates more land than he could cultivate himself without violating the spoilage limitation – and then proceeds to compound this injustice by purchasing, at a price favourable to himself, the labour of other men who have been prevented by his action from appropriating some of this land. But two things might be said in his defence. First – as we earlier noted Locke remarking – it may be pointed out that these labourers may not in fact be *worse off* than they would have been as independent smallholders, because the economies of scale made possible by large estates may enable such labourers to be paid more in wages than they could hope to earn by their independent efforts. Secondly, the great landowner – or his ancestors – may have built up his possessions only gradually, purchasing first the land and then the labour of less industrious or efficient men, without ever violating the Lockean limitations. If he inherited his lands from ancestors who proceeded in this fashion, then this too would appear to be a legitimate way for him to acquire the property, on Lockean principles, unless civil society has enacted positive laws restricting such practices – for Locke does not think that natural law prohibits the free gift or bequest of property, so long as the recipient does not violate the spoilage limitation. It might be urged, perhaps, that a co-operative system of land ownership and production would be fairer, while at the same time being capable of achieving the same economies of scale. But to this it may be replied that Locke does not exclude the possibility of civil society's encouraging such arrangements by means of positive law – by, for example, making it a condition of membership of the state that property in goods and land cannot be inherited. Locke is only concerned to show that it is not contrary to natural law or the character of civil society as such that large inequalities in personal wealth should be permitted.

However, this still leaves unaddressed an issue touched on earlier, namely, how it is that an employer can accrue any wealth from the labour of his employees if he pays them what their labour is truly worth. How, in short, can the employer extract a *profit* from their work without unjustly 'exploiting' them? However, it would seem that this is – at most – only a problem if one advocates a fully fledged 'labour theory of value', according to which the 'true' value of a product is to be quantified in terms of the amount of labour involved in producing it. Locke, it appears, does not go so far as to endorse such a theory – even when he remarks, for instance, that 'when any one hath computed, he will then see, how much *labour makes the far greatest part of the value* of things, we enjoy in this World' (*Second Treatise*, 42). For there is nothing in this remark which implies a strict quantitative relationship between a commodity's 'value' and the amount of labour required to produce it. Indeed, there is nothing here that implies either that a commodity's 'value' is some intrinsic, quantifiable feature of it or that labour may be unambiguously measured in objectively specifiable units.

It is sometimes suggested that Locke writes as an advocate on behalf of the emerging property-owing middle classes of seventeenth-century England and thus an apologist for early modern capitalism (see, for example, Macpherson 1962). In fact, although Locke was notoriously careful with his own relatively modest income from rents and investments, he was by upbringing, education and calling a representative of the minor landed gentry and the scholarly world of academia. It is dangerous to try to read any ulterior motive or propagandist purpose into the text of the *Second Treatise*, beyond those that are evident on its surface and in the immediate circumstances of its composition, as part of a concerted response to Filmer's illiberal monarchist tract.

RIGHTS OF RESISTANCE AND THE LIMITS OF POLITICAL OBLIGATION

In Chapter 29 of *Leviathan*, Hobbes cites a number of 'doctrines' or 'opinions' of a 'seditious' character which, if not stamped upon by the state authorities, are liable to disease the body politic. In particular, he criticizes the following views. (1) That private citizens are competent judges of matters that are subject to the civil law. (2) That conscientious refusal to obey the civil law is sometimes justifiable. (3) That the sovereign power should itself be subject to the civil law. And (4) that private property should be exempt from state interference. Locke, on the other hand, at least implicitly supports all of these views in some form and quite explicitly advocates and defends some of them. This is why his political theory may justly be described as liberal, in contrast with Hobbes's absolutism.

Locke imposes clear restrictions on the rights of government over the private citizen, contending that they cannot override certain individual natural rights. As he puts it, the legislative power

> hath no other end but preservation, and therefore can never have a right to destroy, enslave, or designedly to impoverish the Subjects. The Obligations of the Law of Nature, cease not in Society.
>
> (*Second Treatise*, 135)

He concludes that 'Absolute Arbitrary Power, or Governing without *settled standing Laws*, can neither of them consist with the ends of Society and Government' (*Second Treatise*, 137). Thus he sees the restraints on governmental authority as arising out of the very nature and purpose of the original 'compact', which, he assumes, was entered into by the parties concerned only in order to protect their individual rights and freedoms. His reasoning extends, in particular, to individual *property* rights – which is why he maintains, contrary to Hobbes, that the government is never entitled to appropriate an individual's private goods, land or money without his consent:

> [T]he preservation of Property being the end of Government . . . however it may have power to make Laws for the regulating of *Property* between the Subjects one amongst another, yet can never have a Power to take to themselves the whole or any part of the Subjects *Property*, without their own consent.
>
> (*Second Treatise*, 138–9)

Hence, such consent is, for Locke, a necessary prerequisite for the legitimate raising of taxes:

> 'tis fit every one who enjoys his share of the Protection, should pay out of his Estate his proportion for the maintenance of it. But still it

> must be with his own Consent, *i.e.* the Consent of the Majority,
> giving it either by themselves, or their Representatives chosen by
> them.
>
> (*Second Treatise*, 140)

So here we have a very clear statement of the principle encapsulated, almost one hundred years later, in the famous slogan of the American War of Independence, 'No taxation without representation'.

Locke discusses in some detail – although with an understandable degree of circumspection, in view of the volatile political circumstances of the time – the conditions in which subjects may rightfully employ forcible resistance against the government. Resort to such force, he thinks, is warranted only when the abuse of governmental power is so manifest and general that the government has lost all claim to legitimacy – and even then, only when every avenue of lawful redress has been shut off: '[F]orce is to be *opposed* to nothing, but to unjust and unlawful *Force* . . . [and] is only to be used, where a Man is intercepted from appealing to the Law' (*Second Treatise*, 204–7). Furthermore, Locke implies that forcible resistance to the government cannot legitimately be undertaken by an individual subject simply on his own account, but should be motivated only by the collective oppression of the people. Such resistance is admissible, he suggests, only

> if either [the government's] illegal Acts have extended to the
> Majority of the People; or if the Mischief and Oppression . . . seem to
> threaten all, and they are perswaded in their Consciences, that their
> Laws, and with them their Estates, Liberties, and Lives are in
> danger.
>
> (*Second Treatise*, 209)

The crucial difference between the positions of Hobbes and Locke is that Locke, unlike Hobbes, considers that a government may cease to be legitimate by abusing the trust of the people, whereupon the state of nature is effectively restored and the people 'have a Right to resume their original Liberty, and [establish] a new Legislative' (*Second Treatise*, 222). But who is to be the judge as to whether the government really has abused the trust of the people? Ultimately, the people themselves, in Locke's view:

> *Who shall be Judge* whether the Prince or Legislative act contrary to their Trust? . . . I reply: *The People shall be Judge* . . . But if the Prince . . . decline that way of Determination, the Appeal then lies no where but to Heaven.
>
> (*Second Treatise*, 240–2)

Locke is rather vague concerning the means by which the people's judgement is supposed to emerge, but it is clear that he thinks that a popular uprising or rebellion against an oppressive government can be justified as a last resort. This, in effect, is what he means by an 'appeal to heaven'. And this is one reason why, although the Two Treatises were not originally written to vindicate the Glorious Revolution of 1688, Locke was able to advertise them as serving to

> establish the Throne of our Great Restorer, Our present King William; to make good his Title, in the Consent of the People, which being the only one of all lawful Governments, he has more fully and clearly than any Prince in Christendom: And to justifie to the World, the People of England, whose love of their Just and Natural Rights, with their Resolution to preserve them, saved the Nation when it was on the very brink of Slavery and Ruine.
>
> (*Two Treatises*, the Preface)

RELIGIOUS TOLERATION

In the same year – 1689 – that the Two Treatises were published, Locke's almost equally famous first *Letter Concerning Toleration*, or *Letter on Toleration*, appeared in Latin, under the title *Epistola de Tolerantia*, and in an English translation – although, like the Two Treatises, it was largely composed several years earlier. (Three further *Letters* were to follow, but I shall not discuss them here.) In the first *Letter*, Locke argues vigorously in favour of religious toleration and the separation of church and state. It is worth remarking that his views on these matters were by this time very much more liberal than they had been prior to his association with Shaftesbury in the 1660s (see Chapter 1 above).

Locke's arguments in the first *Letter* may be summed up in the following terms. First, he appeals to the nature and purpose of civil society to argue that the civil magistrate should have no jurisdiction over matters concerning religious practice or observance, pointing out that

> The commonwealth seems to me to be a society of men constituted only for the procuring, preserving, and advancing their own civil interests. Civil interests I call life, liberty, health, and indolency of body; and the possession of outward things, such as money, lands, houses, furniture, and the like.
>
> (*Letter*, p. 128)

He urges that 'the care of souls is not committed to the civil magistrate, any more than to other men' (*Letter*, p. 129) and that, in any case, 'his [the civil magistrate's] power consists only in outward force; but true and saving religion consists in the inward persuasion of the mind' (*Letter*, p. 129). He also points out that the diversity of religious belief all over the world is such that, if it were legitimate for the civil magistrate to enforce specific forms of religious observance, most of the world's population would be condemned to practise a false religion, to the endangerment of their own souls: 'One country alone would be in the right, and all the rest of the world would be put under an obligation of following their princes in the ways that lead to destruction' (*Letter*, p. 130).

Locke next considers what the nature of a 'church' is, taking this to be

a voluntary society of men, joining themselves together of their own
accord in order to the public worshipping of God in such a manner
as they judge acceptable to him, and effectual to the salvation of
their souls.

(Letter, p. 131)

From this definition, he concludes that although a church has a
right to expel members who do not adhere to its established rules,
it has no authority to extend its jurisdiction into the civil sphere:

The end of a religious society . . . is the public worship of God . . .
All discipline ought therefore to tend to that end, and all
ecclesiastical laws to be thereunto confined. Nothing ought or
can be transacted in this society relating to the possession of
civil and worldly goods. No force is here to be made use of upon
any reason whatsoever.

(Letter, p. 133)

Having thus argued for the separation of church and state, with
each being confined to its own proper sphere of authority and
activity, Locke is in a position to mount a defence of religious
toleration and to explain precisely how far, in his view, the duty of
toleration extends. He concludes, first, that while the duty of toleration does not require any church to refrain from expelling recalci-
trant members of its community, 'Excommunication neither does,
nor can, deprive the excommunicated person of any of those civil
goods that he formerly possessed' (Letter, p. 134). Secondly, he
concludes that 'no private person has any right in any manner to
prejudice another person in his civil enjoyments because he is of
another church or religion' (Letter, p. 134). And here he emphasizes
that the civil magistrate, in his capacity of being a member of a
particular church, is no different from anyone else in this respect,
'For the civil government can give no new right to the church, nor
the church to civil government' (Letter, p. 135). His overall conclusion is that

> Nobody, therefore, in fine, neither single persons nor churches, nay,
> nor even commonwealths, have any just title to invade the civil
> rights and worldly goods of each other upon pretence of religion.
>
> (*Letter*, p. 137)

A presumption of Locke's arguments so far is that, in many
matters of religion, infallible knowledge is not available to human
beings – a view fully in line with his more general epistemological
doctrines (see Chapter 2 above). He is, of course, fully aware that
many of his more dogmatic opponents strongly disagree with him
about this. However, against these opponents he has another compelling argument to offer in favour of religious toleration, namely,
that no one can be saved by the true religion who does not
genuinely believe it:

> Although the magistrate's opinion in religion be sound, and the way
> that he appoints be truly evangelical, yet, if I be not thoroughly
> persuaded thereof in my own mind, there will be no safety for me in
> following it. No way whatsoever that I shall walk in against the
> dictates of my conscience will ever bring me to the mansions of the
> blessed.
>
> (*Letter*, p. 143)

Having broached the matter of conscience, Locke now goes on
to raise a very important question when he asks: 'What if the
magistrate should enjoin anything by his authority that appears
unlawful to the conscience of a private person?' (*Letter*, p. 155).
His answer is subtly nuanced, as might be expected in view of
the potentially explosive nature of the problem. On the one
hand, he deems that such a person should follow his conscience
but accept lawful punishment for doing so, 'For the private
judgement of any person concerning a law enacted in political
matters, for the public good, does not take away the obligation
of that law, nor deserve a dispensation' (*Letter*, p. 155). However,
he goes on:

[I]f the law indeed be concerning things that lie not within the verge of the magistrate's authority . . . men are not in these cases obliged by that law, against their consciences . . . [T]he . . . judgement of the magistrate does not give him any new right of imposing laws upon his subjects, which neither was in the constitution of the government granted him, nor ever was in the power of the people to grant.

(*Letter*, p. 156)

Characteristically, Locke steadfastly pursues the issue to the bitter end and asks, finally,

But what if the magistrate believe that he has a right to make such laws, and that they are for the public good, and his subjects believe the contrary? Who shall be judge between them?

(*Letter*, p. 156)

Locke forthrightly replies: 'I answer, God alone' (*Letter*, p. 156). And, while he is emphatic that each person's duty of concern is, first, for the salvation of his own soul and, secondly, for the public peace, he implies that, in extreme circumstances, popular rebellion against the magistrate may be justified – echoing here his cautious remarks in the *Second Treatise* about the legitimacy of an ultimate 'appeal to heaven'.

For all his liberality, Locke sets determinate limits to the extent of due religious toleration. First, he considers that we have no duty of toleration towards Churches which teach that their members are justified in engaging in seditious practices against the state, or which do not themselves recognize a duty of religious toleration. Secondly, he does not consider that toleration should be extended to '[a] church . . . which is constituted upon such a bottom that all those who enter into it do thereby *ipso facto* deliver themselves up to the protection and service of another prince' (*Letter*, p. 158). One implicit target here seems to be the Roman Catholic Church, with the Pope – who had at that time extensive political influence –

being seen as such a 'prince' (but see Waldron 2002, pp. 218–23). Finally, Locke considers that toleration should not be extended to atheists, chiefly on the ground that 'Promises, covenants, and oaths, which are the bonds of human society, can have no hold upon an atheist' (*Letter*, p. 158). This argument may hardly seem compelling, especially to present-day readers. Here, however, we should also recall that Locke held that belief in God is not merely a matter of faith, but also of reason, because he considered that the existence of God is capable of rational demonstration or proof. If – rightly or wrongly – he regarded atheism as irrational, one can at least understand why he should have thought that we have no duty to tolerate attempts to spread it amongst the populace, to the detriment of religious belief of any kind. It would be unfair, I think, simply to accuse Locke of hypocrisy on this score, that is, of failing to extend to atheists a right to toleration that is properly their due by his own lights. We who now live in a largely secular society – partly as a result of that very separation of church and state that Locke recommended – should not forget how very different was the intellectual, political and religious atmosphere in which Locke himself was writing and how deep-seated and widespread religious intolerance then was. That we now live in more enlightened times is due in no inconsiderable degree to Locke's own efforts.

SUMMARY

As a political philosopher, Locke argues forcefully in defence of representative democracy, respect for private property rights, constitutional limitations on the extent of governmental power, the separation of church and state, and religious toleration – grounding all of these liberal principles in the notion that the only justifiable end of civil government is the protection of the life, liberties and possessions of its individual citizens, who alone can authorize its right to rule through their freely given consent. We may find fault with the details of some of Locke's argumentation, but his sincerity and his passionate commitment to individual freedom are unquestionable. Although it is hard to determine exactly what influence any work of political philosophy has on the political culture and institutions of succeeding generations, it seems fair to say that wherever the principles of liberal democracy hold sway in the world today, they do so in no small measure thanks to Locke's courageous and spirited defence of them.

FURTHER READING

Dunn, John 1969: *The Political Thought of John Locke* (Cambridge: Cambridge University Press).

Lloyd Thomas, David A. 1995: *Locke on Government* (London: Routledge).

Marshall, John 1994: *John Locke: Resistance, Religion and Responsibility* (Cambridge: Cambridge University Press).

Simmons, A. John 1992: *The Lockean Theory of Rights* (Princeton, NJ: Princeton University Press).

Simmons, A. John 1993: *On the Edge of Anarchy: Locke, Consent, and the Limits of Society* (Princeton, NJ: Princeton University Press).

Tully, James 1993: *An Approach to Political Philosophy: Locke in Contexts* (Cambridge: Cambridge University Press).

Yolton, John W. (ed.) 1969: *John Locke: Problems and Perspectives* (Cambridge: Cambridge University Press).

Seven

Legacy and Influence

What should be our estimate of the place of John Locke in the history of philosophy and of his influence on succeeding generations of thinkers? What impact has his work had upon society at large and has it been on balance a beneficial one? Big questions like these are tempting to ask and to try to answer, but it would be an illusion to suppose that they can be settled definitively and in a wholly objective fashion. Each succeeding age fashions its own intellectual heroes, often more in order to vindicate its own prejudices than in dispassionate recognition of the true achievements of the individual thinkers who are selected for this purpose. Unsurprisingly, then, the reputation of past philosophers has often been subject to large swings of fashion from one age to the next. David Hume, for example, is now widely admired by academic philosophers, not least because the sceptical, atheistic and naturalistic tendencies of his thought are in tune with recent and current philosophical and scientific attitudes. It is probably true to say that Hume's stock amongst academic philosophers is at present still somewhat higher than Locke's, although I sense that the balance is now shifting. But it was not always so and at various times in the past Hume's philosophy was very much out of fashion. Locke, however, has never really been out of fashion in this way and it is interesting to speculate as to why this should be so.

A significant fact, I think, is that Locke never aspired, as Hume and many other philosophers both major and minor have done, to be admired as a clever or ingenious or strikingly original thinker.

Consequently, those philosophers who especially value such intellectual qualities are often inclined to dismiss Locke as a worthy but
essentially mediocre figure in the history of their subject. But
Locke's real greatness as a philosopher lies not least in his unswerv-
ing determination to pursue the truth to the best of his ability,
irrespective of whether the results of his inquiries should lead him
to endorse or reject fashionable claims. As a result, some of the
claims that he does advance may seem either tediously obvious or
hopelessly mistaken to the fashionable thinkers of any particular
generation. A symptom of his solid worth, however, is that the
fashionable thinkers of different generations typically select different Lockean doctrines for criticism as being either tediously obvious or hopelessly mistaken – depending, of course, upon their own
predilections. Consequently, their verdicts undermine each other. A
doctrine cannot easily be both tediously obvious and hopelessly
mistaken.

The serious philosophers of each succeeding age find that in
revisiting Locke's greatest works they discover a vast storehouse of
important insights into matters of profound importance for a
proper understanding of our own condition and of the world we
inhabit. Since I am better equipped to speak for the philosophers of
the present rather than of any previous generation, I shall briefly
illustrate this fact by citing some prominent examples of philosophical issues whose modern treatment still owes much to Locke.

In the philosophy of perception, for instance, Locke's account of
the distinction between primary qualities – such as shape and size –
and secondary qualities – such as colour and taste – still provides
the starting-point for most present-day discussion (see, for
example, McGinn 1983). In the philosophy of language and the
philosophy of science, his distinction between 'real' and 'nominal'
essences informs current views of the meaning of so-called natural
kind terms – terms denoting naturally occurring types of
substances or biological organisms, such as 'gold' and 'tiger'
(see Putnam 1975). In metaphysics, it was Locke who laid the

foundation of recent debates about the persistence of objects over time and the nature of personal identity (see, for example, Parfit 1984 and Wiggins 2001), for he was the first philosopher to see clearly that before we can say whether something existing at one time and place is or is not identical with something existing at another time and place, we must first determine what sort or kind of thing it is whose identity is in question (see Lowe 1989).

Other important examples of the continuing impact of Locke's thought may be found in the philosophy of action and moral theory. There has recently been a revival of volitionism – the view, favoured by Locke, that voluntary actions are initiated by an 'act of will' on the part of the agent (see, for example, Ginet 1990 and McCann 1998). This, together with renewed attention to the perennial problem of free will and moral responsibility – another major concern of Locke's – has led to increasing engagement with Locke's views by modern philosophers working in these areas (see Yaffe 2000). The same may be said regarding Locke's distinctively liberal-minded political philosophy. Revitalized scholarly interest in this has been connected with a resurgence of Locke's idea that political obligation is founded on an agreement or 'compact' between those who submit themselves to government – an agreement freely entered into by and equally binding upon all parties to it, including those into whose hands governmental authority is entrusted. The highly influential work of the American political philosophers John Rawls and Robert Nozick in the last three decades of the twentieth century cannot be adequately understood without an appreciation of its Lockean resonances (see Rawls 1972 and Nozick 1974).

Nor should we forget epistemology, the central concern of Locke's greatest work, the *Essay Concerning Human Understanding*. One very important unifying element in Locke's thought is his relatively modest conception of the scope of human knowledge – especially in matters of metaphysics – which he combines with a conviction that we may nevertheless establish with certainty the truth of at least some principles of mathematics and morality. Such certainty, according to Locke, is entirely the product of reason and intuition and is in no way indicative of the innateness of the principles in question. Indeed, he emphatically repudiates the doctrine of innate ideas and principles as both unfounded and pernicious, as no doubt it was in the hands of many of his seventeenth-century contemporaries. This combination of views is in considerable measure responsible for Locke's endorsement of toleration in matters of religious belief and his insistence that legitimate civil government rests upon the freely given consent of the governed. For if, as Locke supposes, all human beings have very similar but strictly limited cognitive capacities and each of us demonstrably has a duty to exercise those capacities to the best of our ability in judging what to believe or not to believe, rather than relying blindly on authority or tradition, then none of us is justified in forcing our religious beliefs upon others or in presuming to judge for others where their true political interests lie (see Wolterstorff 1996).

Incidentally, Locke's repudiation of the doctrine of innate ideas, while it does align him with much present-day thinking in epistemology, places him in opposition to some recent views in linguistics and psychology, notably those that see evidence for the doctrine in our language-learning capacities (see Chomsky 1988) and some of those that emphasize the evolutionary roots of human psychology (see Cummins and Allen [eds] 1998). However, these modern trends in favour of innatism – or 'nativism', as it is often now called – have by no means gone unopposed (see Cowie 1999) and at the very least we can say that Locke's contribution to the debate between innatism and empiricism still provides a starting-point for much current discussion of the issues at stake. In any case, we should not forget that Locke wrote long before Charles Darwin developed the modern theory of evolution through natural selection and hence at a time at which innate ideas and principles could only be supposed to have a divine origin, enabling their advocates to claim an unchallengeable status for them as representing God's own ordinances. The kind of innatism that modern theoretical linguists and evolutionary psychologists argue for is quite different and they fully embrace an empiricist methodology in their own scientific work. It is hard to say how Locke himself would have regarded their position, so far removed is it from the innatism of his seventeenth-century contemporaries (for further discussion, see Lowe 1995, pp. 27–33).

Although Locke has never really been out of fashion, there have been times at which he has been set up as something of a straw man whose doctrines – for instance, concerning abstract general ideas, the workings of language, and volitions or acts of will – have been caricatured simply to provide an easy target for opposing views. Thankfully, this sort of cavalier treatment is now largely a thing of the past and Locke's reputation as a serious and important philosopher is probably higher at present than it has been at any time since the eighteenth century. This should not be particularly surprising, because Locke's approach to philosophical questions is, in many ways, in keeping with that of the current age. His respect for empirical science and his naturalistic view of the powers of the human mind exemplify this harmony. Recall here that Locke cast himself in the role of an 'under-labourer' to the great scientists of his day, such as Isaac Newton and Robert Boyle (see Chapter 2 above). Indeed, although Locke deferred to Newton and Boyle in matters concerning physical science, he himself may be said to be the father – or at least the grandfather – of modern empirical psychology. His distrust of words put him out of favour when it was fashionable, during the middle of the twentieth century, to approach philosophical questions almost exclusively through the medium of language. But it sits much more comfortably with many modern views of the development of the human mind and its cognitive capacities – setting aside the issue concerning innatism mentioned earlier. Thus, it is no longer possible to dismiss as naive and wrong-headed Locke's assumption of the priority of thought over language. Even his views about abstract general ideas, once strongly ridiculed, now find an echo in some modern psycho-logical accounts of our ability to categorize and classify objects of perception (see Keil 1989).

In sum, if I were pressed to identify, in just a few sentences, those aspects of Locke's work that have had the most lasting influence on philosophy and the intellectual world in general, this is what I would say. Locke was a pivotal figure in the history of philosophy, helping to forge a naturalistic conception of the human mind and its powers and thereby opening the way to the development of the modern science of empirical psychology. At the same time, he helped to engender the modern division of labour between philosophy – understood as centrally involving a critical inquiry into our own conceptual structures and pretensions to knowledge – and empirical science, seen as underwritten by systematic experimentation and the impartial observation of nature. He also stands out, of course, as the foremost champion of individual liberty in the political sphere and of toleration in matters of religious belief. In all of these respects, Locke's philosophy has been a major force for enlightenment and freedom in human affairs and hence, in my estimation, a major force for good.

Glossary

a priori knowledge   knowledge that is not dependent on empirical evidence.

abstract general idea   according to Locke, an idea of a sort of things, containing only those simple ideas common to the ideas of all particular things of that sort.

abstraction   the mental process by which, according to Locke, abstract general ideas are formed.

agent-causation   causation of an event by an agent or a person.

attribute   a general feature common to all substances of the same category or kind, such as spatial extension in the case of material substances.

bare particular   a particular that is neither a particular quality nor a particular object, supposedly possessing no qualities or properties of its own.

Bradley's regress   an infinite regress that apparently arises if we suppose that a quality needs to be bound to the object that has it by a relation between the quality and the object.

categorical property   a property, such as shape, that is not merely a disposition or power of the object that possesses it.

compatibilism   the doctrine that freedom of the will is compatible with universal causal determinism.

compresence   the co-occurrence of properties as properties of the same object.

concept   a component of thought in virtue of which thoughts containing it are thoughts about a certain thing or kind of thing.

contraposition   the logical transformation of a conditional of the form 'If p, then q' into its equivalent, 'If not q, then not p', or vice versa.

demonstration   a deductively valid proof from premises whose truth is certain.

determinism   the doctrine that every event is causally necessitated by preceding events.

deviant causal chain   a causal chain connecting an intention or volition to act in a certain way to an action of that sort which is, despite that connection, unintentional or non-voluntary.

direct realism   the doctrine that external objects are perceived directly, rather than indirectly via the perception of inner mental objects.

discursive thought   thought that is sequential and syntactically structured in a linguistic or quasi-linguistic fashion.

disposition   a power or capacity of an object to act or behave in some specific way.

efficient causation   the production of an event or sustaining of a state of affairs by something.

empirical   concerning or involving experience.

empiricism   the doctrine that there is no knowledge that is not dependent in some way upon experience.

entity   something, of any kind, that does or could exist.

event-causation   the causation of an event by one or more other events.

idea   for Locke, a component of thought or experience, which may be either simple or itself composed of other ideas.

idealism   the doctrine that nothing exists but minds and the ideas that compose their thoughts and experiences.

ideationism   the doctrine that thought is composed of ideas and that the primary function of words is to serve as signs of ideas.

image   a representation that is pictorial or quasi-pictorial in character.

individualism   the doctrine that individual human beings do not depend for their individuality upon any civil society or community to which they may belong.

innatism   the doctrine that the mind is equipped at birth, and prior to experience of any kind, with certain ideas or the knowledge of certain principles.

intentionality   the property that thoughts and experiences have of being of or about things that are distinct from those thoughts and experiences.

intuition   the mental act of directly apprehending the certain truth of a proposition, or the mental capacity to engage in such acts.

labour theory of value   the doctrine that the true value of a commodity is determined by the amount of labour needed to produce it.

language of thought   a quasi-linguistic symbolic system in which, according to some philosophers, all human thought is constructed by the mind or brain.

law of nature   in political philosophy, a rule of conduct, founded on reason, which has force independently of any laws instituted by political authority.

libertarianism   in the philosophy of action, the doctrine that our free choices are not causally determined by prior events; in political philosophy, the doctrine that the state must respect and protect certain fundamental liberties of its individual citizens.

Lockean proviso   Locke's stipulation that, in appropriating unowned natural resources, we should leave 'enough and as good' for other people.

mode   a particular quality or property, such as the particular colour or shape of an object.

nativism   a modern equivalent or version of innatism.

natural kind   a sort or kind of naturally occurring thing or stuff, such as the kinds *oak tree*, *tiger* and *gold*.

natural right   a right which people possess independently of the legislative authority of any civil society to which they may belong.

necessary condition   a condition in whose absence a given event or state of affairs is guaranteed not to occur or obtain.

nominal essence   for Locke, the abstract general idea by reference to which we classify something as being a thing of a certain sort, signified by a certain general name.

nominalism   the doctrine that only particulars exist and that general names are not names of universals.

object   an entity that possesses properties or qualities.

ontological   concerning existence or what exists.

particular   an entity that is unique and unrepeatable, unlike a universal.

percept   a component of perceptual experience.

plurality   in modern metaphysics, a multiplicity of things, such as the planets of our solar system, or the Tudor monarchs of England.

power   a disposition or capacity of an object to act or behave in some specific way.

predicate   an expression which, when completed by a subject-term, forms a sentence, such as a verb or adjectival phrase.

primary quality   a quality or property, such as shape, which all material objects possess independently of their relations to other things.

property   a feature or characteristic of something.

psychologism   the doctrine that there is a psychological basis to linguistic meaning or rules of logic.

real essence   in the case of a material substance, its inner atomic constitution or structure, according to Locke.

reductio ad absurdum   a deductive argument demonstrating the falsehood of a claim by showing how, in conjunction with accepted truths, it gives rise to a contradiction or other absurdity.

reflection   Locke's term for what is nowadays called introspection, a mental process by which the mind attends to states of itself and its own operations.

relatum   any one of the entities between which a certain relation obtains (plural: relata).

Scholasticism   mediaeval philosophy inspired by the works of Aristotle and deeply concerned with the application of metaphysical and logical doctrines to theological issues.

secondary quality   a quality or property, like redness or bitterness, that is attributable to objects at least partly in virtue of the way in which they affect our senses.

semantics   the study or science of linguistic meaning.

sortal term   a name for a sort of object or kind of stuff.

sovereign   the supreme political authority in a civil society.

spoilage limitation   according to Locke, the principle that denies us a property right in any perishable thing that we allow to spoil or go to waste.

state of nature   an actual or hypothetical condition of people in which they are subject to no political authority or civil laws.

substance   a self-subsistent object or bearer of properties; alternatively, a kind of material stuff, such as gold or water.

substance-causation   causation of an event by a substance.

substratum   a bearer or support of properties (plural: substrata).

sufficient condition   a condition in whose presence a given event or state of affairs is guaranteed to occur or obtain.

syntactical   concerning the formal or grammatical features or structure of language.

trope   in modern metaphysics, a mode or particular property of any object.

universal   a feature or characteristic that is repeatable and may be common to many different particulars.

volition   a mental event that is an act or exercise of the will.

volitionism   the doctrine that all of our voluntary actions involve and proceed from volitions or acts of will.

WORKS BY LOCKE

Correspondence of John Locke, The, 8 volumes, ed. E. S. de Beer (Oxford: Clarendon Press, 1976–89).

Epistola de Tolerantia/A Letter on Toleration, ed. R. Klibansky, trans. J. W. Gough (Oxford: Clarendon Press, 1968).

Essay Concerning Human Understanding, An, ed. P. H. Nidditch (Oxford: Clarendon Press, 1975).

Essays on the Law of Nature, ed. W. von Leyden (Oxford: Clarendon Press, 1954).

Letter Concerning Toleration, A, in *The Second Treatise of Government and A Letter Concerning Toleration*, ed. J. W. Gough, 3rd edn (Oxford: Blackwell, 1966).

Letter to the Right Rev. Edward Lord Bishop of Worcester, A, in *The Works of John Locke*, Volume IV (London: Thomas Tegg, 1823).

Reasonableness of Christianity, The, ed. J. C. Higgins-Biddle (Oxford: Clarendon Press, 1999).

Some Thoughts Concerning Education, ed. J. W. & J. S. Yolton (Oxford: Clarendon Press, 1989).

Two Tracts on Government, ed. P. Abrams (Cambridge: Cambridge University Press, 1967).

Two Treatises of Government, ed. P. Laslett, 2nd edn (Cambridge: Cambridge University Press, 1967).

Works of John Locke, The, 10 volumes (London: Thomas Tegg, 1823).

WORKS BY OTHER AUTHORS

Alexander, Peter 1985: *Ideas, Qualities and Corpuscles: Locke and Boyle on the External World* (Cambridge: Cambridge University Press).

Alston, William & Bennett, Jonathan 1988: 'Locke on People and Substances', *Philosophical Review* 97, pp. 25–46.

Ashcraft, Richard 1986: *Revolutionary Politics and Locke's Two Treatises of Government* (Princeton, NJ: Princeton University Press).

Ashworth, E. J. 1981: ' "Do Words Signify Ideas or Things?" The Scholastic Sources of Locke's Theory of Language', *Journal of the History of Philosophy* 19, pp. 299–326.

Ashworth, E. J. 1984: 'Locke on Language', *Canadian Journal of Philosophy* 14, pp. 45–73.

Ayers, Michael 1975: 'The Ideas of Power and Substance in Locke's Philosophy', *Philosophical Quarterly* 25, pp. 1–27, reprinted in revised form in I. C. Tipton (ed.), *Locke on Human Understanding* (Oxford: Oxford University Press, 1977).

Ayers, Michael 1991: *Locke* (London & New York: Routledge).

Ayers, Michael 1994: 'The Foundations of Knowledge and the Logic of Substance: The Structure of Locke's General Philosophy', in G. A. J. Rogers (ed.), *Locke's Philosophy: Content and Context* (Oxford: Clarendon Press).

Bennett, Jonathan 1987: 'Substratum', *History of Philosophy Quarterly* 4, pp. 197–215.

Berkeley, George 1949: *Alciphron; Or, the Minute Philosopher*, in *The Works of George Berkeley, Bishop of Cloyne*, 9 volumes, ed. T. E. Jessop & A. A. Luce (London: Thomas Nelson & Sons).

Berkeley, George 1975: *Philosophical Works*, ed. M. R. Ayers (London: Dent).

Butler, Joseph 1975: 'Of Personal Identity', in J. Perry (ed.), *Personal Identity* (Berkeley and Los Angeles: University of California Press).

Campbell, Keith 1990: *Abstract Particulars* (Oxford: Blackwell).

Chappell, Vere 1994a: 'Locke on the Freedom of the Will', in G. A. J. Rogers (ed.), *Locke's Philosophy: Content and Context* (Oxford: Clarendon Press).

Chappell, Vere (ed.) 1994b: *The Cambridge Companion to Locke* (Cambridge: Cambridge University Press).

Chappell, Vere (ed.) 1998: *Locke* (Oxford: Oxford University Press).

Chomsky, Noam 1988: *Language and Problems of Knowledge* (Cambridge, MA: MIT Press).

Clarke, Randolph 2003: *Libertarian Accounts of Free Will* (New York: Oxford University Press).

Cowie, Fiona 1999: *What's Within? Nativism Reconsidered* (New York: Oxford University Press).

Cranston, Maurice 1957: *John Locke: A Biography* (London: Longman).

Cromer, Richard F. 1991: *Language and Thought in Normal and Handicapped Children* (Oxford: Blackwell).

Cummins, Denise Dellarosa and Allen, Colin (eds) 1998: *The Evolution of Mind* (New York: Oxford University Press).

Davidson, Donald 1980: 'Freedom to Act', in his *Essays on Actions and Events* (Oxford: Clarendon Press).

Descartes, René 1984: *The Philosophical Writings of Descartes*, ed. J. Cottingham, R. Stoothoof & D. Murdoch (Cambridge: Cambridge University Press).

Dunn, John 1969a: 'The Politics of Locke in England and America in the Eighteenth Century', in J. W. Yolton (ed.), *John Locke: Problems and Perspectives* (Cambridge: Cambridge University Press).

Dunn, John 1969b: *The Political Thought of John Locke* (Cambridge: Cambridge University Press).

Filmer, Robert 1991: *Patriarcha and Other Writings*, ed. J. P. Sommerville (Cambridge: Cambridge University Press).

Fodor, Jerry A. 1975: *The Language of Thought* (New York: Crowell).

Frege, Gottlob 1953: *The Foundations of Arithmetic*, trans. J. L. Austin, 2nd edn (Oxford: Blackwell).

Fuller, Gary, Stecker, Robert and Wright, John P. (eds) 2000: *John Locke: An Essay Concerning Human Understanding in Focus* (London & New York: Routledge).

Ginet, Carl 1990: *On Action* (Cambridge: Cambridge University Press).

Guyer, Paul 1994: 'Locke's Philosophy of Language', in Vere Chappell (ed.), *The Cambridge Companion to Locke* (Cambridge: Cambridge University Press).

Hacking, Ian 1975: *Why Does Language Matter to Philosophy?* (Cambridge: Cambridge University Press).

Hall, Roland (ed.) 1970–2000: *The Locke Newsletter*.

Hall, Roland (ed.) 2000 – : *Locke Studies*.

Hall, Roland & Woolhouse, Roger 1983: *Eighty Years of Locke Scholarship* (Edinburgh: Edinburgh University Press).

Harris, Ian 1998: *The Mind of John Locke*, revised edn (Cambridge: Cambridge University Press).

Hart, H. L. A. 1984: 'Are There Any Natural Rights?', in J. Waldron (ed.), *Theories of Rights* (Oxford: Oxford University Press).

Hobbes, Thomas 1996: *Leviathan*, ed. R. Tuck (Cambridge: Cambridge University Press).

Hornsby, Jennifer 1980: *Actions* (London: Routledge & Kegan Paul).

Hume, David 1978: *A Treatise of Human Nature*, ed. L. A. Selby-Bigge & P. H. Nidditch (Oxford: Clarendon Press).

Hume, David 1985: 'Of the Original Contract', in his *Essays Moral, Political and Literary*, ed. E. F. Miller (Indianapolis, IN: Liberty Classics).

James, William 1890: *Principles of Psychology* (New York: Henry Holt & Co).

Jolley, Nicholas 1999: *Locke: His Philosophical Thought* (Oxford: Oxford University Press).

Kant, Immanuel 1929: *Critique of Pure Reason*, trans. N. Kemp Smith (London: Macmillan).

Keil, Frank C. 1989: *Concepts, Kinds, and Cognitive Development* (Cambridge, MA: MIT Press).

Kim, Halla 2003: 'Locke on Innatism', *Locke Studies* 3, pp. 15–39.

Kosslyn, Stephen M. 1990: 'Mental Imagery', in Daniel N. Osherson et al. (eds), *Visual Cognition and Action* (Cambridge, MA: MIT Press).

Kretzmann, Norman 1968: 'The Main Thesis of Locke's Semantic Theory', *Philosophical Review* 77, pp. 175–96.

Leibniz, G. W. 1981: *New Essays on Human Understanding*, trans. P. Remnant & J. Bennett (Cambridge: Cambridge University Press).

Lloyd Thomas, David A. 1995: *Locke on Government* (London: Routledge).

Losonsky, Michael 1994: 'Locke on Meaning and Signification', in G. A. J. Rogers (ed.), *Locke's Philosophy: Content and Context* (Oxford: Clarendon Press).

Lowe, E. J. 1986: 'Necessity and the Will in Locke's Theory of Action', *History of Philosophy Quarterly* 3, pp. 149–63, reprinted in Udo Thiel (ed.), *Locke: Epistemology and Metaphysics* (Aldershot: Dartmouth, 2002).

Lowe, E. J. 1989: *Kinds of Being: A Study of Individuation, Identity and the Logic of Sortal Terms* (Oxford: Blackwell).

Lowe, E. J. 1995: *Locke on Human Understanding* (London & New York: Routledge).

Lowe, E. J. 1996: *Subjects of Experience* (Cambridge: Cambridge University Press).

Lowe, E. J. 1998: *The Possibility of Metaphysics: Substance, Identity, and Time* (Oxford: Clarendon Press).

Lowe, E. J. 2000: *An Introduction to the Philosophy of Mind* (Cambridge: Cambridge University Press).

Lowe, E. J. 2002: *A Survey of Metaphysics* (Oxford: Oxford University Press).

Macpherson, C. B. 1962: *The Political Theory of Possessive Individualism: Hobbes to Locke* (Oxford: Oxford University Press).

Magri, Tito 2000: 'Locke, Suspension of Desire, and the Remote Good', *British Journal for the Philosophy of History* 8, pp. 55–70, reprinted in Udo Thiel (ed.), *Locke: Epistemology and Metaphysics* (Aldershot: Dartmouth, 2002).

Marshall, John 1994: *John Locke: Resistance, Religion and Responsibility* (Cambridge: Cambridge University Press).

Martin, C. B. 1980: 'Substance Substantiated', *Australasian Journal of Philosophy* 58, pp. 3–10.

McCann, Edwin 1994: 'Locke's Philosophy of Body', in Vere Chappell (ed.), *The Cambridge Companion to Locke* (Cambridge: Cambridge University Press).

McCann, Hugh J. 1998: *The Works of Agency: On Human Action, Will, and Freedom* (Ithaca, NY: Cornell University Press).

McCracken, Charles J. 1983: *Malebranche and British Philosophy* (Oxford: Clarendon Press).

McGinn, Colin 1983: *The Subjective View: Secondary Qualities and Indexical Thoughts* (Oxford: Clarendon Press).

Miller, Alexander 1995: 'Lowe's *Locke on Human Understanding*', *The Locke Newsletter* 26, pp. 141–55.

Morgan, Michael J. 1977: Molyneux's Question: Vision, Touch and the Philosophy of Perception (Cambridge: Cambridge University Press).

Noonan, Harold 2003: Personal Identity, 2nd edn (London & New York: Routledge).

Nozick, Robert 1974: Anarchy, State and Utopia (Oxford: Blackwell).

Ott, Walter R. 2004: Locke's Philosophy of Language (Cambridge: Cambridge University Press).

Parfit, Derek 1984: Reasons and Persons (Oxford: Clarendon Press).

Putnam, Hilary 1975: 'The Meaning of "Meaning" ', in his Mind, Language and Reality (Cambridge: Cambridge University Press).

Rawls, John 1972: A Theory of Justice (Oxford: Oxford University Press).

Reid, Thomas 1975: 'Of Mr Locke's Account of Personal Identity', in J. Perry (ed.), Personal Identity (Berkeley and Los Angeles: University of California Press).

Rogers, G. A. J. (ed.) 1994: Locke's Philosophy: Content and Context (Oxford: Clarendon Press).

Sidney, Algernon 1996: Discourses Concerning Government, ed. T. G. West (Indianapolis, IN: Liberty Fund).

Simmons, A. John 1992: The Lockean Theory of Rights (Princeton, NJ: Princeton University Press).

Simmons, A. John 1993: On the Edge of Anarchy: Locke, Consent, and the Limits of Society (Princeton, NJ: Princeton University Press).

Stewart, M. A. (ed.) 2000: English Philosophy in the Age of Locke (Oxford: Clarendon Press).

Taylor, Daniel M. 1970: Explanation and Meaning (Cambridge: Cambridge University Press).

Thiel, Udo (ed.) 2002: Locke: Epistemology and Metaphysics (Aldershot: Dartmouth).

Tipton, Ian C. (ed.) 1977: Locke on Human Understanding (Oxford: Oxford University Press).

Tully, James 1980: A Discourse on Property: John Locke and his Adversaries (Cambridge: Cambridge University Press).

Tully, James 1993: An Approach to Political Philosophy: Locke in Contexts (Cambridge: Cambridge University Press).

Waldron, Jeremy 2002: God, Locke, and Equality: Christian Foundations in Locke's Political Thought (Cambridge: Cambridge University Press).

Wiggins, David 2001: Sameness and Substance Renewed (Cambridge: Cambridge University Press).

Williams, D. C. 1966: Principles of Empirical Realism (Springfield, IL: Charles C. Thomas).

Wittgenstein, Ludwig 1958: Philosophical Investigations, trans. G. E. M. Anscombe (Oxford: Blackwell).

Wolterstorff, Nicholas 1996: *John Locke and the Ethics of Belief* (Cambridge: Cambridge University Press).

Yaffe, Gideon 2000: *Liberty Worth the Name: Locke on Free Agency* (Princeton, NJ: Princeton University Press).

Yolton, John W. 1956: *John Locke and the Way of Ideas* (Oxford: Clarendon Press).

Yolton, John W. (ed.) 1969: *John Locke: Problems and Perspectives* (Cambridge: Cambridge University Press).

Yolton, John W. 1970: *Locke and the Compass of Human Understanding* (Cambridge: Cambridge University Press).

Yolton, John W. 1984: *Perceptual Acquaintance from Descartes to Reid* (Oxford: Blackwell).

Index

Routledge Philosophy GuideBook to Locke on *Human Understanding*

E.J. Lowe

'An extremely valuable and well-balanced guide. It would be difficult to improve on this in the way of a relatively concise companion to Locke's masterwork.' – *George Botterill, Sheffield University*

198x129: 216pp
Hb: 0-415-10090-9
Pb: 0-415-10091-7

Routledge Philosophy GuideBook to Locke on *Government*

David Lloyd Thomas

'Lloyd Thomas provides an exemplary model of how students should go about this sort of work with a text to hand. He shows how to read a text both scrupulously and open-mindedly.' – *Mind*

198x129: 152pp
Hb: 0-415-09533-6
Pb: 0-415-09534-4

Modern Philosophy

Richard Francks, University of Leeds, Uk

Modern Philosophy is an exploration of the ideas of six major thinkers from Descartes to Hume. It takes a fresh and engaging look at the common themes that dominate this period, as well as examining the differences in the work of the six philosophers.

216x138: 320pp
Hb: 1-85728-762-2
Pb: 1-857-28565-4

Political Philosophy

Dudley Knowles, University of Glasgow, UK

'Throughout there is a masterly grasp of common-sense moral and political thinking which is never at the mercy of the wide range of approaches presented, never falls into unnecessary abstraction which makes the book a firmly reliable source for undergraduate understanding of the subject.'
– *Philosophical Books*

216x138: 408pp
Hb: 1-85728-760-6
Pb: 1-85728-550-6